C-3701 CAREER EXAMINATION SERIES

This is your
PASSBOOK for...

Child Protective Supervisor

Test Preparation Study Guide
Questions & Answers

COPYRIGHT NOTICE

This book is SOLELY intended for, is sold ONLY to, and its use is RESTRICTED to individual, bona fide applicants or candidates who qualify by virtue of having seriously filed applications for appropriate license, certificate, professional and/or promotional advancement, higher school matriculation, scholarship, or other legitimate requirements of education and/or governmental authorities.

This book is NOT intended for use, class instruction, tutoring, training, duplication, copying, reprinting, excerption, or adaptation, etc., by:

1) Other publishers
2) Proprietors and/or Instructors of "Coaching" and/or Preparatory Courses
3) Personnel and/or Training Divisions of commercial, industrial, and governmental organizations
4) Schools, colleges, or universities and/or their departments and staffs, including teachers and other personnel
5) Testing Agencies or Bureaus
6) Study groups which seek by the purchase of a single volume to copy and/or duplicate and/or adapt this material for use by the group as a whole without having purchased individual volumes for each of the members of the group
7) Et al.

Such persons would be in violation of appropriate Federal and State statutes.

PROVISION OF LICENSING AGREEMENTS – Recognized educational, commercial, industrial, and governmental institutions and organizations, and others legitimately engaged in educational pursuits, including training, testing, and measurement activities, may address request for a licensing agreement to the copyright owners, who will determine whether, and under what conditions, including fees and charges, the materials in this book may be used them. In other words, a licensing facility exists for the legitimate use of the material in this book on other than an individual basis. However, it is asseverated and affirmed here that the material in this book CANNOT be used without the receipt of the express permission of such a licensing agreement from the Publishers. Inquiries re licensing should be addressed to the company, attention rights and permissions department.

All rights reserved, including the right of reproduction in whole or in part, in any form or by any means, electronic or mechanical, including photocopying, recording, or by any information storage and retrieval system, without permission in writing from the Publisher.

Copyright © 2024 by
National Learning Corporation

212 Michael Drive, Syosset, NY 11791
(516) 921-8888 • www.passbooks.com
E-mail: info@passbooks.com

PUBLISHED IN THE UNITED STATES OF AMERICA

PASSBOOK® SERIES

THE *PASSBOOK® SERIES* has been created to prepare applicants and candidates for the ultimate academic battlefield – the examination room.

At some time in our lives, each and every one of us may be required to take an examination – for validation, matriculation, admission, qualification, registration, certification, or licensure.

Based on the assumption that every applicant or candidate has met the basic formal educational standards, has taken the required number of courses, and read the necessary texts, the *PASSBOOK® SERIES* furnishes the one special preparation which may assure passing with confidence, instead of failing with insecurity. Examination questions – together with answers – are furnished as the basic vehicle for study so that the mysteries of the examination and its compounding difficulties may be eliminated or diminished by a sure method.

This book is meant to help you pass your examination provided that you qualify and are serious in your objective.

The entire field is reviewed through the huge store of content information which is succinctly presented through a provocative and challenging approach – the question-and-answer method.

A climate of success is established by furnishing the correct answers at the end of each test.

You soon learn to recognize types of questions, forms of questions, and patterns of questioning. You may even begin to anticipate expected outcomes.

You perceive that many questions are repeated or adapted so that you can gain acute insights, which may enable you to score many sure points.

You learn how to confront new questions, or types of questions, and to attack them confidently and work out the correct answers.

You note objectives and emphases, and recognize pitfalls and dangers, so that you may make positive educational adjustments.

Moreover, you are kept fully informed in relation to new concepts, methods, practices, and directions in the field.

You discover that you are actually taking the examination all the time: you are preparing for the examination by "taking" an examination, not by reading extraneous and/or supererogatory textbooks.

In short, this PASSBOOK®, used directedly, should be an important factor in helping you to pass your test.

CHILD PROTECTIVE SUPERVISOR

DUTIES
Supervises child protective workers and caseworkers working in the Child Protective Services Unit; reviews new referrals and assigns responsibility for investigation or supervision; discusses areas of particular concern and suggests possible approaches; reviews under care case records to study worker activity; evaluates and prepares written evaluations on all employees assigned to the unit, recommends methods and strategies for improvement; accompanies workers on field visits to evaluate their competence and to assess the need for further training, or when a situation is serious and the supervisor's presence is warranted.

SUBJECT OF EXAMINATION
The written test will be designed to test for knowledge, skills, and/or abilities in such areas as:
1. Understanding and recognizing the dynamics and effects of child abuse and neglect;
2. Laws, rules, and regulations related to child abuse and neglect;
3. Case investigation and records maintenance;
4. Interviewing;
5. Supervision; and
6. Preparing written material.

HOW TO TAKE A TEST

I. YOU MUST PASS AN EXAMINATION

A. *WHAT EVERY CANDIDATE SHOULD KNOW*

Examination applicants often ask us for help in preparing for the written test. What can I study in advance? What kinds of questions will be asked? How will the test be given? How will the papers be graded?

As an applicant for a civil service examination, you may be wondering about some of these things. Our purpose here is to suggest effective methods of advance study and to describe civil service examinations.

Your chances for success on this examination can be increased if you know how to prepare. Those "pre-examination jitters" can be reduced if you know what to expect. You can even experience an adventure in good citizenship if you know why civil service exams are given.

B. *WHY ARE CIVIL SERVICE EXAMINATIONS GIVEN?*

Civil service examinations are important to you in two ways. As a citizen, you want public jobs filled by employees who know how to do their work. As a job seeker, you want a fair chance to compete for that job on an equal footing with other candidates. The best-known means of accomplishing this two-fold goal is the competitive examination.

Exams are widely publicized throughout the nation. They may be administered for jobs in federal, state, city, municipal, town or village governments or agencies.

Any citizen may apply, with some limitations, such as the age or residence of applicants. Your experience and education may be reviewed to see whether you meet the requirements for the particular examination. When these requirements exist, they are reasonable and applied consistently to all applicants. Thus, a competitive examination may cause you some uneasiness now, but it is your privilege and safeguard.

C. *HOW ARE CIVIL SERVICE EXAMS DEVELOPED?*

Examinations are carefully written by trained technicians who are specialists in the field known as "psychological measurement," in consultation with recognized authorities in the field of work that the test will cover. These experts recommend the subject matter areas or skills to be tested; only those knowledges or skills important to your success on the job are included. The most reliable books and source materials available are used as references. Together, the experts and technicians judge the difficulty level of the questions.

Test technicians know how to phrase questions so that the problem is clearly stated. Their ethics do not permit "trick" or "catch" questions. Questions may have been tried out on sample groups, or subjected to statistical analysis, to determine their usefulness.

Written tests are often used in combination with performance tests, ratings of training and experience, and oral interviews. All of these measures combine to form the best-known means of finding the right person for the right job.

II. HOW TO PASS THE WRITTEN TEST

A. NATURE OF THE EXAMINATION

To prepare intelligently for civil service examinations, you should know how they differ from school examinations you have taken. In school you were assigned certain definite pages to read or subjects to cover. The examination questions were quite detailed and usually emphasized memory. Civil service exams, on the other hand, try to discover your present ability to perform the duties of a position, plus your potentiality to learn these duties. In other words, a civil service exam attempts to predict how successful you will be. Questions cover such a broad area that they cannot be as minute and detailed as school exam questions.

In the public service similar kinds of work, or positions, are grouped together in one "class." This process is known as *position-classification*. All the positions in a class are paid according to the salary range for that class. One class title covers all of these positions, and they are all tested by the same examination.

B. FOUR BASIC STEPS

1) Study the announcement

How, then, can you know what subjects to study? Our best answer is: "Learn as much as possible about the class of positions for which you've applied." The exam will test the knowledge, skills and abilities needed to do the work.

Your most valuable source of information about the position you want is the official exam announcement. This announcement lists the training and experience qualifications. Check these standards and apply only if you come reasonably close to meeting them.

The brief description of the position in the examination announcement offers some clues to the subjects which will be tested. Think about the job itself. Review the duties in your mind. Can you perform them, or are there some in which you are rusty? Fill in the blank spots in your preparation.

Many jurisdictions preview the written test in the exam announcement by including a section called "Knowledge and Abilities Required," "Scope of the Examination," or some similar heading. Here you will find out specifically what fields will be tested.

2) Review your own background

Once you learn in general what the position is all about, and what you need to know to do the work, ask yourself which subjects you already know fairly well and which need improvement. You may wonder whether to concentrate on improving your strong areas or on building some background in your fields of weakness. When the announcement has specified "some knowledge" or "considerable knowledge," or has used adjectives like "beginning principles of…" or "advanced … methods," you can get a clue as to the number and difficulty of questions to be asked in any given field. More questions, and hence broader coverage, would be included for those subjects which are more important in the work. Now weigh your strengths and weaknesses against the job requirements and prepare accordingly.

3) Determine the level of the position

Another way to tell how intensively you should prepare is to understand the level of the job for which you are applying. Is it the entering level? In other words, is this the position in which beginners in a field of work are hired? Or is it an intermediate or advanced level? Sometimes this is indicated by such words as "Junior" or "Senior" in the class title. Other jurisdictions use Roman numerals to designate the level – Clerk I, Clerk II, for example. The word "Supervisor" sometimes appears in the title. If the level is not indicated by the title, check the description of duties. Will you be working under very close supervision, or will you have responsibility for independent decisions in this work?

4) Choose appropriate study materials

Now that you know the subjects to be examined and the relative amount of each subject to be covered, you can choose suitable study materials. For beginning level jobs, or even advanced ones, if you have a pronounced weakness in some aspect of your training, read a modern, standard textbook in that field. Be sure it is up to date and has general coverage. Such books are normally available at your library, and the librarian will be glad to help you locate one. For entry-level positions, questions of appropriate difficulty are chosen -- neither highly advanced questions, nor those too simple. Such questions require careful thought but not advanced training.

If the position for which you are applying is technical or advanced, you will read more advanced, specialized material. If you are already familiar with the basic principles of your field, elementary textbooks would waste your time. Concentrate on advanced textbooks and technical periodicals. Think through the concepts and review difficult problems in your field.

These are all general sources. You can get more ideas on your own initiative, following these leads. For example, training manuals and publications of the government agency which employs workers in your field can be useful, particularly for technical and professional positions. A letter or visit to the government department involved may result in more specific study suggestions, and certainly will provide you with a more definite idea of the exact nature of the position you are seeking.

III. KINDS OF TESTS

Tests are used for purposes other than measuring knowledge and ability to perform specified duties. For some positions, it is equally important to test ability to make adjustments to new situations or to profit from training. In others, basic mental abilities not dependent on information are essential. Questions which test these things may not appear as pertinent to the duties of the position as those which test for knowledge and information. Yet they are often highly important parts of a fair examination. For very general questions, it is almost impossible to help you direct your study efforts. What we can do is to point out some of the more common of these general abilities needed in public service positions and describe some typical questions.

1) General information

Broad, general information has been found useful for predicting job success in some kinds of work. This is tested in a variety of ways, from vocabulary lists to questions about current events. Basic background in some field of work, such as sociology or economics, may be sampled in a group of questions. Often these are principles which have become familiar to most persons through exposure rather than through formal training. It is difficult to advise you how to study for these questions; being alert to the world around you is our best suggestion.

2) Verbal ability

An example of an ability needed in many positions is verbal or language ability. Verbal ability is, in brief, the ability to use and understand words. Vocabulary and grammar tests are typical measures of this ability. Reading comprehension or paragraph interpretation questions are common in many kinds of civil service tests. You are given a paragraph of written material and asked to find its central meaning.

3) Numerical ability

Number skills can be tested by the familiar arithmetic problem, by checking paired lists of numbers to see which are alike and which are different, or by interpreting charts and graphs. In the latter test, a graph may be printed in the test booklet which you are asked to use as the basis for answering questions.

4) Observation

A popular test for law-enforcement positions is the observation test. A picture is shown to you for several minutes, then taken away. Questions about the picture test your ability to observe both details and larger elements.

5) Following directions

In many positions in the public service, the employee must be able to carry out written instructions dependably and accurately. You may be given a chart with several columns, each column listing a variety of information. The questions require you to carry out directions involving the information given in the chart.

6) Skills and aptitudes

Performance tests effectively measure some manual skills and aptitudes. When the skill is one in which you are trained, such as typing or shorthand, you can practice. These tests are often very much like those given in business school or high school courses. For many of the other skills and aptitudes, however, no short-time preparation can be made. Skills and abilities natural to you or that you have developed throughout your lifetime are being tested.

Many of the general questions just described provide all the data needed to answer the questions and ask you to use your reasoning ability to find the answers. Your best preparation for these tests, as well as for tests of facts and ideas, is to be at your physical and mental best. You, no doubt, have your own methods of getting into an exam-taking mood and keeping "in shape." The next section lists some ideas on this subject.

IV. KINDS OF QUESTIONS

Only rarely is the "essay" question, which you answer in narrative form, used in civil service tests. Civil service tests are usually of the short-answer type. Full instructions for answering these questions will be given to you at the examination. But in case this is your first experience with short-answer questions and separate answer sheets, here is what you need to know:

1) Multiple-choice Questions

Most popular of the short-answer questions is the "multiple choice" or "best answer" question. It can be used, for example, to test for factual knowledge, ability to solve problems or judgment in meeting situations found at work.

A multiple-choice question is normally one of three types—
- It can begin with an incomplete statement followed by several possible endings. You are to find the one ending which *best* completes the statement, although some of the others may not be entirely wrong.
- It can also be a complete statement in the form of a question which is answered by choosing one of the statements listed.

- It can be in the form of a problem – again you select the best answer.

Here is an example of a multiple-choice question with a discussion which should give you some clues as to the method for choosing the right answer:

When an employee has a complaint about his assignment, the action which will *best* help him overcome his difficulty is to
   A. discuss his difficulty with his coworkers
   B. take the problem to the head of the organization
   C. take the problem to the person who gave him the assignment
   D. say nothing to anyone about his complaint

In answering this question, you should study each of the choices to find which is best. Consider choice "A" – Certainly an employee may discuss his complaint with fellow employees, but no change or improvement can result, and the complaint remains unresolved. Choice "B" is a poor choice since the head of the organization probably does not know what assignment you have been given, and taking your problem to him is known as "going over the head" of the supervisor. The supervisor, or person who made the assignment, is the person who can clarify it or correct any injustice. Choice "C" is, therefore, correct. To say nothing, as in choice "D," is unwise. Supervisors have and interest in knowing the problems employees are facing, and the employee is seeking a solution to his problem.

2) True/False Questions

The "true/false" or "right/wrong" form of question is sometimes used. Here a complete statement is given. Your job is to decide whether the statement is right or wrong.

SAMPLE: A roaming cell-phone call to a nearby city costs less than a non-roaming call to a distant city.

This statement is wrong, or false, since roaming calls are more expensive.

This is not a complete list of all possible question forms, although most of the others are variations of these common types. You will always get complete directions for answering questions. Be sure you understand *how* to mark your answers – ask questions until you do.

V. RECORDING YOUR ANSWERS

Computer terminals are used more and more today for many different kinds of exams.

For an examination with very few applicants, you may be told to record your answers in the test booklet itself. Separate answer sheets are much more common. If this separate answer sheet is to be scored by machine – and this is often the case – it is highly important that you mark your answers correctly in order to get credit.

An electronic scoring machine is often used in civil service offices because of the speed with which papers can be scored. Machine-scored answer sheets must be marked with a pencil, which will be given to you. This pencil has a high graphite content which responds to the electronic scoring machine. As a matter of fact, stray dots may register as answers, so do not let your pencil rest on the answer sheet while you are pondering the correct answer. Also, if your pencil lead breaks or is otherwise defective, ask for another.

Since the answer sheet will be dropped in a slot in the scoring machine, be careful not to bend the corners or get the paper crumpled.

The answer sheet normally has five vertical columns of numbers, with 30 numbers to a column. These numbers correspond to the question numbers in your test booklet. After each number, going across the page are four or five pairs of dotted lines. These short dotted lines have small letters or numbers above them. The first two pairs may also have a "T" or "F" above the letters. This indicates that the first two pairs only are to be used if the questions are of the true-false type. If the questions are multiple choice, disregard the "T" and "F" and pay attention only to the small letters or numbers.

Answer your questions in the manner of the sample that follows:

32. The largest city in the United States is
    A. Washington, D.C.
    B. New York City
    C. Chicago
    D. Detroit
    E. San Francisco

1) Choose the answer you think is best. (New York City is the largest, so "B" is correct.)
2) Find the row of dotted lines numbered the same as the question you are answering. (Find row number 32)
3) Find the pair of dotted lines corresponding to the answer. (Find the pair of lines under the mark "B.")
4) Make a solid black mark between the dotted lines.

VI. BEFORE THE TEST

Common sense will help you find procedures to follow to get ready for an examination. Too many of us, however, overlook these sensible measures. Indeed, nervousness and fatigue have been found to be the most serious reasons why applicants fail to do their best on civil service tests. Here is a list of reminders:

- Begin your preparation early – Don't wait until the last minute to go scurrying around for books and materials or to find out what the position is all about.
- Prepare continuously – An hour a night for a week is better than an all-night cram session. This has been definitely established. What is more, a night a week for a month will return better dividends than crowding your study into a shorter period of time.
- Locate the place of the exam – You have been sent a notice telling you when and where to report for the examination. If the location is in a different town or otherwise unfamiliar to you, it would be well to inquire the best route and learn something about the building.
- Relax the night before the test – Allow your mind to rest. Do not study at all that night. Plan some mild recreation or diversion; then go to bed early and get a good night's sleep.
- Get up early enough to make a leisurely trip to the place for the test – This way unforeseen events, traffic snarls, unfamiliar buildings, etc. will not upset you.
- Dress comfortably – A written test is not a fashion show. You will be known by number and not by name, so wear something comfortable.

- Leave excess paraphernalia at home – Shopping bags and odd bundles will get in your way. You need bring only the items mentioned in the official notice you received; usually everything you need is provided. Do not bring reference books to the exam. They will only confuse those last minutes and be taken away from you when in the test room.
- Arrive somewhat ahead of time – If because of transportation schedules you must get there very early, bring a newspaper or magazine to take your mind off yourself while waiting.
- Locate the examination room – When you have found the proper room, you will be directed to the seat or part of the room where you will sit. Sometimes you are given a sheet of instructions to read while you are waiting. Do not fill out any forms until you are told to do so; just read them and be prepared.
- Relax and prepare to listen to the instructions
- If you have any physical problem that may keep you from doing your best, be sure to tell the test administrator. If you are sick or in poor health, you really cannot do your best on the exam. You can come back and take the test some other time.

VII. AT THE TEST

The day of the test is here and you have the test booklet in your hand. The temptation to get going is very strong. Caution! There is more to success than knowing the right answers. You must know how to identify your papers and understand variations in the type of short-answer question used in this particular examination. Follow these suggestions for maximum results from your efforts:

1) Cooperate with the monitor

The test administrator has a duty to create a situation in which you can be as much at ease as possible. He will give instructions, tell you when to begin, check to see that you are marking your answer sheet correctly, and so on. He is not there to guard you, although he will see that your competitors do not take unfair advantage. He wants to help you do your best.

2) Listen to all instructions

Don't jump the gun! Wait until you understand all directions. In most civil service tests you get more time than you need to answer the questions. So don't be in a hurry. Read each word of instructions until you clearly understand the meaning. Study the examples, listen to all announcements and follow directions. Ask questions if you do not understand what to do.

3) Identify your papers

Civil service exams are usually identified by number only. You will be assigned a number; you must not put your name on your test papers. Be sure to copy your number correctly. Since more than one exam may be given, copy your exact examination title.

4) Plan your time

Unless you are told that a test is a "speed" or "rate of work" test, speed itself is usually not important. Time enough to answer all the questions will be provided, but this does not mean that you have all day. An overall time limit has been set. Divide the total time (in minutes) by the number of questions to determine the approximate time you have for each question.

5) Do not linger over difficult questions

If you come across a difficult question, mark it with a paper clip (useful to have along) and come back to it when you have been through the booklet. One caution if you do this – be sure to skip a number on your answer sheet as well. Check often to be sure that you have not lost your place and that you are marking in the row numbered the same as the question you are answering.

6) Read the questions

Be sure you know what the question asks! Many capable people are unsuccessful because they failed to *read* the questions correctly.

7) Answer all questions

Unless you have been instructed that a penalty will be deducted for incorrect answers, it is better to guess than to omit a question.

8) Speed tests

It is often better NOT to guess on speed tests. It has been found that on timed tests people are tempted to spend the last few seconds before time is called in marking answers at random – without even reading them – in the hope of picking up a few extra points. To discourage this practice, the instructions may warn you that your score will be "corrected" for guessing. That is, a penalty will be applied. The incorrect answers will be deducted from the correct ones, or some other penalty formula will be used.

9) Review your answers

If you finish before time is called, go back to the questions you guessed or omitted to give them further thought. Review other answers if you have time.

10) Return your test materials

If you are ready to leave before others have finished or time is called, take ALL your materials to the monitor and leave quietly. Never take any test material with you. The monitor can discover whose papers are not complete, and taking a test booklet may be grounds for disqualification.

VIII. EXAMINATION TECHNIQUES

1) Read the general instructions carefully. These are usually printed on the first page of the exam booklet. As a rule, these instructions refer to the timing of the examination; the fact that you should not start work until the signal and must stop work at a signal, etc. If there are any *special* instructions, such as a choice of questions to be answered, make sure that you note this instruction carefully.

2) When you are ready to start work on the examination, that is as soon as the signal has been given, read the instructions to each question booklet, underline any key words or phrases, such as *least, best, outline, describe* and the like. In this way you will tend to answer as requested rather than discover on reviewing your paper that you *listed without describing*, that you selected the *worst* choice rather than the *best* choice, etc.

3) If the examination is of the objective or multiple-choice type – that is, each question will also give a series of possible answers: A, B, C or D, and you are called upon to select the best answer and write the letter next to that answer on your answer paper – it is advisable to start answering each question in turn. There may be anywhere from 50 to 100 such questions in the three or four hours allotted and you can see how much time would be taken if you read through all the questions before beginning to answer any. Furthermore, if you come across a question or group of questions which you know would be difficult to answer, it would undoubtedly affect your handling of all the other questions.

4) If the examination is of the essay type and contains but a few questions, it is a moot point as to whether you should read all the questions before starting to answer any one. Of course, if you are given a choice – say five out of seven and the like – then it is essential to read all the questions so you can eliminate the two that are most difficult. If, however, you are asked to answer all the questions, there may be danger in trying to answer the easiest one first because you may find that you will spend too much time on it. The best technique is to answer the first question, then proceed to the second, etc.

5) Time your answers. Before the exam begins, write down the time it started, then add the time allowed for the examination and write down the time it must be completed, then divide the time available somewhat as follows:
    - If 3-1/2 hours are allowed, that would be 210 minutes. If you have 80 objective-type questions, that would be an average of 2-1/2 minutes per question. Allow yourself no more than 2 minutes per question, or a total of 160 minutes, which will permit about 50 minutes to review.
    - If for the time allotment of 210 minutes there are 7 essay questions to answer, that would average about 30 minutes a question. Give yourself only 25 minutes per question so that you have about 35 minutes to review.

6) The most important instruction is to *read each question* and make sure you know what is wanted. The second most important instruction is to *time yourself properly* so that you answer every question. The third most important instruction is to *answer every question*. Guess if you have to but include something for each question. Remember that you will receive no credit for a blank and will probably receive some credit if you write something in answer to an essay question. If you guess a letter – say "B" for a multiple-choice question – you may have guessed right. If you leave a blank as an answer to a multiple-choice question, the examiners may respect your feelings but it will not add a point to your score. Some exams may penalize you for wrong answers, so in such cases *only*, you may not want to guess unless you have some basis for your answer.

7) Suggestions
    a. Objective-type questions
        1. Examine the question booklet for proper sequence of pages and questions
        2. Read all instructions carefully
        3. Skip any question which seems too difficult; return to it after all other questions have been answered
        4. Apportion your time properly; do not spend too much time on any single question or group of questions

5. Note and underline key words – *all, most, fewest, least, best, worst, same, opposite*, etc.
6. Pay particular attention to negatives
7. Note unusual option, e.g., unduly long, short, complex, different or similar in content to the body of the question
8. Observe the use of "hedging" words – *probably, may, most likely*, etc.
9. Make sure that your answer is put next to the same number as the question
10. Do not second-guess unless you have good reason to believe the second answer is definitely more correct
11. Cross out original answer if you decide another answer is more accurate; do not erase until you are ready to hand your paper in
12. Answer all questions; guess unless instructed otherwise
13. Leave time for review

b. Essay questions
   1. Read each question carefully
   2. Determine exactly what is wanted. Underline key words or phrases.
   3. Decide on outline or paragraph answer
   4. Include many different points and elements unless asked to develop any one or two points or elements
   5. Show impartiality by giving pros and cons unless directed to select one side only
   6. Make and write down any assumptions you find necessary to answer the questions
   7. Watch your English, grammar, punctuation and choice of words
   8. Time your answers; don't crowd material

8) Answering the essay question

Most essay questions can be answered by framing the specific response around several key words or ideas. Here are a few such key words or ideas:

M's: manpower, materials, methods, money, management
P's: purpose, program, policy, plan, procedure, practice, problems, pitfalls, personnel, public relations
   a. Six basic steps in handling problems:
      1. Preliminary plan and background development
      2. Collect information, data and facts
      3. Analyze and interpret information, data and facts
      4. Analyze and develop solutions as well as make recommendations
      5. Prepare report and sell recommendations
      6. Install recommendations and follow up effectiveness

   b. Pitfalls to avoid
      1. *Taking things for granted* – A statement of the situation does not necessarily imply that each of the elements is necessarily true; for example, a complaint may be invalid and biased so that all that can be taken for granted is that a complaint has been registered

2. *Considering only one side of a situation* – Wherever possible, indicate several alternatives and then point out the reasons you selected the best one
3. *Failing to indicate follow up* – Whenever your answer indicates action on your part, make certain that you will take proper follow-up action to see how successful your recommendations, procedures or actions turn out to be
4. *Taking too long in answering any single question* – Remember to time your answers properly

IX. AFTER THE TEST

Scoring procedures differ in detail among civil service jurisdictions although the general principles are the same. Whether the papers are hand-scored or graded by machine we have described, they are nearly always graded by number. That is, the person who marks the paper knows only the number – never the name – of the applicant. Not until all the papers have been graded will they be matched with names. If other tests, such as training and experience or oral interview ratings have been given, scores will be combined. Different parts of the examination usually have different weights. For example, the written test might count 60 percent of the final grade, and a rating of training and experience 40 percent. In many jurisdictions, veterans will have a certain number of points added to their grades.

After the final grade has been determined, the names are placed in grade order and an eligible list is established. There are various methods for resolving ties between those who get the same final grade – probably the most common is to place first the name of the person whose application was received first. Job offers are made from the eligible list in the order the names appear on it. You will be notified of your grade and your rank as soon as all these computations have been made. This will be done as rapidly as possible.

People who are found to meet the requirements in the announcement are called "eligibles." Their names are put on a list of eligible candidates. An eligible's chances of getting a job depend on how high he stands on this list and how fast agencies are filling jobs from the list.

When a job is to be filled from a list of eligibles, the agency asks for the names of people on the list of eligibles for that job. When the civil service commission receives this request, it sends to the agency the names of the three people highest on this list. Or, if the job to be filled has specialized requirements, the office sends the agency the names of the top three persons who meet these requirements from the general list.

The appointing officer makes a choice from among the three people whose names were sent to him. If the selected person accepts the appointment, the names of the others are put back on the list to be considered for future openings.

That is the rule in hiring from all kinds of eligible lists, whether they are for typist, carpenter, chemist, or something else. For every vacancy, the appointing officer has his choice of any one of the top three eligibles on the list. This explains why the person whose name is on top of the list sometimes does not get an appointment when some of the persons lower on the list do. If the appointing officer chooses the second or third eligible, the No. 1 eligible does not get a job at once, but stays on the list until he is appointed or the list is terminated.

X. HOW TO PASS THE INTERVIEW TEST

The examination for which you applied requires an oral interview test. You have already taken the written test and you are now being called for the interview test – the final part of the formal examination.

You may think that it is not possible to prepare for an interview test and that there are no procedures to follow during an interview. Our purpose is to point out some things you can do in advance that will help you and some good rules to follow and pitfalls to avoid while you are being interviewed.

What is an interview supposed to test?

The written examination is designed to test the technical knowledge and competence of the candidate; the oral is designed to evaluate intangible qualities, not readily measured otherwise, and to establish a list showing the relative fitness of each candidate – as measured against his competitors – for the position sought. Scoring is not on the basis of "right" and "wrong," but on a sliding scale of values ranging from "not passable" to "outstanding." As a matter of fact, it is possible to achieve a relatively low score without a single "incorrect" answer because of evident weakness in the qualities being measured.

Occasionally, an examination may consist entirely of an oral test – either an individual or a group oral. In such cases, information is sought concerning the technical knowledges and abilities of the candidate, since there has been no written examination for this purpose. More commonly, however, an oral test is used to supplement a written examination.

Who conducts interviews?

The composition of oral boards varies among different jurisdictions. In nearly all, a representative of the personnel department serves as chairman. One of the members of the board may be a representative of the department in which the candidate would work. In some cases, "outside experts" are used, and, frequently, a businessman or some other representative of the general public is asked to serve. Labor and management or other special groups may be represented. The aim is to secure the services of experts in the appropriate field.

However the board is composed, it is a good idea (and not at all improper or unethical) to ascertain in advance of the interview who the members are and what groups they represent. When you are introduced to them, you will have some idea of their backgrounds and interests, and at least you will not stutter and stammer over their names.

What should be done before the interview?

While knowledge about the board members is useful and takes some of the surprise element out of the interview, there is other preparation which is more substantive. It *is* possible to prepare for an oral interview – in several ways:

1) Keep a copy of your application and review it carefully before the interview

This may be the only document before the oral board, and the starting point of the interview. Know what education and experience you have listed there, and the sequence and dates of all of it. Sometimes the board will ask you to review the highlights of your experience for them; you should not have to hem and haw doing it.

2) Study the class specification and the examination announcement

Usually, the oral board has one or both of these to guide them. The qualities, characteristics or knowledges required by the position sought are stated in these documents. They offer valuable clues as to the nature of the oral interview. For example, if the job involves supervisory responsibilities, the announcement will usually indicate that knowledge of modern supervisory methods and the qualifications of the candidate as a supervisor will be tested. If so, you can expect such questions, frequently in the form of a hypothetical situation which you are expected to solve. NEVER go into an oral without knowledge of the duties and responsibilities of the job you seek.

3) Think through each qualification required

Try to visualize the kind of questions you would ask if you were a board member. How well could you answer them? Try especially to appraise your own knowledge and background in each area, *measured against the job sought*, and identify any areas in which you are weak. Be critical and realistic – do not flatter yourself.

4) Do some general reading in areas in which you feel you may be weak

For example, if the job involves supervision and your past experience has NOT, some general reading in supervisory methods and practices, particularly in the field of human relations, might be useful. Do NOT study agency procedures or detailed manuals. The oral board will be testing your understanding and capacity, not your memory.

5) Get a good night's sleep and watch your general health and mental attitude

You will want a clear head at the interview. Take care of a cold or any other minor ailment, and of course, no hangovers.

What should be done on the day of the interview?

Now comes the day of the interview itself. Give yourself plenty of time to get there. Plan to arrive somewhat ahead of the scheduled time, particularly if your appointment is in the fore part of the day. If a previous candidate fails to appear, the board might be ready for you a bit early. By early afternoon an oral board is almost invariably behind schedule if there are many candidates, and you may have to wait. Take along a book or magazine to read, or your application to review, but leave any extraneous material in the waiting room when you go in for your interview. In any event, relax and compose yourself.

The matter of dress is important. The board is forming impressions about you – from your experience, your manners, your attitude, and your appearance. Give your personal appearance careful attention. Dress your best, but not your flashiest. Choose conservative, appropriate clothing, and be sure it is immaculate. This is a business interview, and your appearance should indicate that you regard it as such. Besides, being well groomed and properly dressed will help boost your confidence.

Sooner or later, someone will call your name and escort you into the interview room. *This is it.* From here on you are on your own. It is too late for any more preparation. But remember, you asked for this opportunity to prove your fitness, and you are here because your request was granted.

What happens when you go in?

The usual sequence of events will be as follows: The clerk (who is often the board stenographer) will introduce you to the chairman of the oral board, who will introduce you to the other members of the board. Acknowledge the introductions before you sit down. Do not be surprised if you find a microphone facing you or a stenotypist sitting by. Oral interviews are usually recorded in the event of an appeal or other review.

Usually the chairman of the board will open the interview by reviewing the highlights of your education and work experience from your application – primarily for the benefit of the other members of the board, as well as to get the material into the record. Do not interrupt or comment unless there is an error or significant misinterpretation; if that is the case, do not hesitate. But do not quibble about insignificant matters. Also, he will usually ask you some question about your education, experience or your present job – partly to get you to start talking and to establish the interviewing "rapport." He may start the actual questioning, or turn it over to one of the other members. Frequently, each member undertakes the questioning on a particular area, one in which he is perhaps most competent, so you can expect each member to participate in the examination. Because time is limited, you may also expect some rather abrupt switches in the direction the questioning takes, so do not be upset by it. Normally, a board member will not pursue a single line of questioning unless he discovers a particular strength or weakness.

After each member has participated, the chairman will usually ask whether any member has any further questions, then will ask you if you have anything you wish to add. Unless you are expecting this question, it may floor you. Worse, it may start you off on an extended, extemporaneous speech. The board is not usually seeking more information. The question is principally to offer you a last opportunity to present further qualifications or to indicate that you have nothing to add. So, if you feel that a significant qualification or characteristic has been overlooked, it is proper to point it out in a sentence or so. Do not compliment the board on the thoroughness of their examination – they have been sketchy, and you know it. If you wish, merely say, "No thank you, I have nothing further to add." This is a point where you can "talk yourself out" of a good impression or fail to present an important bit of information. Remember, *you close the interview yourself*.

The chairman will then say, "That is all, Mr. _____, thank you." Do not be startled; the interview is over, and quicker than you think. Thank him, gather your belongings and take your leave. Save your sigh of relief for the other side of the door.

How to put your best foot forward

Throughout this entire process, you may feel that the board individually and collectively is trying to pierce your defenses, seek out your hidden weaknesses and embarrass and confuse you. Actually, this is not true. They are obliged to make an appraisal of your qualifications for the job you are seeking, and they want to see you in your best light. Remember, they must interview all candidates and a non-cooperative candidate may become a failure in spite of their best efforts to bring out his qualifications. Here are 15 suggestions that will help you:

1) Be natural – Keep your attitude confident, not cocky

If you are not confident that you can do the job, do not expect the board to be. Do not apologize for your weaknesses, try to bring out your strong points. The board is interested in a positive, not negative, presentation. Cockiness will antagonize any board member and make him wonder if you are covering up a weakness by a false show of strength.

2) Get comfortable, but don't lounge or sprawl

Sit erectly but not stiffly. A careless posture may lead the board to conclude that you are careless in other things, or at least that you are not impressed by the importance of the occasion. Either conclusion is natural, even if incorrect. Do not fuss with your clothing, a pencil or an ashtray. Your hands may occasionally be useful to emphasize a point; do not let them become a point of distraction.

3) Do not wisecrack or make small talk

This is a serious situation, and your attitude should show that you consider it as such. Further, the time of the board is limited – they do not want to waste it, and neither should you.

4) Do not exaggerate your experience or abilities

In the first place, from information in the application or other interviews and sources, the board may know more about you than you think. Secondly, you probably will not get away with it. An experienced board is rather adept at spotting such a situation, so do not take the chance.

5) If you know a board member, do not make a point of it, yet do not hide it

Certainly you are not fooling him, and probably not the other members of the board. Do not try to take advantage of your acquaintanceship – it will probably do you little good.

6) Do not dominate the interview

Let the board do that. They will give you the clues – do not assume that you have to do all the talking. Realize that the board has a number of questions to ask you, and do not try to take up all the interview time by showing off your extensive knowledge of the answer to the first one.

7) Be attentive

You only have 20 minutes or so, and you should keep your attention at its sharpest throughout. When a member is addressing a problem or question to you, give him your undivided attention. Address your reply principally to him, but do not exclude the other board members.

8) Do not interrupt

A board member may be stating a problem for you to analyze. He will ask you a question when the time comes. Let him state the problem, and wait for the question.

9) Make sure you understand the question

Do not try to answer until you are sure what the question is. If it is not clear, restate it in your own words or ask the board member to clarify it for you. However, do not haggle about minor elements.

10) Reply promptly but not hastily

A common entry on oral board rating sheets is "candidate responded readily," or "candidate hesitated in replies." Respond as promptly and quickly as you can, but do not jump to a hasty, ill-considered answer.

11) Do not be peremptory in your answers

A brief answer is proper – but do not fire your answer back. That is a losing game from your point of view. The board member can probably ask questions much faster than you can answer them.

12) Do not try to create the answer you think the board member wants

He is interested in what kind of mind you have and how it works – not in playing games. Furthermore, he can usually spot this practice and will actually grade you down on it.

13) Do not switch sides in your reply merely to agree with a board member

Frequently, a member will take a contrary position merely to draw you out and to see if you are willing and able to defend your point of view. Do not start a debate, yet do not surrender a good position. If a position is worth taking, it is worth defending.

14) Do not be afraid to admit an error in judgment if you are shown to be wrong

The board knows that you are forced to reply without any opportunity for careful consideration. Your answer may be demonstrably wrong. If so, admit it and get on with the interview.

15) Do not dwell at length on your present job

The opening question may relate to your present assignment. Answer the question but do not go into an extended discussion. You are being examined for a *new* job, not your present one. As a matter of fact, try to phrase ALL your answers in terms of the job for which you are being examined.

Basis of Rating

Probably you will forget most of these "do's" and "don'ts" when you walk into the oral interview room. Even remembering them all will not ensure you a passing grade. Perhaps you did not have the qualifications in the first place. But remembering them will help you to put your best foot forward, without treading on the toes of the board members.

Rumor and popular opinion to the contrary notwithstanding, an oral board wants you to make the best appearance possible. They know you are under pressure – but they also want to see how you respond to it as a guide to what your reaction would be under the pressures of the job you seek. They will be influenced by the degree of poise you display, the personal traits you show and the manner in which you respond.

ABOUT THIS BOOK

This book contains tests divided into Examination Sections. Go through each test, answering every question in the margin. We have also attached a sample answer sheet at the back of the book that can be removed and used. At the end of each test look at the answer key and check your answers. On the ones you got wrong, look at the right answer choice and learn. Do not fill in the answers first. Do not memorize the questions and answers, but understand the answer and principles involved. On your test, the questions will likely be different from the samples. Questions are changed and new ones added. If you understand these past questions you should have success with any changes that arise. Tests may consist of several types of questions. We have additional books on each subject should more study be advisable or necessary for you. Finally, the more you study, the better prepared you will be. This book is intended to be the last thing you study before you walk into the examination room. Prior study of relevant texts is also recommended. NLC publishes some of these in our Fundamental Series. Knowledge and good sense are important factors in passing your exam. Good luck also helps. So now study this Passbook, absorb the material contained within and take that knowledge into the examination. Then do your best to pass that exam.

EXAMINATION SECTION

EXAMINATION SECTION
TEST 1

DIRECTIONS: Each question or incomplete statement is followed by several suggested answers or completions. Select the one the BEST answers the question or completes the statement. *PRINT THE LETTER OF THE CORRECT ANSWER IN THE SPACE AT THE RIGHT.*

1. In most states, minors must be at least _____ and able to prove to the court that they can provide their own support and make mature decisions before the court will emancipate them.

    A. 10
    B. 12
    C. 14
    D. 16

    1._____

2. An initial report contains allegations of environmental neglect, but no claim of abuse or any other form of neglect. Generally, the investigating worker is required to
    I. interview all subjects of the report and the reporter
    II. contact local law enforcement
    III. visit the home
    IV. establish a collateral contact with a professional person

    A. I only
    B. I and III
    C. II and IV
    D. I, II, III and IV

    2._____

3. The first use of the "best interests of the child" standard in a custody decision occurred in

    A. *Chapsky v. Wood (1881)*
    B. *Meyer v. Nebraska (1923)*
    C. *In re Gault (1967)*
    D. *Wisconsin v. Yoder (1972)*

    3._____

4. Many states and localities have established a priority system for responding to initial reports of abuse or neglect. In a system based primarily on the type of allegation reported, which of the following would be given "priority three" status--a non-emergency situation that may not require CPS intervention?

    A. Excessive corporal punishment
    B. Torture
    C. Drug/alcohol abuse
    D. Chronic truancy

    4._____

5. Each of the following is a potential sign of neglect in a school-age child, <u>except</u>

    A. poor self-discipline
    B. unreceptiveness to concepts of caring and respect for peers
    C. delayed language development
    D. bullying

    5._____

6. The confidentiality provisions of the Child Abuse Prevention and Treatment Act require states to make unauthorized disclosures of child abuse and neglect reports a criminal offense. These provisions apply to
    I. physicians
    II. CPS caseworkers
    III. step-parents
    IV. divorce attorneys

    A. I and IV
    B. II, III and IV
    C. III and IV
    D. I, II, III and IV

7. During an interactional assessment of parents and their children, a questioner wants to assess the parents' current life satisfaction. The issue is best addressed by the question

    A. If you could change one thing in your lives right now, what would it be?
    B. Do you ever wish you'd never had children?
    C. Why do you think you're here answering these questions?
    D. Are you both happy right now?

8. Signs of neglect in infants and toddlers include each of the following, except

    A. delayed gross motor development
    B. behavioral abnormalities
    C. poor self-discipline
    D. growth failure

9. A CPS agency is attempting to prioritize its caseload. In general, which of the following types of cases should be addressed first?

    A. Reabuse cases, after initial report and intervention
    B. Foster care considered or indicated
    C. Chronic neglect families
    D. Mentally ill/mentally retarded parents

10. When interviewing a child who is suspected to be a victim of sexual abuse, it is important to remember that developmentally, after a child is able to answer questions regarding who and what happened to them, the next question to which children will be able to express an answer is

    A. Why did this happen?
    B. Where did this happen?
    C. For how long has this been happening?
    D. When did this happen

11. In a typical risk assessment instrument, which of the following variables would most likely be classified as constituting an intermediate risk?

    A. An injury that does not require medical attention
    B. A home environment in which a perpetrator has complete access to a child
    C. An injury to a child's knees
    D. A family that has recently experienced the birth of a child

12. Physical discipline by a parent is permitted in all states, provided that it is reasonable and not excessive. The "reasonableness" standard is largely dependent on   12.____

    A. the size of the child
    B. whether the child is seriously hurt
    C. the culture in which the parent was raised
    D. the age of the child

13. In an official sense, "lack of supervision" usually refers to children _____ or younger who are left without an adult or babysitter in attendance.   13.____

    A. 8
    B. 12
    C. 14
    D. 16

14. Among CSP workers, the inability of a child to make eye contact with an adult interviewer is often cited as a sign of neglect. Workers should be careful when applying this to children from some cultures, however--especially those of _____ heritage.   14.____

    A. Hispanic
    B. African-American
    C. Native American
    D. Asian

15. Which of the following statements about dependency and neglect proceedings is true?   15.____

    A. The court issues interim orders for child custody and care pending resolution
    B. It can directly result in the termination of parental rights
    C. The child is represented by the parents' attorney
    D. A trial takes place immediately after a dependency or neglect action is filed

16. Most states have a(n) _____ -month time frame for reunification efforts before a petition is filed to terminate parental rights.   16.____

    A. 6
    B. 12
    C. 18
    D. 24

17. The legal term for a person over whom a guardian is appointed to manage his or her affairs is   17.____

    A. dependent
    B. curate
    C. ward
    D. protege

18. In cases involving out-of-home placement, a worker's planning for reunification begins   18.____

    A. coincident with the placement
    B. as soon as the parents accept the prescribed services
    C. as soon as the parents demonstrate a willingness to be reunited with the child
    D. 30 days after the placement

19. In a typical risk assessment instrument, which of the following variables would most likely be classified as constituting a high risk?

    A. A caretaker with a moderate mental handicap
    B. A minor unexplained injury
    C. An inconsistent display of necessary parenting skills by a caretaker
    D. A child younger than 5

20. Which of the following living arrangements is generally considered to be most restrictive?

    A. Group home
    B. Specialized foster care
    C. Supervised independent living
    D. Adoptive home

21. In cases of neglect, authorized state intervention must be based clearly on

    A. living conditions demonstrably inferior to the local standard
    B. the availability of a service or services to meet the particular needs of the child
    C. a substantial need to protect the child from specific harm by a parent
    D. reasonable suspicion

22. If a priority system is established for responding to initial reports, workers should use it primarily to determine

    A. the level of intervention required
    B. the relative risk to the child
    C. the parties guilty of the abuse or neglect
    D. whether a home visit is justified

23. Generally, the time a child stays in foster care may be litigated under each of the following, except

    A. section 1983 of the Federal Civil Rights Act
    B. the Child Abuse Prevention and Treatment Act
    C. Titles IV and XX of the Social Security Act
    D. common law principles

24. In cases involving placement, it is generally believed that a span of _____ gives most parents motivating time pressure to respond to interventions or court orders before the next court hearing.

    A. 30 days
    B. 3 months
    C. 6 months
    D. 12 months

25. An initial report, coming from a school, alleges that a child frequently comes to school with both burns and bruises, and recently suffered a sprained wrist. Viewing this a "priority two" report, the worker must do each of the following, except

A. interview all other persons who may have interviewed the abuse or neglect
B. notify the State's Attorney of the existence and content of the report
C. interview each adult and child subject of the report
D. interview at least two other professional persons (school personnel, nurse, etc.) who are believed to have first-hand knowledge of the child's situation

---

KEY (CORRECT ANSWERS)

1.	C	11.	D
2.	B	12.	D
3.	A	13.	B
4.	D	14.	A
5.	D	15.	A
6.	C	16.	C
7.	A	17.	C
8.	C	18.	A
9.	C	19.	D
10.	B	20.	A

21. C
22. B
23. B
24. B
25. B

TEST 2

DIRECTIONS: Each question or incomplete statement is followed by several suggested answers or completions. Select the one the BEST answers the question or completes the statement. *PRINT THE LETTER OF THE CORRECT ANSWER IN THE SPACE AT THE RIGHT.*

1. Examples of parental behaviors that would be classified as emotional abuse include
   I. Burning a child as a form of punishment
   II. Locking a child in a dark closet for several hours as a form of punishment
   III. Grounding a disobedient child for an extended period of several months for a relatively minor offense
   IV. Leaving a preschooler alone in the home

   A. I and II
   B. I, II and IV
   C. II and III
   D. I, II, III and IV

1.____

2. The clinical definition of "failure to thrive" refers simply to a child's failure to

   A. perform academically at grade level
   B. respond to normal nurturing behaviors
   C. gain weight adequately
   D. develop physically and socially

2.____

3. Of the following, the most likely reason for out-of-home placement is

   A. physical abuse
   B. severe general neglect
   C. sexual abuse
   D. absent or incapacitated caretaker

3.____

4. Which of the following factors is LEAST important in determining whether or not a parent or guardian is guilty of physical endangerment?

   A. Whether the child was injured or not
   B. The child's age
   C. The child's maturity level, subjectively assessed
   D. The danger involved in the situation

4.____

5. Most of the U.S. agencies established prior to 1980 to respond to the problems of abuse and neglect were based on the _____ model.

   A. Social-political
   B. Psychoanalytical
   C. Ecological
   D. Medical-legal

5.____

6. The Child Abuse Prevention and Treatment Act provides a definition of mental injury to a child that serves as a general guideline for states to follow if they want to receive federal funding for child protective services. The definition includes each of the following specifications, except

6.____

A. The parent's behavior must cause or perpetuate the mental difficulty of the child
B. A connection exists between the parent's behavior and the child's mental problems
C. "Mental" refers to emotional, intellectual, or psychological functioning
D. The parent's behavior must be obvious or explicit

7. For a 12-year-old child who is sexually abused, the most likely presentation would be

   A. abdominal pain
   B. eating disturbances
   C. regressive behavior
   D. fear of falling asleep

8. According to Summit (1983), child sexual abuse accommodation syndrome includes each of the following characteristics, except

   A. delayed disclosure
   B. regression
   C. secrecy
   D. helplessness

9. In making judgements about clients, which of the following would a worker typically do last?

   A. Speculate about causes of a child's behavior
   B. Investigating the child's and the family's medical and social history
   C. Observing a series of different interactions
   D. Determining which factors and behaviors are related in family interactions

10. In an infant who has learned to crawl, the type of fracture that is almost certainly diagnostic of abuse is

    A. a comminuted fracture of the fingertip
    B. a transverse fracture of the radius
    C. a chip fracture of the cheekbone
    D. a spiral fracture of the femur

11. What is the legal term used to denote any conduct that may imply consent?

    A. Capitulation
    B. Sufferance
    C. Surrender
    D. Acquiescence

12. In most cases, the worker's first assessment of a child's risk for abuse or neglect is made

    A. when the initial report is taken
    B. after interviews with members of the household
    C. after the first home visit
    D. upon conclusion of a prescribed number of home visits

13. When the doctrine of informed consent is applied to the treatment of children, it must include the elements of

    A. voluntariness, coincidence, and nonsolicitation
    B. selectivity, legitimacy, and documentation
    C. legitimacy, capacity, and nonsolicitation
    D. capacity, voluntariness, and relevancy

14. When a worker has insufficient knowledge about a situation or its possible consequences for a child, he or she may fail to alter the ordinary course of assessment because there is no perceived risk. This is an example of

    A. Learned helplessness
    B. Unconflicted change
    C. Defensive avoidance
    D. Unconflicted inertia

15. Which of the following features is not commonly associated with Munchausen syndrome by proxy?

    A. Perpetrator is the father
    B. Most victims are infants and toddlers
    C. Perpetrator is in a medical-related line of work
    D. Perpetrator has a history of symptoms and signs similar to those which are simulated or produced in the child

16. An initial report alleges that a child who is three years old is inadequately cared for. Viewing this as a "priority one" report, the worker must
    I. immediately contact the police
    II. notify the State's Attorney of the existence and content of the report
    III. interview each adult and child subject of the report
    IV. interview all other persons who may have interviewed the abuse or neglect

    A. I only
    B. I, II and III
    C. III and IV
    D. I, II, III, and IV

17. In the last two decades or so, the orientation of foster care has changed its orientation from child welfare to

    A. family treatment
    B. alternative living arrangements
    C. crisis intervention
    D. punishment of perpetrators

18. Each of the following criteria are useful in assessing the reliability of a child's statements regarding sexual abuse, except

    A. drawings or play with retrieval props (dolls, etc.) is consistent with the child's verbal history
    B. the association of the child's statements with an appropriate affect

C. the ability of a child to answer questions consistently, using the same words each time
D. the ability of the child to give specific details about what took place

19. In most states, the age of assent for treatment begins at 19.____

   A. 7
   B. 9
   C. 12
   D. 14

20. Which of the following cases established tort liability for professionals who fail to report suspected child abuse? 20.____

   A. *Canterbury v. Spence (1972)*
   B. *Landers v. Flood (1976)*
   C. *Krikorian v. Barry (1987)*
   D. *White v. North Carolina State Board of Examiners of Practicing Psychologists (1990)*

21. In cases of emotional abuse, the severity of the abuse is typically determined by each of the following, except 21.____

   A. the willingness of the parents to cooperate and make progress in treatment
   B. the nature of the child's psychopathology or disturbed behavior
   C. the nature of the child's physical environment
   D. the age of the child

22. Many states and localities have established a priority system for responding to initial reports of abuse or neglect. In a system based primarily on the type of allegation reported, which of the following would be given "priority one" status? 22.____

   A. Sexual abuse
   B. Bone fractures
   C. Poisoning
   D. Human bite marks

23. In an investigation of an initial report, a worker visits the home of the family and makes observations about the child, the incident described in the report, and the parents; Usually, the worker should then focus on 23.____

   A. locating available community resources
   B. determining the risk of future harm to the child
   C. listing applicable agency policies and procedures
   D. identifying family stressors

24. Generally, when a worker begins an investigation of an initial report of abuse or neglect, the first question that must be investigated is 24.____

   A. How serious is the current situation?
   B. What level of intervention in indicated?
   C. What has actually happened to the child or children in question?
   D. What is the risk of future harm to the child?

25. The family treatment model, a placement-prevention model,
    A. is generally least successful with neglectful families
    B. generally makes use of fewer concrete support services than other models
    C. provides in-home services for a period of about 90 days
    D. provides a corrective intervention

KEY (CORRECT ANSWERS)

1.	A	11.	D
2.	C	12.	A
3.	B	13.	D
4.	A	14.	D
5.	D	15.	A
6.	D	16.	D
7.	D	17.	A
8.	B	18.	C
9.	A	19.	A
10.	D	20.	B

21. C
22. A
23. D
24. C
25. A

TEST 3

DIRECTIONS: Each question or incomplete statement is followed by several suggested answers or completions. Select the one the BEST answers the question or completes the statement. *PRINT THE LETTER OF THE CORRECT ANSWER IN THE SPACE AT THE RIGHT.*

1. In a hearing to decide the termination of parental rights, 1.____

    A. the parents are represented by a defense attorney
    B. the applicable law is embodied in the state's criminal codes
    C. the child is represented by a guardian *ad litem*
    D. the burden of proof is evidence beyond a reasonable doubt

2. In general, courts have the authority to sever the legal relationship between a parent and child 2.____
    I. as part of the finding of a dependency and neglect hearing
    II. as the conclusion of a termination hearing
    III. in criminal cases involving wrongs against children

    A. I only
    B. II only
    C. II and III
    D. I, II and III

3. Typically, when a case of neglect has resulted in an emergency placement, a period of _____ is assigned as the time period by which parents must be ready for the return of the child or children into an improved environment. 3.____

    A. 3 months
    B. 6 months
    C. 1 year
    D. 2 years

4. Which of the following items of information is most relevant to a dependency and neglect hearing? 4.____

    A. Other children in home and their probable safety
    B. Comparison of parents
    C. Recommendation regarding custody
    D. Information regarding alleged perpetrator(s)

5. The Homebuilders model of family preservation 5.____

    A. has been found to be most successful with children who have not suffered physical abuse
    B. is motivated primarily by the goal of correction
    C. uses long-term interventions of 90-180 days
    D. is based on social learning theory

6. Which of the following items of federal legislation provides for services aimed to reduce foster care placement?

    A. Child Abuse Prevention and Treatment Act
    B. Adoption Assistance and Child Welfare Act
    C. Uniform Reciprocal Enforcement of Support Act
    D. Omnibus Budget Reconciliation Act of 1993

7. If a child is placed under the supervision of dependency court, or in custody of the county or state, court reviews are generally mandated every

    A. 3 months
    B. 6 months
    C. 1 year
    D. 2 years

8. Of the following, the most appropriate choice for a family preservation effort would be a

    A. case involving a child older than 2 in which there is not a strong likelihood of further risk
    B. family who resists in-home services
    C. case of sexual abuse in which the perpetrator cannot be removed from access to the child victim
    D. family in which the parent is severely developmentally or psychiatrically disabled

9. As a general rule, children who have been in an emergency shelter for _____ or more should be evaluated by a mental health professional.

    A. 3 months
    B. 6 months
    C. 1 year
    D. 2 years

10. The decision to confirm a report of child abuse or neglect is likely to rely on each of the following, except

    A. the intent of the perpetrator
    B. the availability of community resources that may help reduce the risk of abuse or neglect
    C. the degree to which the worker is certain that an injury was caused by willful or negligent acts of the caretaker or perpetrator
    D. information regarding past incidents or reports

11. Accidental bruises or cuts on the _____ of a child are extremely rare, and should always be looked upon with suspicion by an investigating worker.

    A. lower extremities
    B. shoulder
    C. back
    D. neck

12. Courts generally define _____ as intentional conduct by a parent showing an intent to forgo all parental duties.   12.____

    A. acquiescence
    B. abandonment
    C. emancipation
    D. neglect

13. For a 4-year-old child who is sexually abused, the most likely presentation would be   13.____

    A. nightmares
    B. thumb-sucking
    C. eating disturbances
    D. sleeping unusually long hours

14. Which of the following is a guideline that should be followed in the oversight of parental visitations of a child who has been placed in foster care?   14.____

    A. Visitations should be irregularly spaced
    B. The caseworker should take a passive role in promoting regular contact once visitation rights have been granted
    C. In general, visitations should be monitored closely at first
    D. Recommendations for visitation should be as specific as possible regarding duration and frequency

15. In a typical risk assessment instrument, which of the following variables would most likely be classified as constituting a high risk?   15.____

    A. A recent change in marital or relationship status
    B. Water and/or electricity inoperative
    C. A child between 5 and 9 years of age
    D. Family does not belong to a church or social group

16. Which of the following elements is generally common to all family preservation programs?   16.____

    A. Staff members are not required to have a degree in social work.
    B. They focus their efforts on the symptomatic family member or members.
    C. Workers carry a small caseload at any given time.
    D. They accept families of any status, regardless of the perceived risk of placement.

17. A CPS agency is attempting to prioritize its caseload. In general, which of the following types of cases would be addressed after the others have been considered?   17.____

    A. Resistant or uncooperative parents
    B. Children with emotional/psychological disorders
    C. Recommendations of different professionals or agencies are in conflict
    D. Children with moderate to severe physical injuries

18. According to the Adoption Assistance and Child Welfare Act of 1980, a placement can be made

    A. completely at the discretion of the courts
    B. only after a worker makes a real effort to seek out alternative resources and to avoid placement
    C. only if all living relatives at the age of majority or older agree
    D. completely at the discretion of the investigating agency

19. The most frequently used protocol for interactional assessments of parents and children includes eight major areas of inquiry. Which of the following is one of these?

    A. Previous legal troubles
    B. Records from family of origin
    C. Education and work experience
    D. Feeding experiences from newborn to present

20. Which of the following is LEAST likely to be a long-term consequence of emotional maltreatment of a child?

    A. Apathy
    B. Extreme violence
    C. Impaired physical development
    D. Anxiety and anger

21. Absent special circumstances, long-term foster care is generally considered an inappropriate plan for any child aged _____ or under.

    A. 19
    B. 12
    C. 15
    D. 18

22. When interviewing a child who is suspected to be a victim of sexual abuse, it is important to remember that younger children--children under the age of 3--are generally able to answer questions regarding
    I. who the perpetrator was
    II. where the abuse happened
    III. when the abuse happened
    IV. why the abuse happened

    A. I only
    B. I and III
    C. I, II and III
    D. I, II, III and IV

23. The length of time children remain in foster care in the United States is broadly limited under the provisions of the federal

    A. Child Abuse Prevention and Treatment Act
    B. Adoption Assistance and Child Welfare Act
    C. Uniform Reciprocal Enforcement of Support Act
    D. Omnibus Budget Reconciliation Act of 1993

24. The first home visit of a CSP worker reveals a physical environment that presents imminent danger to the children of the house: there is no heat (the visit occurs in a cold winter month); no functional plumbing; and several windows are broken. The worker should

    A. seek immediate placement for all children in the household
    B. seek immediate placement for children in the household younger than 3
    C. try to find temporary alternative housing for the entire family
    D. begin the application process for financial aid that might help fix these problems

24._____

25. Which of the following conditions is most likely to necessitate the attempt to place a child outside of his or her home and away from parents?

    A. Child is extremely fearful of parents
    B. Unhealthy or unlivable physical environment
    C. Child exhibits seductive and sexualized behavior
    D. Failure to thrive

25._____

KEY (CORRECT ANSWERS)

1.	C	11.	D
2.	B	12.	B
3.	B	13.	B
4.	A	14.	D
5.	D	15.	A
6.	D	16.	C
7.	B	17.	C
8.	A	18.	B
9.	A	19.	D
10.	B	20.	B

21. C
22. A
23. B
24. C
25. A

EXAMINATION SECTION
TEST 1

DIRECTIONS: Each question or incomplete statement is followed by several suggested answers or completions. Select the one the BEST answers the question or completes the statement PRINT THE LETTER OF THE CORRECT ANSWER IN THE SPACE AT THE RIGHT.

1. In general, the most serious decision a CPS agency (or inter-agency board) can be called upon to make is

    A. when to intervene in a case of neglect
    B. whether to make a home visit in response to a report
    C. when to return a child from a foster home to a natural home
    D. whether to begin termination of parental rights

2. Which of the following is/are defined by the Child Abuse Prevention and Treatment Act as a form of child neglect?
    I. Failure to seek periodic medical and dental check-ups that have the potential to prevent disease
    II. Punishment involving close confinement
    III. Failure to seek necessary health care for a sick child
    IV. Failure to enroll a school-age child in an educational program

    A. I only
    B. II and III
    C. III and IV
    D. I, II, III and IV

3. The first task that a worker faces in making judgements about clients is

    A. predicting the likelihood of abuse or neglect
    B. determining relationships between events
    C. describing the general situation and family interactions
    D. testing theories about assumptions

4. Inflicted bruises on a child are so common at certain body sites that discovering them there is diagnostic of abuse. Which of the following is LEAST likely to be the site of an inflicted bruise?

    A. Forehead
    B. Neck
    C. Genitals
    D. Buttocks and lower back

5. The most frequently reported type of child maltreatment is

    A. physical abuse
    B. physical endangerment
    C. sexual abuse
    D. neglect

6. The final phase of an interview with a child who has suffered sexual abuse should be devoted to

   A. gathering as much concrete evidence as possible against the perpetrator
   B. making sure the child understands that he or she should never let the abuse happen again
   C. telling the child emphatically that the abuse was not his or her fault
   D. compiling a list of physical and behavioral symptoms

7. What is the legal term for an individual who assumes parental obligations and status without a formal, legal adoption?

   A. Parens patriae
   B. In loco parentis
   C. Ad litem
   D. In re

8. Of the forms of maltreatment listed below, the one that generally causes the greatest number of child fatalities is

   A. emotional abuse
   B. physical abuse
   C. neglect
   D. sexual abuse

9. Major indications that an agency should initiate the termination of parental rights include
   I. Voluntary placement of a child without visits, correspondence, or other contact for one year
   II. Repetitive moderate injuries
   III. Untreatable psychopathology in the child
   IV. Untreatable psychopathology in one or both parents

   A. I and II
   B. I, II and IV
   C. II, III and IV
   D. I, II, III and IV

10. Which of the following is the minimum required to trigger the mandatory reporting requirements of the Child Abuse Prevention and Treatment Act?

    A. Reasonable suspicion
    B. Suspicion shared by at least one other witness
    C. Clear and convincing evidence
    D. A preponderance of evidence

11. When a child is abandoned or orphaned and the state must step in, it is usually the case that an attempt is made to first place the child

    A. in a suitable institution
    B. with an adoption agency
    C. with foster parents
    D. with relatives

12. Which of the following parties is generally not involved in the pretrial or trial stages of a dependency and neglect proceeding?   12.____

    A. CPS or social services agency
    B. Child through guardian *ad litem*
    C. Concerned party seeking custody
    D. Parents or custodians

13. In a typical risk assessment instrument, which of the following variables would most likely be classified as constituting no risk or a low risk?   13.____

    A. Family is geographically isolated from community services
    B. A caretaker who is overly compliant with the investigator
    C. An injury on the child's torso
    D. One previous report of abuse

14. Once a placement has occurred, the worker's next immediate responsibility is generally to   14.____

    A. conduct observations at the foster home
    B. make a post-placement family assessment
    C. begin the implementation of in-home services
    D. develop an individual case plan

15. Which of the following cases would typically require the most time for review by a CPS board or staff?   15.____

    A. Failure to thrive
    B. A child younger than 1 year old in an unheated home
    C. School-age child exhibiting antisocial behavior
    D. A child younger than 1 year old with physical abuse

16. In taking a child's history of alleged sexual abuse, it's important to remember that there's little evidence to suggest that children's reports are unreliable. In the rare instances that a child makes a false accusation, it's usually for one of a limited number of reasons. Which of the following is not one of these?   16.____

    A. The child wants to please or anger the parents
    B. The child has misinterpreted innocent behavior by the alleged perpetrator
    C. The child hopes to obtain an objective (dating, custody change
    D. The child perceives him/herself to be in trouble, and wants to protect him/herself from incrimination

17. During the first year of a child's life, about _____% of all serious intracranial injuries that occur are the result of abuse.   17.____

    A. 15
    B. 45
    C. 75
    D. 95

18. Often, the task of determining an appropriate level of intervention in cases of child neglect tends to be most difficult in cases where _____ is/are a main factor in the family's inability to maintain safe housing and adequate food.

   A. drug abuse
   B. poverty
   C. an abusive family of origin
   D. differing cultural values

19. Each of the following elements is generally common to all family preservation programs, except

   A. services are delivered according to routinely designated case categories
   B. they are crisis-oriented
   C. length of involvement is typically limited to between 2 and 5 months
   D. the staff maintains flexible hours, 7 days a week

20. Adequate foster care standards were established in the United States by

   A. *Miller v. Youakim* (1979)
   B. *G.L. v. Zumwalt* (1980)
   C. the Child Abuse Prevention Treatment Act
   D. the Adoption Assistance and Child Welfare Act

21. A worker begins an investigation of a report by visiting the home of a family and observing that a child has several bruises on her back, arms, and legs. In order to maintain an objective stance, the worker should describe the child as

   A. self-destructive
   B. clumsy
   C. abused
   D. bruised

22. A CPS agency based in an institutional or resident-care facility must meet requirements for minimally adequate care. Which of the following is generally not one of these requirements?

   A. Individualized treatment plans
   B. A sufficient number of qualified staff
   C. Planned therapeutic programs and activities
   D. Planned educational instruction

23. During an interview with a 3-year-old child who is suspected to be a victim of sexual abuse, the interview asks a series of questions, each of which the child immediately answers *Yes* while playing with some dolls that have been placed in front her. The child does not appear to be paying attention to the interviewer's questions. The interviewer should then

   A. abruptly terminate the interview and begin again later
   B. explain to the child how important it is that she pay attention and answer the questions as truthfully as she can
   C. ask another question to which the answer is known
   D. ask the child to demonstrate the abuse using the dolls with which she is playing

24. Which of the following is true of a guardianship?

    A. A guardianship obtained outside dependency court does not require reunification efforts.
    B. A guardian is eligible for federal AFDC, regardless of familial relation to the child.
    C. Parents permanently lose their right to a child.
    D. A guardian of the child's person is automatically considered to be the guardian of the child's estate.

25. Generally, incorporating emotional abuse and neglect into juvenile codes is made especially difficult because

    A. neglect is almost always a civil rather than criminal matter
    B. there is a lack of agreement on whether certain forms of neglect require treatment
    C. they can result from a lack of interaction as often as an interaction
    D. the terms that define cause, treatment and consequences are vague

KEY (CORRECT ANSWERS)

1.	C	11.	D
2.	C	12.	C
3.	C	13.	C
4.	A	14.	B
5.	D	15.	D
6.	C	16.	B
7.	B	17.	D
8.	C	18.	B
9.	B	19.	A
10.	A	20.	B

21.	D
22.	D
23.	C
24.	A
25.	D

TEST 2

DIRECTIONS: Each question or incomplete statement is followed by several suggested answers or completions. Select the one the BEST answers the question or completes the statement. *PRINT THE LETTER OF THE CORRECT ANSWER IN THE SPACE AT THE RIGHT.*

1. Research has demonstrated that probably the greatest benefit involved in group classes focusing on child development and care is   1.____

    A. the learning of a few concrete skills
    B. an improvement in families' overall living environment
    C. the alleviation of social isolation
    D. acquisition of new insights and attitudes

2. Programs such as individual behavior therapy, group therapy, and therapeutic day care have been found to be especially beneficial to families when they can continue for at least _____ months   2.____

    A. 3-6
    B. 6-18
    C. 12-24
    D. 18-36

3. Which of the following conditions is most likely to necessitate the attempt to place a child outside of his or her home and away from parents?   3.____

    A. Child is younger than 2
    B. Munchausen syndrome by proxy
    C. Both parents unemployed
    D. Sibling suffered severe past abuse

4. Signs exhibited by a child that may be indicative of sexual abuse include   4.____
    I. Headaches
    II. Wetting/soiling of underwear
    III. Seductive behavior
    IV. Impulsiveness

    A. I and III
    B. II and III
    C. II, III and IV
    D. I, II, III and IV

5. An initial report contains allegations of educational neglect, but no claim of abuse or other forms of neglect. Generally, the investigating worker is required to   5.____

    A. interview only the child and the primary caretaker
    B. interview all involved child and adult subjects of the report, along with the reporter
    C. establish a collateral contact with another professional
    D. visit the home

6. An accidental fall will generally not cause a bruise on the

   A. soft tissue of the cheek
   B. forehead
   C. cheekbone
   D. elbow

7. Under federal law, an individual case plan for a child must be developed within _____ after the initial removal of a child or after an emergency in-person response.

   A. 48 hours
   B. 10 days
   C. 30 days
   D. 60 days

8. In forming judgements about clients, a worker should generally use information or behaviors that are most

   A. recent
   B. vivid
   C. consistent
   D. available

9. In general, which of the following factors has been demonstrated to be the most influential in determining whether a report of abuse or neglect will be confirmed, and whether placement will be initiated?

   A. The nature of the incident
   B. The age of the child
   C. Agency staffing patterns
   D. Parental characteristics

10. In general, what is the likelihood that a report of child abuse or neglect will be confirmed by a worker's investigation?

    A. 10-20%
    B. 25-50%
    C. 40-60%
    D. 60-80%

11. Which of the following is true of child custody petitions initiated by a CPS worker?

    A. It is generally filed by a named individual
    B. The child is generally removed from the home pending a hearing
    C. Preliminary hearings on the need to take immediate custody are generally held within 24 hours
    D. Only one copy of the petition is served to a set of parents

12. In most states, professionals who are required to report the possibility of child maltreatment to the proper authority include
    I. Law enforcement personnel, such as police officers
    II. Child care providers
    III. Medical or hospital personnel
    IV. Attorneys

A. I and II
B. I, II and III
C. III only
D. I, II, III and IV

13. As a general rule, children who have been in foster care for _____ or more should be evaluated by a mental health professional.

    A. 3 months
    B. 6 months
    C. 1 year
    D. 2 years

14. The most commonly encountered hand marks left on a child in cases of physical abuse are

    A. hand prints
    B. linear marks-parallel bruises marking the edges of fingers
    C. grab marks-oval-shaped bruises resembling fingerprints
    D. pinch marks-crescent-shaped bruises facing each other

15. According to the National Center on Child Abuse and Neglect, emotional abuse includes each of the following, except

    A. threatened harm
    B. close confinement
    C. refusal to provide essential care
    D. verbal assault

16. In the Families model of home-based intervention,

    A. very few, if any, support services are involved
    B. the main objective is to eliminate the symptom
    C. the average intervention period is just over 4 months
    D. a strategic therapist assesses the family for a period of 30 days

17. Which of the following is LEAST likely to be an area of particular concern regarding the decision-making processes of child welfare workers?

    A. Lack of training in methods for predicting behavior
    B. Inability to predict client behavior with accuracy
    C. Lack of consistency over time
    D. Lack of agreement between workers on the same case information

18. Many states and localities have established a priority system for responding to initial reports of abuse or neglect. In a system based primarily on the type of allegation reported, which of the following would be given *priority two* status-dangerous and perhaps requiring emergency services?

    A. Internal injuries
    B. Suicidal child
    C. Sprains/dislocations
    D. Malnutrition/failure to thrive

19. In general, until more information is known, CPS workers should avoid the initiation of a criminal investigation of the perpetrator in cases involving

    A. Munchausen syndrome by proxy
    B. deliberate poisoning with intent to kill
    C. premeditated by not potentially lethal physical abuse
    D. nonsevere physical abuse, but where a previous sibling was killed or died under suspicious circumstances

19.____

20. The surrender of care, custody and earnings of a child, as well as the renunciation of parental duties, is known by the legal term

    A. Emancipation
    B. Quitclaim
    C. Surrender
    D. Relinquishment

20.____

21. Generally, infants who have been placed in foster care should be visited at least _____ by their biological parents.

    A. once a day
    B. 3 times a week
    C. weekly
    D. every two weeks

21.____

22. A parent or guardian fails to provide necessary physical, affectional, medical, or institutional care for a child is guilty of neglect if that failure is due to
    I. financial inability
    II. mental incapacity
    III. immorality
    IV. cruelty

    A. I, III and IV
    B. II, III and IV
    C. III and IV
    D. I, II, III, and IV

22.____

23. When faced with a situation requiring the immediate alleviation of risks, a worker may rush to pace a child without considering possible alternatives. This is an example of

    A. Hypervigilance
    B. Unconflicted change
    C. Unconflicted inertia
    D. Defensive avoidance

23.____

24. Approximately what percentage of children living in foster care are adopted each year?

    A. 10
    B. 25
    C. 45
    D. 60

24.____

25. Which of the following is LEAST likely to be included in the behavioral profile of an abused or neglected child?

   A. Excessive attention to physical appearance
   B. Immaturity
   C. Self-hatred
   D. Sexual sophistication (beyond age level)

KEY (CORRECT ANSWERS)

1. C
2. B
3. D
4. D
5. B

6. A
7. C
8. C
9. A
10. C

11. C
12. B
13. C
14. C
15. C

16. C
17. A
18. C
19. A
20. A

21. B
22. B
23. B
24. A
25. A

TEST 3

DIRECTIONS: Each question or incomplete statement is followed by several suggested answers or completions. Select the one the BEST answers the question or completes the statement. *PRINT THE LETTER OF THE CORRECT ANSWER IN THE SPACE AT THE RIGHT.*

1. The most important factor in determining whether a parent or guardian is guilty of child neglect is

   A. the degree of the child's suffering
   B. whether the negligent behavior is intentional or the consequence of other factors such as financial trouble
   C. whether the child's suffering is physical or emotional
   D. whether the child has suffered an injury as a result of the neglect

   1.____

2. When burns are inflicted on a child, the most commonly-used agent is

   A. hot water
   B. a cigarette
   C. a stove or hot plate
   D. a lighter or match

   2.____

3. Which of the following legal terms refers to the role of the state as guardian of legally disabled individuals?

   A. Parens patriae
   B. Vis major
   C. Eminent domain
   D. In loco parentis

   3.____

4. When documenting the effects of intervention in a case of child neglect, the worker's records must include
   I. notations on the child's progress
   II. assessments of other concerned professionals regarding the child's situation
   III. the parents' cooperation and compliance with requests regarding problems

   A. I only
   B. I and II
   C. I and III
   D. I, II and III

   4.____

5. A worker who feels that an agency's resources are not adequate to help a particular child is at risk for performing the unproductive behavior known as

   A. Defensive avoidance
   B. Unconflicted inertia
   C. Hypervigilance
   D. Unconflicted change

   5.____

6. Which of the following items of information is most relevant to a domestic hearing?

    A. Treatment plan for all members of household
    B. Statement of child
    C. Why safety of the child can't be insured in the home
    D. Comparison of parents

7. Among the general population, regardless of other factors, the chances that a person will exhibit abusive behavior is about _____%.

    A. 0-1
    B. 1-10
    C. 5-15
    D. 10-25

8. For an 8-year-old child who is sexually abused, the most likely presentation would be

    A. stranger anxiety
    B. baby talk
    C. a significant change in attitude or grades
    D. separation anxiety

9. A CPS worker may avoid the placement of a child by making use of certain emergency services. Which of the following is generally not available in such situations?

    A. Emergency shelters for families about to be separated as a result of evictions, condemned housing, etc.
    B. Emergency homemakers available 24 hours a day both to maintain children at home and to teach parents
    C. Outreach and follow-through with immediate casework assistance in the crisis and follow-through beyond the crisis stage
    D. Emergency short-term employment for out-of-work parents, accompanied by qualified day-care services

10. If parents are assigned to parenting classes in cases of neglect, it should be expected that those who benefit from the classes will benefit after remaining with a group for at least

    A. 3 months
    B. 6 months
    C. 1 year
    D. 2 years

11. The use of objective risk-assessment instruments in the investigation of reports has proven difficult for each of the following reasons, except

    A. the assignment of weights to scale factors based solely on professional judgement
    B. the difficulty in making scales sensitive enough to identify all true cases of abuse or neglect
    C. overbroad or vague classifications of situations and behaviors
    D. the fact that incidence of abuse and neglect in the general population is not a very frequent occurrence

12. When launching an investigation of an initial report, a worker usually focuses first on the   12.____

    A. parental characteristics
    B. characteristics of the child or children subjects of the report
    C. incident and presenting problem
    D. physical environment in which the child lives

13. The purposes of a civil child abuse proceeding include   13.____

    I. Punishment
    II. Treatment
    III. Protection
    IV. Deterrence

    A. I and IV
    B. II and III
    C. III and IV
    D. I, II, III and IV

14. What is the approximate risk that a sibling of a physically abused child has also been abused at the same time?   14.____

    A. 20%
    B. 40%
    C. 60%
    D. 80%

15. If a worker decides to use a rating scale to determine the risk to a child, which of the following factors would be LEAST likely to be included in the scale?   15.____

    A. Age of parents
    B. Age of the child
    C. Parental attitude
    D. Health of the child

16. Which of the following cases would typically require the most time for review by a CPS board or staff?   16.____

    A. Aggressive behavior by a school-age child
    B. Re-abuse or failure
    C. Developmental delays in a 3-year-old
    D. Temporary abandonment of an 8-year-old

17. Probably the most pervasive and long-term consequence of sexual abuse for a child is   17.____

    A. phobic behaviors
    B. a poor self-image
    C. over-assertiveness
    D. nightmares

18. A home visit to a client's house reveals an environment that is less than ideal, but there isn't enough evidence to support a finding of abuse or neglect. Which of the following are options for the case worker?   18.____

    I. Closing the file with no referrals
    II. Referring the family to voluntary protective services
    III. Emergency placement
    IV. Solicitation of the police to conduct surveillance for evidentiary purposes

A. I and II
B. II only
C. II or III
D. I, II, III and IV

19. In general, parental alcohol and/or drug abuse is present in about_____% of all cases of child neglect.

    A. 20-30
    B. 40-60
    C. 70-80
    D. 90-100

20. In a dependency and neglect proceeding,

    A. the purpose is to rehabilitate the offending parent or custodian
    B. the burden of proof is a preponderance of evidence
    C. the issue is whether a specific individual injured the child at a specific time
    D. the maximum penalty may involve imprisonment

21. During an interactional assessment of a parent and children, the questioner should

    A. adopt a formal style
    B. focus on issues rather than specific inquiries
    C. only question the parent after the children have been removed
    D. use closed-ended questions

Questions 22 and 23 and refer to the information below.

A 12-year-old girl reports that her stepfather has fondled her. A physical examination revealed no evidence, and the father denied any misconduct. In an interview with the CPS worker, the girl repeated her account of what happened. The mother is unsure whom to believe. She reports that the girl has been having trouble in school lately, and that she suspects the girl might be using drugs. The whole family has been under strain because of a recent move. The mother and stepfather both work full time, and interviews with co-workers reveal no evidence of family trouble.

22. Each of the following items of information is needed to make a decision about the risk to the girl, except

    A. the girl's account of family interaction and the stepfather's ongoing behavior
    B. concrete proof (urinalysis or blood test) confirming or disproving drug use by the girl
    C. previous reports on stepfather from last state of residence
    D. the mother's attitudes toward her daughter, the stepfather, and the reported incident

23. In order to accurately assess this situation, a worker must have knowledge about each of the following, except

    A. demographics which are predictive of sexual abuse
    B. child development
    C. family dynamics in sexual abuse
    D. risk factors for sexual abuse

24. Which of the following is LEAST likely to be included in the behavioral profile of an abused or neglected child?

    A. Anxiety
    B. Withdrawal
    C. Extreme aggression
    D. Arrogance

25. In general, criminal filing in cases of child abuse should be strongly considered as a way of enforcing treatment when the offender is

    A. a sibling
    B. an unrelated adult such as a teacher or boyfriend
    C. a single parent
    D. mentally or emotionally impaired

KEY (CORRECT ANSWERS)

1. B	11. C
2. A	12. B
3. A	13. B
4. D	14. A
5. A	15. A
6. D	16. B
7. B	17. B
8. C	18. A
9. D	19. C
10. D	20. B

21. B
22. B
23. A
24. D
25. B

EXAMINATION SECTION
TEST 1

DIRECTIONS: Each question or incomplete statement is followed by several suggested answers or completions. Select the one that BEST answers the question or completes the statement. *PRINT THE LETTER OF THE CORRECT ANSWER IN THE SPACE AT THE RIGHT.*

1. Of the following clinical situations, which is MOST suspicious of child abuse on the basis of physical signs and patient history? 1.____

    A. A 6-month old with many facial scratches that go in different directions.
    B. A year-old Native American child with a livid, irregularly shaped spot on her lower back. The parents say the mark has been there since birth.
    C. A 2-month old who is constantly crying and passing gas. Her mother says the baby will not nurse.
    D. A 4-month old infant with several bruises on his back. The child's mother says he is always crying.

2. In terms of child abuse, "tertiary prevention" is 2.____
    I. targeted to families that have confirmed or unconfirmed reports of child abuse and neglect
    II. is considered to be the same as treatment by most prevention advocates
    III. targeted to the community at large
    IV. targeted to families that have one or more risk factors

    A. I and II
    B. II only
    C. III only
    D. I, II, III or IV

3. A nurse is taking a history for a child with pediatric growth failure and malnutrition. For the purpose of evaluating whether child neglect ought to be suspected, the most important part of the history will be the 3.____

    A. environmental and psychosocial history
    B. medical-based history
    C. growth and developmental progress
    D. feeding and nutritional history

4. The health care evaluation of suspected child physical or sexual abuse includes each of the following, EXCEPT a 4.____

    A. physical examination
    B. laboratory assessment
    C. history
    D. forensic interview

5. Among children who are younger than 1 year of age, about _____ percent of fractures are likely to have been inflicted by someone else. 5.____

    A. 10   B. 25   C. 50   D. 75

33

6. The minimum circumstance required to invoke the mandatory reporting requirements of the Child Abuse Prevention and Treatment Act (CAPTA) as reauthorized by the Keeping Children and Families Safe Act of 2003, is

   A. reasonable cause to suspect abuse
   B. suspicion of abuse that is shared by at least one other mandatory reporter
   C. clear and convincing evidence
   D. a preponderance of evidence

7. The "Primary Target Zone" for child abuse on a child's body includes the
   I. thighs
   II. cheeks
   III. backside of the hands
   IV. shoulders

   A. I only
   B. I and III
   C. I, II and IV
   D. I, II, III and IV

8. When burns are inflicted on a child, the most commonly used burn agent is

   A. a cigarette
   B. household chemicals
   C. hot water
   D. a lighter or match

9. The American Academy of Pediatrics (AAP) views _____ as "suggestive," rather than "diagnostic," of child abuse.

   A. gonorrhea
   B. HIV
   C. T. vaginalis
   D. syphilis

10. Parental behaviors that would be classified as emotional abuse include
    I. leaving a kindergartner alone in the home
    II. burning a child as a form of punishment
    III. locking a child in a bathroom for several hours as a form of punishment
    IV. grounding a child for several months as punishment for a relatively minor offens

    A. I only
    B. I or II
    C. II or III
    D. II, III or IV

11. In most states, a mandated reporter of child abuse is subject to civil liability
    I. if it can be proven that he or she did not act in good faith
    II. if the suspicion turns out to be unfounded
    III. if the parent or caretaker is penalized
    IV. under no circumstances

    A. I only   B. I or II   C. I, II or IV   D. IV only

12. Of the following types of burns, the one LEAST likely to be regarded suspicious for an inflicted injury is a burn

    A. on the child's back
    B. that is in a small-area and penetrates deeply
    C. that covers the complete circumference of the hand and extends to the wrist (a "glove" burn)
    D. on the fingertip or palm of the dominant hand

13. An infant who has suffered a head injury may present with nonspecific symptoms such as
    I. hyperactivity
    II. irritability
    III. persistent, unexplained vomiting
    IV. apnea

    A. I and II   B. II only   C. II, III and IV   D. I, II, III and IV

14. Failure to thrive is a condition that is more likely to be correlated with each of the following, EXCEPT

    A. female children
    B. child neglect
    C. interactional failures or dysfunctions between the child and caretaker
    D. poverty

15. Of the following, the _____ of a parent or caretaker is the factor that is MOST likely to be correlated with the occurrence of child maltreatment.

    A. sexual orientation   B. national origin
    C. annual income   D. religion

16. Children who are suspected of being sexually abused may need an examination emergently, urgently, or electively scheduled for a later time with their own physician. Indications for an urgent examination include each of the following, EXCEPT

    A. the possibility of STD
    B. pregnancy, if the child is pubertal
    C. severe psychological shock
    D. vaginal discharge

17. The Child Abuse Prevention and Treatment Act (CAPTA), as reauthorized by the Keeping Children and Families Safe Act of 2003, provides a specific definition for
    I. sexual abuse
    II. physical abuse
    III. neglect
    IV. emotional abuse

    A. I only
    B. I and II
    C. I, II and III
    D. I, II, III and IV

18. Characteristics common to Munchausen-by-proxy syndrome (MBPS) include each of the following, EXCEPT that the

    A. victim is an infant or toddler
    B. perpetrator is the father
    C. perpetrator has a history of symptoms and signs similar to those being simulated or produced in the child
    D. case occurs in outpatient, rather than inpatient setting

19. A health care professional is attempting to closely observe the hymen and labia minora of a young girl. This can generally be done by applying gentle _____ traction to the labia majora.

    A. medial
    B. lateral
    C. anterior
    D. posterior

20. The Childhelp National Child Abuse Hotline (1-800-4-A-CHILD) may be useful for
    I. mandatory reporters who seek a single place to report suspected child abuse, without having to worry about state guidelines
    II. mandatory reporters who want advice about how to proceed with a report
    III. parents who seek crisis intervention
    IV. any professional who wants a referral for a child

    A. I or II
    B. II only
    C. III or IV
    D. I, II, III or IV

21. It was estimated in the early 21st century that child sexual abuse affects at least _____ children every year.

    A. 5,000   B. 10,000   C. 100,000   D. 1 million

22. Of the following, the child at greatest risk for becoming a victim of child abuse would be one who

    A. is physically, emotionally, or mentally disabled
    B. remains silent when interacting with authority figures
    C. has a habit of talking back to authority figures
    D. is shy and introverted to begin with

23. Most-but certainly not all-children who are victims of abuse

    A. refuse to talk about the situation with other adults
    B. are younger than three years of age
    C. exhibit no signs or symptoms
    D. have been abused by someone they know and trust

24. Looking at children 5 years after presentation for sexual abuse and comparing them to a similarly aged group of children who were not abused, one study found that the children who were sexually abused displayed
    I. increased tendency for depression
    II. lower self-esteem
    III. more disturbed behavior
    IV. increased tendency for anxiety disorder

    A. I only
    B. I and II
    C. I, II and IV
    D. I, II, III and IV

25. Which of the following is NOT a characteristic that is typically associated with the phenomenon known as child sexual abuse accommodation syndrome?

    A. Helplessness
    B. Delay or retraction of disclosure
    C. Secrecy
    D. Regressive behavior

KEY (CORRECT ANSWERS)

1. D
2. A
3. A
4. D
5. D

6. A
7. C
8. C
9. C
10. C

11. A
12. D
13. C
14. A
15. C

16. C
17. A
18. B
19. B
20. C

21. C
22. A
23. D
24. D
25. D

TEST 2

DIRECTIONS: Each question or incomplete statement is followed by several suggested answers or completions. Select the one that BEST answers the question or completes the statement. *PRINT THE LETTER OF THE CORRECT ANSWER IN THE SPACE AT THE RIGHT.*

1. Of the following early interventional strategies, which can improve the outcome in a case of non-organic or psychosocial failure to thrive?
    I. Support groups for new mothers
    II. Education about how to recognize an infant's behavioral cues
    III. Counseling for parents who say they wanted a child of another gender
    IV. Breast-feeding/nutrition education

    A. I only
    B. I and II
    C. III only
    D. I, II, III and IV

2. While taking a medical history, a nurse may become alerted to possible warning signs regarding sexual abuse in the child's home environment. Of the following, the LEAST suspicious would be parents who

    A. know little about the child's health or have vague recollections of past medical history
    B. share intimate feelings and emotions in front of their children
    C. appear overly concerned with custody issues
    D. bicker or quarrel openly in front of the nurse

3. It would be considered "reasonable cause to suspect" abuse or maltreatment if a nurse

    A. feels it is possible that an injury was caused by neglect or nonaccidental means
    B. was told when reporting to the intake that the child's injury was most likely a case of abuse
    C. sees a case of recurrent fractures in a child
    D. has seen the child in the emergency department on several occasions

4. Physically abused children often have peer relationships characterized by

    A. withdrawal and shyness
    B. over-optimism
    C. anger and aggression
    D. over-dependence and "clinginess"

5. The risk that the sibling of a physically abused child will suffer abuse at the same time is about _____ percent.

    A. 20
    B. 40
    C. 60
    D. 80

6. When a child who is a suspected victim of physical or sexual abuse is transitioning from the intake history to the physical examination, the health care professional should
    I. if a colposcope is used, describe it as a special camera that will not touch the child
    II. assure the child that needles will not be used
    III. leave the room to allow the caretaker to help the child disrobe and put on a gown for the exam
    IV. use a genital swab gently before the child is aware that one will be used

    A. I and III
    B. II, III and IV
    C. III and IV
    D. I, II, III and IV

7. A child who is being sexually abused is more likely than others to
    I. act out sexually explicit acts in play or depict sexual content in artwork
    II. express that they have secrets they are unable to tell
    III. touch themselves in private parts more than normal
    IV. use sexual words in appropriate to his or her age

    A. I and II
    B. I and IV
    C. II and III
    D. I, II, III and IV

8. Guidelines to be considered in determining whether to hospitalize an abused child include:
    I. It is not medically appropriate to hospitalize a child simply for the reason of guaranteeing his or her safety.
    II. Most seriously injured children are best monitored in an intensive care setting.
    III. Hospitalization may offer time to sort out difficult diagnostic and therapeutic decisions.
    IV. The sole determining factor for hospitalization should be the seriousness of the child's injuries.

    A. I and II
    B. I, II and IV
    C. II and III
    D. I, II, III and IV

9. The Muram diagnostic categorization system offers insight into how a variety of prepubertal genital examinations may assist in the diagnosis of child sexual abuse. In the Muram system, a finding of semen in the child's vagina would be classified as a Category _____ finding.

    A. I
    B. II
    C. III
    D. IV

10. Child victims of Munchausen-by-proxy syndrome (MBPS) are usually

   A. of higher socioeconomic status
   B. from an ethnic minority
   C. boys
   D. about 3 years of age

11. Which of the following is true in most states?

   A. Child abuse cannot be reported anonymously.
   B. In nearly all cases, a person who reports child abuse cannot be sued.
   C. By law, abused children must be removed from their homes immediately.
   D. The person reported for abuse is entitled to know who made the report.

12. Common presentations for the abused, head-injured child include each of the following, EXCEPT

   A. lethargy
   B. bradycardia
   C. irritability
   D. aphasia

13. Historical characteristics of abusive injuries include
   I. a significant an inexplicable delay in seeking treatment
   II. unexplained or vaguely explained injuries
   III. changing history
   IV. injuries incompatible with the stated history

   A. I only
   B. I, II and IV
   C. III and IV
   D. I, II, III and IV

14. For an 11-year-old child who is sexually abused, the most likely sign would be

   A. chest pains
   B. a fear of falling asleep
   C. an eating disorder
   D. regressive behaviors

15. The bruising pattern most frequently observed in cases of child abuse includes
   I. injuries on multiple edges of a child's body
   II. injuries confined to bony prominences
   III. multiple resolving injuries (i.e., those that occurred at different times and in different areas of the body)

   A. I only
   B. I and II
   C. I and III
   D. I, II and III

16. During the intake, the key to differentiating between accidental and nonaccidental injury lies primarily in the

    A. evidence of previous injuries
    B. appearance of bruises in unusual areas
    C. history and physical examination
    D. type of fracture

17. Health care providers are mandated reporters in all 50 states. The American Academy of Pediatrics recommends reporting a case of suspected sexual abuse when
    I. the child presents with an STD
    II. the child shows more than one of the behavioral indicators of sexual abuse
    III. the child makes a clear disclosure of abusive sexual contact, with or without specific physical findings
    IV. physical examination findings are believed to be the result of abusive sexual contact

    A. I, II and III
    B. I, III and IV
    C. III and IV
    D. I, II, III and IV

18. One behavioral indicator of child abuse is a child that

    A. tends to avoid contact with adults
    B. exhibits an unusual fear of going to school
    C. exhibits unpredictable mood swings or extreme behaviors
    D. is overly critical of parents or caretakers

19. In addition to the genital area, an examination of a girl for whom sexual abuse is suspected should include the
    I. conjunctiva
    II. oral pharynx
    III. extremities

    A. I and II
    B. II and III
    C. III only
    D. I, II and III

20. Ideally, the multidisciplinary team that handles the health care evaluation of suspected child physical or sexual abuse includes each of the following, EXCEPT a

    A. law enforcement officer
    B. physician
    C. social worker
    D. nurse

21. Among children who are younger than 1 year of age, about _____ percent of all serious intracranial injuries are caused by physical abuse.

    A. 35   B. 55   C. 75   D. 95

22. Demographic statistics suggest that incidents of child abuse and neglect

    A. occur mostly in urban areas
    B. occur mostly in rural areas
    C. occur mostly in ethnic inner-city areas
    D. are distributed among all areas and socioeconomic groups

23. Many of the acute signs of sexual abuse are likely to resemble a child's reaction to

    A. stress
    B. infection
    C. fatigue
    D. grief/mourning

24. As part of a history for an infant with pediatric growth failure and malnutrition, a nurse is conducting a detailed history of food intake from infancy through the current period. This part of the history should include
    I. a first-hand observation of the mother and infant during feeding
    II. the parents' or caretakers' perception of the problem
    III. a 72-hour diet diary
    IV. opinions from other family members about what might be the problem

    A. I only
    B. I, II and III
    C. II only
    D. I, II, III and IV

25. The term "emotional abuse"
    I. is not included in every state's definition of child abuse
    II. refers to the act of one person (a caretaker or parent) using his or her power or influence to adversely affect the mental well-being of a child
    III. may include rejection, corruption, and degradation
    IV. generally refers to a long-term situation

    A. I and II
    B. II and III
    C. II, III and IV
    D. I, II, III and IV

KEY (CORRECT ANSWERS)

1.	D	11.	B
2.	D	12.	D
3.	A	13.	D
4.	C	14.	B
5.	A	15.	C
6.	A	16.	C
7.	D	17.	B
8.	C	18.	C
9.	D	19.	B
10.	D	20.	A

21. D
22. D
23. A
24. B
25. D

TEST 3

DIRECTIONS: Each question or incomplete statement is followed by several suggested answers or completions. Select the one that BEST answers the question or completes the statement. *PRINT THE LETTER OF THE CORRECT ANSWER IN THE SPACE AT THE RIGHT.*

1. Which of the following is viewed by the American Academy of Pediatrics to be "diagnostic," rather than "suggestive," of child abuse?   1.____

    A. T. vaginalis
    B. Herpes
    C. Condyloma acuminata
    D. Chlamydia

2. If a nurse mistrusts or doubts what he or she has observed or has been told about an injury, the nurse has   2.____

    A. reasonable cause to suspect abuse
    B. suspicion of abuse
    C. testimonial evidence of abuse
    D. documentary evidence of abuse

3. Most normal childhood injuries occur on the _____ and, by themselves, are probably not indicators of child abuse.   3.____

    A. the backs of the arms
    B. front of the body
    C. wrist and upper arm
    D. back of the body

4. Rapid laboratory tests, such as the rapid plasma reagin test, are generally not appropriate in the diagnosis of child sexual abuse because of their   4.____

    A. requirement of caretaker consent
    B. higher potential for false positives
    C. higher potential for causing infection
    D. inherent invasiveness

5. An accidental fall is LEAST likely to cause a bruise on the   5.____

    A. cheekbone
    B. elbow
    C. soft tissue of the cheek
    D. forehead

6. The best way for health professionals to improve the outcomes in child abuse cases is to   6.____

    A. focus their diagnostic efforts on lower socioeconomic groups, in which most child abuse cases occur
    B. recognize abusers as criminals from the beginning of the process, and view the problem as a law enforcement issue
    C. participate in education and training programs that will help them to recognize child abuse
    D. work with social service professionals to do everything possible to remove an abused child from the custody of the abuser

7. According to the American Psychiatric Association's Diagnostic and Statistical Manual of Mental Disorders (DSM-IV), the most common conditions and symptoms that are created or faked by parents or caretakers with Munchausen-by-proxy syndrome (MBPS) include

    I. diarrhea
    II. failure to thrive
    III. infections
    IV. asthma

    A. I and II
    B. I, II and III
    C. III and IV
    D. I, II, III and IV

8. Of the following, which should most clearly raise a nurse's suspicions about the possibility of child physical abuse?

    A. Inconsistent explanations about the sustained injuries
    B. Parents who are overindulgent and act as if the child can do no wrong
    C. A child who is irritable and frequently complains
    D. A child with skin abrasions all over her forearms, knees and elbows

9. As of 2007, physical discipline is permitted in all states, provided that it is reasonable and not excessive. The standard for reasonableness is largely dependent on the

    A. child's age
    B. seriousness of the child's injury
    C. child's size
    D. culture in which the parent or caretaker was raised

10. Indicators of child emotional abuse typically include each of the following, EXCEPT

    A. fastidiousness about appearance
    B. severe anxiety
    C. avoidance of eye contact
    D. extreme dependence

11. Symptoms of abdominal trauma secondary to perforation, obstruction, or bleeding include

    I. sepsis
    II. vomiting
    III. pain
    IV. shock

    A. I and II
    B. I, III and IV
    C. II and III
    D. I, II, III and IV

12. Which of the following environmental variables generally constitutes the highest risk potential for child maltreatment?

    A. A child who is between 5 and 9 years of age
    B. A denial of water or electricity services to the home
    C. The family does not belong to a church or social group
    D. Recent changes in parental/caregiver marriage or relationship status

13. A child's reaction to physical or sexual abuse is influenced by
    I. their cognitive ability
    II. their treatment by medical personnel
    III. their social and family support system
    IV. how Child Protective Services handles the case

    A. I and III
    B. II and III
    C. II, III and IV
    D. I, II, III and IV

14. Which of the following warning signs for emotional abuse is LEAST common?

    A. Hostility
    B. Apathy
    C. Lack of concentration
    D. Depression

15. When a health care professional suspects child sexual abuse, the medical history should include questions regarding possible behavioral indicators of abuse. These typically include
    I. self-destructive behaviors such as drug abuse
    II. sexualized behavior inappropriate for the child's developmental level
    III. any abrupt behavioral changes
    IV. unreasonably high self-esteem

    A. I or II
    B. I, II and III
    C. II and IV
    D. I, II, III and IV3

16. Multiple bruises at various stages of healing can be associated with repetitive inflicted injuries in children, but are also symptomatic of

    A. achondroplasia
    B. melanoma
    C. eczema
    D. coagulopathy

17. Which of the following statements regarding environmental risk factors for abuse is TRUE?

    A. Children of single parents are at greater risk of abuse
    B. The risk for abuse is not affected by yearly household income
    C. Children from urban areas are at a greater risk of abuse
    D. Child abuse is most common among African American families

18. Children from _____ families are at significantly greater risk for both physical abuse and neglect.

    I. poor
    II. single-parent
    III. large
    IV. racially mixed

    A. I and II
    B. I, II and III
    C. II, III and IV
    D. I, II, III and IV

19. Fractures that are "highly specific" for inflicted injury include each of the following, EXCEPT _____ fractures.

    A. posterior rib
    B. metaphyseal or "bucket handle"
    C. scapular
    D. ulnar

20. Children who allegedly have been exposed to HIV-positive perpetrators must begin HIV postexposure prophylaxis within _____ of exposure.

    A. 12 hours
    B. 36 hours
    C. 7-10 days
    D. 15-30 days

21. If called to court in a case of alleged child abuse, a nurse should generally adhere to each of the following guidelines, EXCEPT

    A. Be sure to check with the CPS caseworker or attorney to see if there will be a briefing before the court appearance
    B. Offer as many opinions as the court and the defense attorney will allow on the record.
    C. Speak slowly and offer concise answers.
    D. If you do not know the answer, don't guess; simply say you don't know.

22. Each of the following behaviors on the part of parents or caretakers is likely to be viewed suspiciously as suggestive of child abuse or molestation, EXCEPT

    A. insistence on personally driving/escorting the child to and from school
    B. constant attempts to be alone with the child
    C. the persistent habit of buying gifts for the child, for no apparent reason
    D. a pattern of wanting or attempting to take the child places

23. When a nurse makes a report to Child Protective Services, it is most important for the nurse to remember that in his role as a mandatory reporter,

    A. he has likely made the decision to bring criminal charges upon the child's caretaker
    B. the burden of proof is on him
    C. CPS has total responsibility for investigating and proving whether child maltreatment has occurred
    D. his name may be made available to the people he suspects of maltreatment

24. If child sexual abuse is suspected, general guidelines for the taking of the child's history include 24._____
    I. formulating the interview in a way that allows the child to view it as a healing process in which they are able to gain some control over the situation
    II. encouraging the child to use the medical term for all body parts, in order to make the details seem more clinical and less personal
    III. relying on non-leading questions as much as possible
    IV. asking direct questions and completing the interview in as brief a time as possible

    A. I only
    B. I and III
    C. I, II and III
    D. I, II, III and IV

25. In most states, mandatory reporters who failed to report child maltreatment 25._____
    I. can be found guilty of a misdemeanor
    II. can be found guilty of a felony
    III. can be held liable for civil damages for any subsequent injury to the child

    A. I and III
    B. II and III
    C. III only
    D. I, II and III

KEY (CORRECT ANSWERS)

1. D	11. D
2. B	12. D
3. B	13. D
4. B	14. A
5. C	15. B
6. C	16. D
7. D	17. A
8. A	18. B
9. B	19. D
10. A	20. B

21. B
22. A
23. C
24. B
25. A

EXAMINATION SECTION
TEST 1

DIRECTIONS: Each question or incomplete statement is followed by several suggested answers or completions. Select the one that BEST answers the question or completes the statement. *PRINT THE LETTER OF THE CORRECT ANSWER IN THE SPACE AT THE RIGHT.*

1. According to the United States Centers for Disease Control and Prevention (CDC), the neglect of children is generally about _____ as common as physical abuse and _____ as common as sexual abuse.

    A. one-fourth; half
    B. twice; twice
    C. three times; six times
    D. ten times; twenty times

    1.____

2. Which of the following is LEAST likely to be observed in a child with post-traumatic stress disorder?

    A. Increased physical arousal
    B. Diminished interest in home and school environments
    C. Aggression
    D. Exaggerated startle response

    2.____

3. The most common weapons in physical child abuse cases are

    A. belts or cords
    B. paddles, spoons, or similar implements
    C. knives or other cutting instruments
    D. hands and fists

    3.____

4. Informing a caretaker or family members that Child Protective Services has been notified in a case of suspected child maltreatment is

    A. required by law in all cases of child maltreatment
    B. required by law only in cases in which the caretakers or family members are implicated
    C. not usually required by law, but it recommended in all cases of child maltreatment
    D. not usually required by law and is not recommended

    4.____

5. Of the following, children are most likely to be abused or neglected by

    A. day care staff
    B. their natural parents
    C. a mother's boyfriend
    D. foster parents

    5.____

6. Key characteristics of Munchausen-by-proxy syndrome (MBPS) include
    I. involves the presentation of a child for frequent medical care and evaluation
    II. a need for the parent or caretaker to assume the "patient" role through the child

    6.____

III. a child illness that is intentionally induced, simulated, or exagerated
IV. short-term symptoms that stop when the caretaker isn't around

    A. I and II
    B. II and III
    C. II and IV
    D. I, II, III and IV

7. In cases of child sexual abuse, the collection of forensic evidence via rape kit may be indicated if the child presents within _____ hours of the last sexual contact with the perpetrator, and if a belief exists that the perpetrator may have left evidence on the child's body.

    A. 24
    B. 48
    C. 72
    D. 96

8. Children who are neglected tend to have peer relationships marked by

    A. dependence and "clinginess"
    B. overinvestment in relationships
    C. avoidance and withdrawal
    D. anger and aggression

9. The average age of a child sexual abuser in the incident of a first attack is

    A. in their teens
    B. in their early 20s
    C. between 25 and 45
    D. between 46 and 65

10. Dissociation is a psychological defense mechanism that serves as an adaptive mechanism in abusive situations. However, if left unchecked, it may develop into

    A. borderline personality disorder
    B. schizophrenia
    C. bipolar disorder
    D. post-traumatic stress disorder

11. During a physical examination, a child spontaneously discloses that she was abused. Ideally, the medical record should clearly document
    I. the exact words spoken by the child, recorded in quotation marks
    II. what question or activity prompted the disclosure
    III. who was present when the child disclosed the information
    IV. any prior suspicions held by the health care professional about the possibility of abuse

    A. I only
    B. I and III
    C. I, II and III
    D. I, II, III and IV

12. Of the following, which environmental or historical factor tends to involve the LOWEST risk for child abuse?

    A. Foster care
    B. Ethnic minority status
    C. Developmental disabilities
    D. Premature infant

13. The differential diagnosis for child sexual abuse involves 4 key physical findings. Which of the following is NOT one of these findings?

    A. Vaginal discharge
    B. Genital bleeding
    C. Anogenital redness
    D. Abdominal bruising

14. Of the following types of burns, the one MOST likely to be regarded suspicious for an inflicted injury is a burn

    A. caused by chemicals
    B. on the back of the hand
    C. that covers the entire foot and stops at a distinct line above the ankle (a "stocking" burn)
    D. with an irregular, splattered pattern

15. Many states and localities have established a priority system for responding to initial reports of abuse or neglect. Of the following, the child most likely receive a "Priority Two" designation by CPS, as dangerous and perhaps requiring emergency services would be one

    A. who has been sexually abused and is in danger of being abused again.
    B. with internal injuries
    C. with a sprain or dislocation
    D. who is malnourished or failing to thrive

16. When a child tells an adult that they have been abused or molested, the most appropriate first response is to

    A. clearly register your disapproval of the abuser's behavior
    B. press the child to reveal as many specifics as possible in order to gather evidence
    C. let the child know that you believe and trust them
    D. approach it matter-of-factly, as if it is no great crisis

17. Because child abuse and neglect frequently occur in concert with other forms of family violence, reportable incidents to Child Protective Services typically include violence
    I. by the father against the mother
    II. between two or more siblings other than the reporting child
    III. by the mother against the father
    IV. by one sibling against the reporting child

    A. I only
    B. I and III
    C. I, II, III and IV
    D. None of the above

18. The Muram diagnostic categorization system offers insight into how a variety of prepubertal genital examinations may assist in the diagnosis of child sexual abuse. In the Muram system, "Category I" refers to

    A. strongly suggestive findings that have a high likelihood of being caused by sexual abuse
    B. nonspecific findings that are minimally suggestive of sexual abuse but also may be caused by other etiologies
    C. genitalia with no observable abnormalities
    D. definitive findings that have no possible cause other then sexual contact

19. The clinical definition of "failure to thrive" refers to a child's failure to

    A. fit in socially with peers
    B. achieve important milestones for mental and social development
    C. respond to normal nurturing behaviors
    D. gain weight

20. Which of the following types of head injuries in a child is most likely to be the result of a fall, rather than an inflicted injury?

    A. Subdural hematoma
    B. Skull fracture
    C. Epidural hematoma
    D. Subarachnoid hemorrhage

21. In which of the following situations would a nurse NOT be mandated to file a report of suspected abuse?

    A. Hearing a parent or caretaker state from personal knowledge that the child has been abused
    B. As supervisor, being notified by a staff member who suspects abuse and ultimately agreeing with the suspicion
    C. Seeing the same patient in the emergency room several times in a span of several weeks
    D. Having reasonable cause to suspect that a child is abused

22. When communicating with a suspected child victim, it is important for the health care professional to remember that

    I. "old" and "young" classifications are not recommended in conversations with child victims
    II. children usually don't care about the impression they make on adults
    III. young children tend to repeat the end of a prior sentence if they are unsure of an answer
    IV. the use of pronouns is often confusing to children

    A. I only
    B. I, III, and IV
    C. II and III
    D. All of the above

23. Preparation of the child and family should be a part of every examination for sexual abuse, and the discussion may generally include each of the following, EXCEPT 23.____

   A. the health care professional's opinion about the likely cause of such injuries
   B. the fact that almost all prepubertal children do not need a speculum or internal examination
   C. the need for photographs for legal documentation
   D. an explanation of why an external examination of the genitalia is necessary

24. Which of the following is LEAST likely to be a behavioral presentment of a child who suffers from abuse or neglect? 24.____

   A. Generalized anxiety
   B. Extreme aggression
   C. Withdrawal and timidity
   D. Intellectual precociousness or arrogance

25. When determining whether a child is suspicious for maltreatment, it is important to consider 25.____

   I. evidence of other past injuries
   II. the child's developmental level
   III. the parent's or caretaker's explanation
   IV. the nature of the injury

   A. I and III
   B. I and IV
   C. I, III and IV
   D. I, II, III and IV

KEY (CORRECT ANSWERS)

1.	C	11.	C
2.	C	12.	B
3.	D	13.	D
4.	C	14.	C
5.	B	15.	C
6.	D	16.	C
7.	C	17.	C
8.	C	18.	C
9.	A	19.	D
10.	A	20.	C

21. C
22. B
23. A
24. D
25. D

TEST 2

DIRECTIONS: Each question or incomplete statement is followed by several suggested answers or completions. Select the one that BEST answers the question or completes the statement. *PRINT THE LETTER OF THE CORRECT ANSWER IN THE SPACE AT THE RIGHT.*

1. The most frequent result of child maltreatment in the victim is　　　　1.___

   A. low self-esteem
   B. phobias
   C. post-traumatic stress disorder
   D. attention deficit disorder

2. Shaken-baby syndrome may typically present with several symptoms. Which of the following is LEAST likely to be one of these symptoms?　　　　2.___

   A. Retinal hemorrhage
   B. Fractures of posterior or anterolateral ribs
   C. Diffuse axonal injury
   D. Oral lacerations

3. Boys are more likely to be sexually abused by:　　　　3.___

   A. siblings
   B. their mothers
   C. their fathers
   D. male non-family members

4. Of the following behaviors, which is most likely to be an indicator of possible child neglect?　　　　4.___

   A. Obsessive behaviors
   B. Offering food from home to friends at school
   C. Enjoying school more than other classmates
   D. Wearing clothing inappropriate for existing weather conditions

5. Which of the following is LEAST likely to be a medical sequela of child sexual abuse?　　　　5.___

   A. neurologic conditions
   B. cardiovascular disorders
   C. functional gastrointestinal disorders
   D. STDs

6. Bruising or other skin manifestations of child abuse　　　　6.___
   I. are always very conspicuous and strongly suggest physical abuse
   II. often are clearly hand-shaped in cases of spanking or swatting
   III. should be investigated if they leave marks that are unusual or have the shape of a specific object
   IV. should be considered suspicious if they are vertical marks that appear on the child's back

   A. I and II
   B. II, III and IV

C. II and IV
D. I, II, III and IV

7. During a physical examination, a 5-year-old child makes a statement that strongly suggests he was sexually abused. As the health care professional, you are taught in such situations to ask questions that are focused but not leading. The best example of this type of question is

   A. Did he touch you with his fingers?
   B. Did he really touch you?
   C. Did his touching make you uncomfortable?
   D. What did he touch you with?

7.____

8. Child Protective Services is usually compelled to take a case to court when

   A. the mandated reporter believes that the parent or caretaker poses an immediate threat to the child
   B. a parent or caretaker is older than 21 years of age
   C. parents or caretakers refuse services or are uncooperative
   D. the abuse is a repeat occurrence

8.____

9. Which of the following statements about child abuse is TRUE?

   A. Boys are slightly more likely to be sexually abused than girls.
   B. Girls are more likely to be abused by women within the family.
   C. Boys are more likely to be killed or seriously injured as a result of abuse.
   D. Boys are more likely to be physically abused by males outside the family.

9.____

10. Apathy-futility syndrome is a disorder that is
    I. seen among children who are chronically neglected
    II. often indicated by children who are very attached to their parents, but inhibited in their emotional responses
    III. often indicated by a total lack of normal separation response when separated from caretakers

    A. I and II
    B. II only
    C. I and III
    D. I, II and III

10.____

11. Physical findings in sexually abused prepubertal girls may include bleeding and lacerations of the genital area. Though most such findings are inconclusive for abuse, which of the following would most strongly suggest sexual abuse in a prepubertal girl?

    A. A healed transection of the hymen
    B. A fresh laceration of the hymen without a history of accidental trauma
    C. A fimbnated hymen
    D. A labial hymen

11.____

12. Which of the following is NOT a criterion that should be used in assessing the reliability of a child's statements regarding sexual abuse?

    A. The child's ability to answer questions consistently and in the same words
    B. The child's ability to give specific details about what happened

12.____

C. The association of the child's statements with an appropriate affect or facial expression
D. Drawings or enactments with props consistent with the child's verbal history

13. Admission laboratory tests for a child in which the health care professional suspects Munchausen-by-proxy syndrome (MBPS) should always include a(n)

    A. complete toxicology screen
    B. MRI or PET scan
    C. rape kit examination
    D. urine culture

14. In diagnosing suspected child sexual abuse, a colposcope can be used to _____ the genital area.
    I. magnify
    II. light
    III. photograph
    IV. examine the recessed portions of

    A. I and II
    B. I, II and III
    C. II and III
    D. I, II, III and IV

15. Which of the following is LEAST likely to be a characteristic of a parent or caretaker who is at risk for perpetrating child abuse?

    A. Close association with one or more abusers
    B. Poor impulse control
    C. Unmet emotional needs
    D. Isolation

16. Which of the following is included in the definition of "child sexual abuse?"
    I. Penetrative sex
    II. Fondling
    III. Sexualized kissing
    IV. Exposing oneself or masturbating in front of the child

    A. I only
    B. I and II
    C. I, II and IV
    D. I, II, III and IV

17. In most states, the legal standard for neglect applies when a parent or caretaker's failure to provide care is due to any of the following, EXCEPT

    A. antisocial personality disorder
    B. cruelty
    C. mental incapacity
    D. financial inability

18. Which of the following is LEAST likely to be the site of an inflicted bruise?

    A. Genitals
    B. Forehead
    C. Upper back
    D. Buttocks

19. Of the reported sexual assaults on children in the United States, about _____ percent are committed by perpetrators who were previously known to the victim.

    A. 30
    B. 50
    C. 70
    D. 90

20. When abuse is likely or strongly suspected by a health care professional, the medical history
    I. may be coordinated with a forensic interview by representatives from Child Protective Services and law enforcement
    II. should be confrontational
    III. should focus on questions that are clearly related to law enforcement
    IV. should allow the health care professional a chance to share an opinion with the child's caretakers about the believed etiology of the child's injury or condition

    A. I only
    B. I or II
    C. III or IV
    D. I, II, III or IV

21. According to the U.S. Department of Health and Human Services, a child from a single-parent family is about _____ likely to be abused or neglected than those from two-parent families.

    A. 87 percent more
    B. 36 percent more
    C. 55 percent less
    D. 12 percent less

22. The Muram diagnostic categorization system offers insight into how a variety of prepubertal genital examinations may assist in the diagnosis of child sexual abuse. In the Muram system, a finding of a transected hymen would be classified as a Category _____ finding.

    A. I
    B. II
    C. III
    D. IV

23. In infants and toddlers, signs of possible child neglect may include each of the following, EXCEPT

    A. poor self-discipline
    B. growth failure

- C. behavioral abnormalities
- D. delayed gross motor development

24. Of the following, a victim of child abuse is MOST likely to be   24.____

    A. needy and demanding
    B. cold and withdrawn
    C. talkative and outgoing
    D. passive and compliant

25. Typically, "child neglect" could be legally substantiated in cases in which a parent or caregiver   25.____

    I. fails to provide adequate clothing for a dependent child
    II. does not provide shelter for a child
    III. used physical punishment on a child
    IV. does not compel a child to attend school

    A. I only
    B. I, II or IV
    C. II or III
    D. I, II, III or IV

KEY (CORRECT ANSWERS)

1.	A	11.	B
2.	D	12.	A
3.	D	13.	A
4.	D	14.	B
5.	B	15.	A
6.	B	16.	D
7.	D	17.	D
8.	C	18.	B
9.	C	19.	D
10.	C	20.	A

21.	A
22.	B
23.	A
24.	A
25.	B

TEST 3

DIRECTIONS: Each question or incomplete statement is followed by several suggested answers or completions. Select the one that BEST answers the question or completes the statement. *PRINT THE LETTER OF THE CORRECT ANSWER IN THE SPACE AT THE RIGHT.*

1. Abnormal physical findings that are suspicious for sexual abuse

    A. are most often caused by something else
    B. are rare
    C. include a crescent-shaped hymen in prepubertal girls
    D. are visible in about half the cases

2. Physical warning signs of child emotional abuse include

    A. below-average weight
    B. speech disorders
    C. unexplained bruises
    D. hypersexualized play

3. The role of law enforcement in child abuse investigations is to

    A. evaluate the credibility of the reporter
    B. determine whether a crime has been committed
    C. determine placement of the child
    D. prosecute abusers

4. Which of the following is a frequent contributing factor to child abuse?

    A. History of family violence
    B. Spousal encouragement
    C. Overworked parents
    D. Academic underperformance

5. In making a report of suspected child abuse, a nurse or other health care practitioner should

    A. avoid mentioning the identity of the suspected perpetrator
    B. make his or her best guess as to the identity of the perpetrator
    C. document the suspected perpetrator, if known, for the purposes of ensuring the safety of the child
    D. document the suspected perpetrator, if known, and provide detailed information substantiating his or her suspicions

6. Children who are suspected of being sexually abused may need an examination emergently, urgently, or electively scheduled for a later time with their own physician. Emergent examinations should be conducted for a child
    I. in severe emotional or psychological crisis
    II. with a history of sexual contact within 96 hours of presentation
    III. with acute bleeding or injury
    IV. who may be pregnant

A. I and II
B. I, II, and III
C. II and III
D. I, II, III and IV

7. Of the following, which is LEAST likely to be a behavioral sign exhibited by an abused or neglected child?

    A. Self-loathing
    B. Sexual precocity
    C. Immaturity
    D. Overfamiliarity with strangers

8. Excessive bruising may be a sign of multiple inflicted injuries, or it may be a sign of an underlying medical condition. Which of the following medical conditions is LEAST likely to present with this symptom?

    A. Keratosis pilaris
    B. Thrombocytopenia
    C. Leukemia
    D. Hemophilia

9. If a child has been taken into protective custody, which of the following typically occurs?

    A. Efforts are made to inform the parent/caretaker about the child's location along with written notice.
    B. The child is taken to family court within 24 hours for disposition to a foster home
    C. The alleged abuser is taken into immediate police custody
    D. The parent or caretaker is informed that they may not visit the child under any circumstances

10. Of the following, which is LEAST likely to be a long-term consequence of emotional maltreatment of a child?

    A. Anxiety and anger
    B. Apathy/lethargy
    C. Impaired physical development
    D. Extreme violence

11. Most of the morbidity associated with sexual abuse is related to

    A. emotional and psychological trauma
    B. perforated and torn tissues
    C. sexually transmitted diseases (STDs)
    D. bruising

12. Which of the following is LEAST likely to be the reason why a child who has been sexually abused is reluctant to tell others about the incident?

    A. The child was a willing participant in the activity
    B. The child does not understand what happened.
    C. The child is afraid that the person involved will withdraw and break up the family
    D. The child is too young to be able to verbalize what happened.

13. Which of the following is LEAST characteristic of parents who maltreat their children?

    A. Mental or physical disability
    B. Lack of familiarity with developmentally appropriate expectations for children
    C. Difficulty in processing information
    D. Lack of familiarity with parenting role

14. Overall, about _____ percent of the injuries to the back of a child's body turn out to be child abuse.

    A. 10
    B. 30
    C. 50
    D. 70

15. In the anogenital examination of a child suspicious for sexual abuse, it is important for the health care professional to

    A. note the child's emotional status
    B. begin by visualizing the more recessed genital structures
    C. end with a general observation and inspection
    D. begin by noting the presence and character of pubic hair

16. Which of the following warning signs of physical abuse is LEAST common?

    A. Problems in school
    B. Unexplained burns, cuts, bruises or welts.
    C. Bite marks
    D. Fear of adults

17. Among children of all ages, approximately _____ percent of bone fractures are inflicted.

    A. 10
    B. 30
    C. 50
    D. 70

18. In the United States, many helping professionals consider the reluctance of a child to make eye contact with an adult to be a sign of possible child neglect. Any professional who interviews a child generally should be more cautious about applying this criterion to children who are of _____ cultural heritage.
    I. African American
    II. Latino
    III. Native American
    IV. Asian

    A. I and II
    B. I, II and IV
    C. II and III
    D. I, II, III and IV

19. In incidents of child sexual abuse, the most valuable component of the medical evaluation is usually the

    A. physical examination
    B. laboratory results
    C. interview with the child
    D. interview with the caretaker(s)

20. Which of the following is a disease that causes multiple fractures and whose symptoms may be mistaken for child abuse?

    A. Osteogenesis imperfecta
    B. Klippel-Feil syndrome
    C. Osteomyelitis
    D. Juvenile rheumatoid arthritis

21. Statistically, most abusers involved in Munchausen-by-proxy syndrome (MBPS) are

    A. fathers
    B. mothers
    C. caretakers outside the family
    D. step-parents

22. Acute findings attributable to recent sexual abuse may include each of the following, EXCEPT

    A. scars on genital skin and mucous membranes
    B. friability
    C. subtle erythema (inflammation)
    D. bleeding

23. Health care providers may wonder, in cases that involve custody disputes, whether an allegation of sexual abuse by one parent or caretaker against another may warrant the same degree of comprehensive evaluation. A study conducted and reported in the journal Pediatrics in 1988, it was found that in cases of custody disputes, allegations of sexual abuse were substantiated _____ percent of the time.

    A. 3
    B. 33
    C. 50
    D. 67

24. Nonaccidental hot water immersion burns typically
    I. are bilateral
    II. are symmetrical
    III. have well-demarcated lines
    IV. have splash marks or speckling patterns

    A. I and II
    B. I, II and III
    C. II and III
    D. IV only

25. A child is admitted to the emergency department after suffering a sudden trauma. 25.____
Regarding the physiological response to trauma, a child who _____ in the period soon after the trauma is more likely to develop post-traumatic stress disorder.

    A. bleeds profusely
    B. suffers digestive problems
    C. is unconscious
    D. has an elevated heart rate

KEY (CORRECT ANSWERS)

1.	B	11.	A
2.	B	12.	A
3.	B	13.	A
4.	A	14.	D
5.	C	15.	A
6.	B	16.	C
7.	D	17.	B
8.	A	18.	C
9.	A	19.	C
10.	D	20.	A

21. B
22. A
23. D
24. B
25. D

EXAMINATION SECTION
TEST 1

DIRECTIONS: Each question or incomplete statement is followed by several suggested answers or completions. Select the one that BEST answers the question or completes the statement. *PRINT THE LETTER OF THE CORRECT ANSWER IN THE SPACE AT THE RIGHT.*

1. Child risk factors for abuse and neglect include
    I. behavior problems
    II. attention deficits
    III. internal locus of control
    IV. anti-social peer group

    A. I only
    B. I, II and IV
    C. II and III
    D. I, II, III and IV

2. Bums account for about _____ percent of all cases of child physical abuse.

    A. 3-5
    B. 10-20
    C. 30-40
    D. 50-60

3. General somatic complaints that are often associated with child sexual abuse include each of the following, EXCEPT

    A. encopresis
    B. tinnitus
    C. headaches
    D. abdominal pain

4. Depending on their age at the time of maltreatment, children who are maltreated generally have

    A. a decreased ability to achieve important developmental milestones
    B. hypochondriasis
    C. a larger social network in adulthood because of the perceived need for stronger, stable relationships
    D. average IQ scores

5. Excluding environmental and adult factors, the only child characteristic that has been associated with a higher risk of sexual abuse is

    A. temperament
    B. gender
    C. conduct problems
    D. age

6. A health care professional suspects that a child's injuries were caused by abuse. During a medical history, if the health care professional offers an opinion about the etiology of the child's injuries to the caretakers, the encounter could
    I. serve as a warning to the caretakers to be more cautious in their handling of the child
    II. cause unnecessary family distress in cases where the etiology ultimately is other than abuse
    III. impede later law enforcement interrogation
    IV. expose the health care professional to civil liability if the etiology is other than abuse

    A. I only
    B. I or IV
    C. II or III
    D. I, II, III or IV

6.____

7. Several studies suggest that among U.S. children who are abused and maltreated, about ____ percent exhibit symptoms of reactive attachment disorder.

    A. 10 to 30
    B. 25 to 40
    C. 50 to 80
    D. 75 to 95

7.____

8. Which of the following is LEAST likely to be a characteristic of an abusive parent or household?

    A. A large number of children in a relatively confined space
    B. Emotional withdrawal from spouse and children
    C. Disorganized household
    D. Marital problems 3.

8.____

9. Most cases of suspected or substantiated sexual abuse of prepubertal girls have physical examination findings that are

    A. normal
    B. in the anal area
    C. in the vaginal area
    D. distributed among several locations

9.____

10. Chronic findings attributable to ongoing sexual abuse may include each of the following, EXCEPT

    A. open lacerations
    B. disrupted vascular patterns in translucent tissues
    C. remodeled hymenal tissue
    D. scarred mucous membranes

10.____

11. In cases of physical abuse, the most commonly encountered hand marks left on a child are

    A. grab marks: oval-shaped bruises resembling fingerprints
    B. pinch marks: two symmetrical crescent-shaped bruises
    C. linear marks: parallel bruises marking the edges of the fingers
    D. hand prints

11.____

12. Of the following child behaviors, which is most likely to be an indicator of possible physical abuse?

    A. Avoiding or withdrawing from physical contact
    B. Wearing lighter clothing than is appropriate for existing conditions
    C. Frequent hugging of other children
    D. Appearing anxious to return home after school

13. Of the following types of fractures, the one most strongly suggestive of physical abuse in an infant who has learned to crawl would be a

    A. spiral fracture of the femur
    B. comminuted fracture of the fingertip
    C. chip fracture of the cheekbone
    D. transverse fracture of the ulna

14. If child sexual abuse is suspected, general guidelines for the medical intake include

    I. interviewing the child first
    II. interviewing the child and the caretaker(s) together before they are interviewed separately
    III. allowing the caretaker to join the child for the physical examination
    IV. to the extent possible, documenting specific quotes the child makes about how any injuries or conditions were caused

    A. I only
    B. I, II and IV
    C. III and IV
    D. I, II, III and IV

15. The examination position most often used for boys when diagnosing sexual abuse is the

    A. left lateral decubitus
    B. prone
    C. frog-leg supine
    D. knee-chest

16. Generally, about ____ percent of child neglect cases involve parental/caretaker drug or alcohol abuse.

    A. 10-30
    B. 30-50
    C. 50-70
    D. 70-80

17. Perpetrators of Munchausen-by-proxy syndrome (MBPS) are MOST likely to have a background in

    A. law enforcement
    B. health care
    C. education
    D. child care

18. When a nonaccidental injury is caused by someone other than the child's parent or legal guardian, the health care professional should

    A. contact law enforcement, but not report to CPS
    B. contact law enforcement and report to CPS
    C. file a report to CPS, but leave law enforcement out of it
    D. leave the decision about contacting law enforcement or CPS up to the parent or legal guardian

19. Which of the following is a symptom of disinhibited reactive attachment disorder?

    A. excessive familiarity with unknown persons
    B. underdeveloped motor coordination
    C. an apparent lack of familiarity with normal body language
    D. avoidance of eye contact

20. What is the leading cause of death in abused children?

    A. Burns
    B. Blunt trauma
    C. Head trauma
    D. Blood loss

21. A child has disclosed the incidence of physical abuse to a nurse. The nurse should generally

    A. express a strongly negative opinion of the perpetrator
    B. express shock
    C. promise confidentiality
    D. reassure the child that he or she has done the right thing in reporting

22. In the year 2000, child abuse fatalities occurred at the rate of _____ in the United States.

    A. 40 per day
    B. 4 per day
    C. 5 per week
    D. 50 per month

23. According to the U.S. Department of Health and Human Services, approximately _____ percent of young adults who have been abused will meet the diagnostic criteria for at least one psychiatric disorder by the age of 21.

    A. 33
    B. 60
    C. 80
    D. 99

24. Which of the following is MOST likely to be a sign that a baby has been violently shaken?

    A. Subdural hematoma
    B. Bruising at the base of the neck
    C. Bulging fontanel
    D. A skull fracture

25. In cases of suspected child maltreatment, the role of the nurse typically includes each of the following, EXCEPT

    A. conducting the forensic interview
    B. reporting to Child Protective Services
    C. assisting in the treatment of any medical conditions
    D. securing the safety of the child

25.____

KEY (CORRECT ANSWERS)

1.	B		11.	A
2.	B		12.	A
3.	B		13.	A
4.	A		14.	C
5.	B		15.	A
6.	C		16.	D
7.	C		17.	B
8.	B		18.	A
9.	A		19.	A
10.	A		20.	C

21. D
22. B
23. C
24. A
25. A

TEST 2

DIRECTIONS: Each question or incomplete statement is followed by several suggested answers or completions. Select the one that BEST answers the question or completes the statement. *PRINT THE LETTER OF THE CORRECT ANSWER IN THE SPACE AT THE RIGHT.*

1. Which of the following is a primary prevention activity?

    A. Parenting classes that are open to the community at large
    B. Assertiveness training for at-risk children
    C. Medical screenings for children in foster care
    D. Psychological screenings for low-income parents

1.____

2. The written report to CPS or a state central registry (SCR) in cases of suspected abuse typically contains

    A. a description of the nature and the extent of the child's injuries
    B. the home phone number of the person making the report
    C. an explanation of why abuse is suspected
    D. a list of previous incidents

2.____

3. Of the U.S. children who are abused each year, about _____ percent are under the age of four.

    A. 10
    B. 25
    C. 50
    D. 75

3.____

4. Child sexual abuse is most often committed by

    A. child care providers or people who work in educational settings
    B. fathers
    C. someone who is known and trusted by the child
    D. complete strangers

4.____

5. Early 21st-century estimates projected that 1 in _____ girls and 1 in _____ boys will have experienced an episode of sexual abuse while younger than 18 years.

    A. 2; 4
    B. 4; 6
    C. 5; 10
    D. 10; 40

5.____

6. Which of the following types of skeletal injuries is LEAST suspicious for child physical abuse?

    A. Long bone fractures at various stages of healing
    B. A compound fracture of the ulna
    C. Spiral, chip, or corner fractures of the metaphysis
    D. Unusual fractures of the ribs, scapula or lateral clavicle

6.____

7. The single leading cause of death for children aged four and younger in the United States is

    A. motor vehicle accidents
    B. falls
    C. child abuse and neglect
    D. residential fires

8. Child neglect would include the
    I. use of close confinement as a punishment
    II. failure to seek necessary medical care for a sick child
    III. failure to enroll a school-age child in an educational program
    IV. failure to seek periodic medical and dental examinations that may prevent disease

    A. I and II
    B. I, II and III
    C. II and III
    D. I, II, III and IV

9. Environmental risk factors for child sexual abuse include each of the following, EXCEPT

    A. caretaker or parent with multiple sexual partners
    B. caretaker or parent who was abused as a child
    C. being raised by a single male parent
    D. poverty

10. Of the following, the most likely warning sign of child physical abuse is

    A. Hyperactivity
    B. Chronic fatigue
    C. Suggesting harsh punishment for other children
    D. Confabulation or the telling of "tall tales"

11. Studies suggests that about _____ percent of abusive parents were themselves abused as children.

    A. 8
    B. 33
    C. 50
    D. 67

12. The Muram diagnostic categorization system offers insight into how a variety of prepubertal genital examinations may assist in the diagnosis of child sexual abuse. In the Muram system, a finding of T. vaginalis would be classified as a Category _____ finding.

    A. I
    B. II
    C. III
    D. IV

13. In a 4-year-old child who is being sexually abused, the most likely behavioral presentation would be

    A. sleeping for extended periods
    B. nightmares
    C. thumb-sucking
    D. eating disturbances

14. In cases of child physical or sexual abuse, the forensic interview
    I. is mostly concerned with detailed answers to who, what, where, and when the abuse occurred
    II. can take the place of the medical history obtained by the health care provider for the child
    III. can be conducted by anyone who is qualified to take a medical history
    IV. for legal reasons, should be conducted in the presence of the child's caretakers

    A. I and II
    B. I, II and III
    C. II and IV
    D. I, II, III and IV

15. Of the following, a bruise on the _____ is LEAST likely to be accidental

    A. thigh
    B. knee
    C. forehead
    D. chin

16. Physical or behavioral indicators of child abuse should be considered to be

    A. warning signals
    B. forensic evidence
    C. testimonial evidence
    D. documented facts

17. Generally, the likelihood that a report of child maltreatment will be confirmed by a CPS investigation is about _____ percent

    A. 5-15
    B. 10-30
    C. 40-60
    D. 60-80

18. When working with child who has recently divulged that he is being abused, an important guideline is to

    A. discuss the situation with colleagues to raise their awareness
    B. offer some kind of physical comfort to the child, such as a warm hug
    C. react immediately and negatively to the idea that the child has been abused
    D. praise the child for his courage and reassure him that there are adults who care

19. Most jurisdictions hold that in order to be considered an "abused child," a child must be   19._____

    A. in a position of dependence on the parent or caretaker, regardless of age
    B. younger than 21 and the biological child of the abuser
    C. younger than 18
    D. younger than 18, or older than 18 with a disability that limits their autonomy

20. Caretakers of Munchausen-by-proxy syndrome (MBPS) victims usually appear to be   20._____

    A. suspicious of others, almost to the point of paranoia
    B. loving and overprotective
    C. angry and confrontational
    D. overbearing and aggressive

21. Among the following factors or events, shaken-baby syndrome is MOST likely to be precipitated by   21._____

    A. uncontrollable crying by the infant
    B. disciplinary problems
    C. parental/caretaker drug or alcohol abuse
    D. the refusal of an infant to feed

22. Which of the following is LEAST likely to be a behavioral sign of neglect in a school-age child?   22._____

    A. Unresponsiveness to the concept of caring
    B. Bullying
    C. Poor self-discipline
    D. Delayed language development

23. Reviews of physical examinations performed on evaluated for suspected child sexual abuse have revealed that about _____ percent of the girls who are victims of sexual abuse have abnormal physical findings.   23._____

    A. 5
    B. 25
    C. 50
    D. 75

24. The initial step of Child Protective Services' intake of a reported case of suspected abuse typically involves each of the following, EXCEPT a (n)   24._____

    A. assessment of the urgency of the response
    B. removal of the child from the environment in which the abuse is alleged to have occurred
    C. determination of whether the report meets statutory and agency guidelines
    D. decision whether to investigate

25. When called to court in a case of child abuse, the health care provider generally serves in the role of   25.____

   I. a lay fact witness to provide first-hand information about what occurred during he child's evaluation
   II. an expert witness, if the provider has advanced training or considerable experience with child physical and/or sexual abuse, on the specifics of the evaluations that were performed as well as general interpretations of issues related to the case
   III. a character witness to offer impressions of the people involved in the case

   A. I only
   B. I and II
   C. II and III
   D. I, II and III

KEY (CORRECT ANSWERS)

1. A
2. A
3. D
4. C
5. B

6. B
7. C
8. C
9. C
10. C

11. B
12. C
13. C
14. A
15. A

16. A
17. C
18. D
19. D
20. B

21. A
22. A
23. A
24. B
25. B

TEST 3

DIRECTIONS: Each question or incomplete statement is followed by several suggested answers or completions. Select the one that BEST answers the question or completes the statement. *PRINT THE LETTER OF THE CORRECT ANSWER IN THE SPACE AT THE RIGHT.*

1. Among children who have been abused, it is most accurate to say that they

    A. tend to develop attention deficit disorders
    B. exhibit a wide range of behaviors
    C. most often have some kind of physical finding that suggests abuse
    D. tend toward aggression in their behavioral responses

    1.____

2. Which of the following signs most strongly suggests the forced feeding of a child?

    A. Bruises on the outside of the mouth
    B. Lacerations of the tongue or frenula
    C. Tearing or braising of the outer ear
    D. Bruising under the eyes

    2.____

3. In order to report suspicions of child abuse to law enforcement and social service authorities, the person who reports must have

    A. reason to suspect that abuse has occurred
    B. the child's permission to report
    C. documented proof that abuse has occurred
    D. circumstantial evidence that abuse has occurred

    3.____

4. For optimal visualization of the genital structures and a fair degree of comfort for the child, the best viewing position would be the

    A. right lateral
    B. knee-chest
    C. frog-leg supine
    D. Trendelenburg

    4.____

5. Pre-school-aged children who have been sexually abused are likely to

    A. run away from home
    B. have nightmares
    C. exhibit clear physical signs of sexual abuse
    D. be hyperactive

    5.____

6. When taking a medical history of a child in whom a health care professional suspects child abuse, guidelines include
    I. using open ended, nonleading questions particularly with younger children
    II. asking not only about physical abuse, but also about sexual abuse, domestic violence, and witnessed abuse
    III. obtaining all historical information from everyone separately, including children

    A. I only
    B. II and III
    C. III only
    D. I, II and III

    6.____

77

7. When a person reports suspected child abuse, his or her name

   A. is told to the child
   B. is reported to the family
   C. remains anonymous only if the report is substantiated
   D. can remain anonymous regardless of the outcome

8. Which of the following is NOT an example of emotional abuse?

   A. Verbal assault
   B. Failure to provide essential care
   C. Close confinement
   D. Threatening physical harm

9. In prepubescent girls, the most common hymenal configuration is

   A. crescent-shaped
   B. septate
   C. annular
   D. imperforate

10. Each of the following is considered to be a key factor in the improvement of outcomes in the area of child maltreatment, EXCEPT the

    A. improvement of access to early intervention and primary prevention programs
    B. provision of social support programs to new parents
    C. focus on tertiary prevention
    D. education of health care professionals in recognizing and intervening appropriately in cases of maltreatment

11. Nationwide, CPS investigations reveal that about ___ percent of the cases of child maltreatment in the United States are cases of physical abuse.

    A. 10   B. 25   C. 50   D. 75

12. When conducting a child interview in the medical evaluation of suspected child sexual abuse, the full potential of the interview can be realized by a reliance on questions or responses such as

    I. "Tell me more."
    II. "How did you feel when that was done to you?"
    III. "And then what happened?"
    IV. "Where was everyone else when this happened?"

    A. I only
    B. I and III
    C. II and III
    D. I, II, III and IV

13. It is most accurate to say that _____ abused children go on to abuse their own children.

    A. very few   B. some   C. about half   D. most3

14. Accidental bruises or cuts on the _____ are extremely rare and should almost always be regarded with suspicion

    A. back   B. neck   C. shoulder   D. legs

15. Which of the following is NOT a secondary prevention activity?
    A. Home visiting programs for new parents
    B. Parent education classes for parents with a history of alcohol and/or drug abuse
    C. Family counseling for families with a history of violence
    D. Respite care for parents with disabled children

16. For a 7-year-old child who has been sexually abused, the most likely behavioral presentation would be

    A. a regression to baby talk
    B. separation anxiety
    C. extreme stranger anxiety
    D. a significant change in attitude or academic performance

17. Which of the following would NOT be a guideline for conducting a lab workup with a child who is suspected to be a victim of sexual abuse?

    A. Place clothing in a plastic bag to preserve any forensic evidence
    B. Maintain and document a clear chain of custody
    C. Collect pubic hairs found on the child's body; if the child has pubic hair, sample 510 hairs.
    D. Consider cultures to be the criterion standard for STD tests

18. Of the following types of maltreatment, the one most likely to cause a child fatality is

    A. physical abuse
    B. emotional abuse
    C. neglect
    D. sexual abuse

19. Which of the following is LEAST likely to be a behavioral indicator of child sexual abuse?

    A. encopresis or enuresis
    B. sleep disturbances
    C. withdrawal from friends or family
    D. excessive familiarity with strangers

20. In most situations, when a case of suspected abuse or neglect turns out to be unfounded,

    A. all the information identifying the subjects is expunged
    B. the health care institution is given written notice that it must be more careful about reporting
    C. the reporter cannot be prosecuted but is subject to civil liability
    D. the reporter is placed on administrative leave but is otherwise unpunished

21. Which of the following is a protective factor in a child (one that reduces the risk for abuse)?

    A. Good social skills
    B. External locus of control
    C. Passive coping style
    D. Bold, fiery temperament

22. Which of the following involves symptoms that approximate the appearance of a cigarette burn? 22.____
    A. Eczema
    B. Impetigo
    C. Keratosis pilaris
    D. Melanoma

23. In about _____ of the households where the mother is a victim of physical abuse, at least one child is a victim as well. 23.____
    A. 10
    B. 30
    C. 50
    D. 70

24. Of the substantiated cases of child maltreatment in the United States, most victims suffer from 24.____
    A. physical abuse
    B. sexual abuse
    C. emotional abuse
    D. neglect

25. Children who are suspected of being sexually abused may need an examination emergently, urgently, or electively scheduled for a later time with their own physician. Generally, urgent examination may take place within of an incident of sexual abuse. 25.____
    A. 8-12 hours
    A. 12-24 hours
    C. 2-3 Days
    D. 7-10 days

KEY (CORRECT ANSWERS)

1. B	11. B
2. B	12. B
3. A	13. B
4. C	14. B
5. B	15. C
6. D	16. D
7. D	17. A
8. B	18. C
9. A	19. D
10. C	20. A

21. A
22. B
23. C
24. D
25. C

EXAMINATION SECTION
TEST 1

DIRECTIONS: Each question or incomplete statement is followed by several suggested answers or completions. Select the one that BEST answers the question or completes the statement. *PRINT THE LETTER OF THE CORRECT ANSWER IN THE SPACE AT THE RIGHT.*

1. A supervisor should consider a social worker to be skilled in diagnosis if, of the following, the worker excels in

    A. categorizing behavior, personality, and social problems in syndrome classes using a standardized nomenclature
    B. relating diagnoses to a theoretical system such as Freudian, Adlerian, Rogerian, etc.
    C. describing the person, problem, and setting as related to the casework situation
    D. determining the genesis of the problems for which the client seeks help

2. The one of the following which is the BASIC difference between the function of a supervisor and the function of a consultant in a large social agency is that the supervisor

    A. is a permanent staff member, while the consultant is a person brought in from the outside
    B. trains young and experienced workers, while the consultant trains those who no longer need supervision
    C. has administrative responsibility for agency operation, while the consultant has no direct administrative responsibility
    D. has a personal relationship with the worker, while the consultant provides administrative controls for evaluating the supervisor

3. Experts in social work supervision have stated that the role of the supervisor should be *authoritative* rather than *authoritarian*.
Of the following, this means MOST NEARLY that the supervisor's authority should come from

    A. his superior skill and competence
    B. his ability to exercise democratic control
    C. responsibility delegated through administrative channels
    D. differences in role perception of the worker and the supervisor

4. Assume that a supervisor who finds himself immobilized in the face of a difficult problem complains because his subordinates are confused and indecisive.
Of the following, it is MOST probable that the supervisor

    A. needs to give more guidance to his subordinates so that they will be able to make decisions within their sphere of responsibility
    B. is projecting his own state of mind on to his subordinates and is venting his feelings of frustration on their incompetence
    C. requires professional help for a personality problem which may make him unsuited for supervisory responsibility
    D. should arrange for his subordinates to get special training in decision-making within their areas of responsibility

5. A supervisor in a large agency with a recent graduate of a school of social work on his staff should be aware that the one of the following which is a common problem of the new professional worker is a tendency to

   A. interpret agency rules and regulations literally because of the desire for supervisory approval
   B. feel frustrated because agency rules and regulations prevent him from making independent decisions based on his professional training
   C. make independent decisions without calling upon the supervisor for expert advice and guidance
   D. protect himself from situations of stress by working with his clients in a routine, uninspired manner

6. Assume that your agency has a serious shortage of professional staff. However, an analysis of the daily tasks of professional social workers reveals that many of the tasks performed are of a clerical or administrative nature.
   Of the following, the MOST appropriate step to take FIRST in order to alleviate the shortage is to

   A. hire indigenous paraprofessionals from the community to take over part of the job load
   B. assign clerical and administrative staff to take over these non-professional tasks
   C. survey professional social workers in order to determine whether some of these clerical or administrative tasks are superfluous
   D. determine how many additional professional social workers are needed and arrange for recruitment in accordance with requirements

7. Experts have made a distinction between the formal and the informal organization of a large agency.
   Of the following, the informal organization has been described as

   A. dysfunctional due to its inevitable conflict with the basic objectives of the agency
   B. those levels of the agency which are separate from the administrative units which have direct responsibility for policy formulation
   C. including only those positions within the agency which have no direct responsibility for its service delivery function
   D. those relationships and channels of communication that resourceful employees develop and use in order to get the work done

8. The term *bureaucracy* has invidious implications for the general public. To the social scientist, however, *bureaucracy* is a technical term for a large, complex organization.
   Of the following, according to the social scientist, a *bureaucracy* is structured on rational principles and characterized by

   A. a democratic system in which each person has maximum freedom to make his own decisions
   B. a strict and well-defined hierarchy of authority functioning on the basis of clear-cut chain of command principles
   C. the assignment of independent responsibility to administrative and professional personnel responsible for delivery of services
   D. equal accessibility of all personnel within program units of the agency to personnel at the level where decisions are made

9. In the hierarchical administrative organization which is characteristic of a large agency, levels of authority emanate from the top downward.
   Of the following, this structure has a tendency toward

   A. decreasing opportunities for staff participation in areas beyond their immediately circumscribed responsibilities
   B. easing the communications flow between departmental lines at the lower levels of the hierarchy
   C. permitting the flow of communication from the top downward, but not from the bottom upward
   D. structural flexibility which adapts readily to changing demands upon the organization

10. Of the following, adherence to *democratic* principles in the administration of a large agency means MOST NEARLY

    A. the feeling of all employees that they are participating in planning and policy making
    B. an equal voice for all employees in planning and policy making
    C. relevant participation of all employees according to their special competence
    D. friendliness, regardless of rank, among all employees at all levels

11. The one of the following which is the MOST important reason that all social workers who work in large agencies should be well-oriented to the administrative process is that they will

    A. be better qualified to participate in planning, decision-making, and formulation of policies
    B. be more sensitive to the needs of extra-agency components in the agency administrative system
    C. have a greater capacity to contribute to the agency and to accept their responsibilities within the system of cooperative effort
    D. be qualified for appointment to positions which do not include direct involvement in service

12. By virtue of training and orientation, social workers are well aware of personality traits that enhance or diminish administrative competence. Social agencies are becoming increasingly conscious, however, of the importance of understanding the effects of different forms of agency organization and structure, not only in relation to staff performance but also in relation to the service the agency performs.
    Of the following, this statement means MOST NEARLY that

    A. administrative difficulties can be analyzed and resolved, not only in terms of personality shortcomings of given individuals but also in terms of organizational arrangements
    B. such factors in agency organization as size, physical arrangements, and organizational roles can be more important than personality traits of administrators in influencing effective delivery of services
    C. agency organization and structure can have a significant effect on staff performance
    D. social workers should give more emphasis to the importance of understanding the effects of agency organization and structure, rather than personality traits

13. According to the task-centered concept of administrative organization, attention is focused on the problem or task at hand, involving all persons who may have a contribution to make, regardless of their professional status or rank in the organization.
Of the following, the MOST probable result of such an approach to agency administration would be to

    A. increase delegation of responsibility from the top downward
    B. increase promotion opportunities for non-professionals
    C. enhance the opportunities for staff to participate in policy formulations
    D. interfere with hierarchical distribution of authority from the top downward

14. The one of the following which CORRECTLY describes the change of focus in social work today is:

    A. New psychological studies and research on human behavior have resulted in increased emphasis on personality problems and the need to change individual dependency patterns
    B. The psychoanalytic orientation and the emphasis on personality problems are being challenged by social science perspectives which stress the environmental causes of individual maladjustment
    C. Emphasis on giving clients supportive assistance with personal problems and on changing individual behavior patterns has shifted to heightened attention to decreasing dependency through required work programs
    D. Sociological studies and other research in the social sciences have resulted in a new emphasis on changing family life and substituting communal ways of living for obsolete institutions

15. The one of the following which is an important distinction between the profession of social work and many other professions is that

    A. there is a basic conflict between social workers' professional interests and the interests of the agency in which they are employed
    B. there is little activity by social workers in the direction of private practice
    C. the claim for recognition of social work as a profession arose when it was practiced mainly within administrative organizations
    D. social workers have a tendency to move from private practice to practice within administrative organizations

16. As the supervisor for the After Hours Emergency Child Care Services, you have been asked by a group of home aides whether they could go out in pairs to areas of the city where they feel uneasy and where some of them have had unpleasant experiences. They point out that caseworkers have approval for this although they usually visit these neighborhoods during daytime hours, while home aides are in the field at all hours of the night. Of the following, your BEST response would be to

    A. remind the home aides that they knew the working conditions when they were hired
    B. question the statement that caseworkers have approval to go in the field in pairs
    C. sympathize with the home aides' fears and agree that their work presents many challenges
    D. indicate that you will consider each such request on an individual basis so that all possible protective measures can be taken

17. At a meeting of your supervisory staff, several supervisors inform you that they lack staff to provide coverage for all service requests. Some units are more overburdened than others because some kinds of service requests are more numerous. A group of caseworkers have suggested to their supervisors that all service requests be distributed throughout the units, instead of continuing the present system of sending requests to specialized units.
Of the following, your BEST immediate response to this proposal would be to

    A. indicate that assignment of work is not a decision to be made by casework staff, but that you will forward the suggestion to your supervisor
    B. point out that, although you have made this serious situation known at higher levels, you do not have the authority to reorganize your units in the manner suggested
    C. ask the supervisors to submit more factual data on volume, distribution of cases, and staff available, along with their recommendations as to the feasibility of the caseworkers' proposal
    D. draft a memo to your supervisor stating that staff shortages are now so serious that caseworkers cannot cover all service requests, and ask for instructions

18. An institution or group home is usually the BEST placement for

    A. children who are committed by the court because of neglect or abuse by their parents
    B. adolescents and school-age children who have temporarily lost their ability to relate to parent substitutes
    C. pre-school age children whose parents cannot care for them temporarily
    D. children who have difficulty relating to their peers

19. Foster homes must be periodically re-examined as a requirement for continued licensing. Of the following, the MOST important reason for this requirement is that

    A. homes that have been used for many years tend to deteriorate and may need to be closed
    B. child welfare workers often do not see the foster fathers at any other time
    C. foster parents may become overwhelmed by too many placements and may desire to have their homes closed
    D. changes in the composition and competence of a foster family should be evaluated and reported regularly

20. A child welfare agency can USUALLY expect that new foster parents who have children of their own will

    A. take on the role of foster parents with very little difficulty
    B. need more help than childless couples in adjusting to their new roles
    C. need to have their responsibilities to their foster children clearly differentiated from their responsibilities to their own children
    D. have a good understanding of the needs of foster children and adjust quickly to the agency's role in providing care for them

21. When a young child makes repeated attempts to break through the reasonable limits which his foster parents have set on his behavior, it is PROBABLY a sign that

    A. the foster parents are not punishing him appropriately for his misbehavior
    B. he does not respect parental authority

C. he is testing whether his foster parents care enough about him to discipline him
D. the foster parents should be more lenient with him

22. Adoptive parents should be provided with factual information about the child's natural parents MAINLY

    A. in order to be able to answer his questions about his natural parents
    B. because they would try to obtain this information anyway
    C. so that they can be prevented from worrying about the child's background
    D. to encourage them to tell the child about his natural parents

23. Foster parents are usually responsible for transporting and accompanying their foster children to various appointments arranged by the child welfare worker.
    When a foster parent informs the worker that he is unable to keep a specific appointment, the worker should

    A. accompany the child to the appointment himself
    B. insist that the foster parent keep the appointment
    C. reschedule the appointment for a time more convenient for the foster parent
    D. evaluate whether cancellation of the appointment would be harmful, and act accordingly

24. After spending several months in a congregate shelter, John is to be placed in a foster home with his younger siblings. However, the discharge physical reveals that he needs a tonsillectomy.
    In this situation, the child welfare worker should FIRST

    A. ask the shelter to arrange for John's tonsillectomy and postpone the placement until after the operation
    B. ask the doctor if he considers the tonsillectomy to be urgent so the worker can decide whether or not to postpone the placement
    C. arrange for the tonsillectomy at once and have John hospitalized
    D. tell the prospective foster mother about the need for the tonsillectomy so she can decide when the surgery should be done

25. An eight-month-old baby, born with withdrawal symptoms and abandoned by her drug-addicted mother, is being made ready for placement in a foster home.
    In this situation, the child welfare worker should

    A. not tell the prospective foster parents about the natural mother's drug addiction so that they won't become unduly worried
    B. tell the prospective foster parents about the natural mother's addiction but assure them that the child has been treated and cured
    C. inform the prospective foster parents of the child's background, explain that she may have a convulsion, and tell them what to do if this should happen
    D. not tell the prospective foster parents about the child's background unless they ask

KEY (CORRECT ANSWERS)

1. C
2. C
3. A
4. B
5. B

6. B
7. D
8. B
9. A
10. C

11. C
12. A
13. C
14. B
15. C

16. D
17. C
18. B
19. D
20. C

21. C
22. A
23. D
24. B
25. C

TEST 2

DIRECTIONS: Each question or incomplete statement is followed by several suggested answers or completions. Select the one that BEST answers the question or completes the statement. *PRINT THE LETTER OF THE CORRECT ANSWER IN THE SPACE AT THE RIGHT.*

1. Of the following, the BEST placement for a twelve-year-old boy who has been diagnosed as having a severe behavior disorder would probably be in a(n)

    A. small group home which is programmed to offer a permissive living atmosphere and home instruction from the State Department of Education
    B. institution geared to treat pre-delinquent children
    C. foster home where his acting out behavior would be understood and accepted
    D. institution where his behavior would be controlled through routines, discipline, and relationships with adults and peers

    1._____

2. In planning services for a young woman expecting an out-of-wedlock child, the child welfare worker should be PRIMARILY concerned with

    A. obtaining as much information as possible about the young woman's ethnic background and health history
    B. determining how the young woman's family is reacting to the situation and whether they will help plan for the unborn child
    C. making up a list of suitable adoption agencies to which the young woman can be referred
    D. providing the young woman with information about all the various arrangements she can make for her unborn child

    2._____

3. A foster mother who has been caring for two retarded preschool children, and receiving a special board rate for the foster care, has become very tired. Her doctor has told her that she needs a vacation, and she so informs the child welfare worker. However, she does not wish to give up caring for the children.
    Of the following, the BEST approach for the worker to take is to

    A. recognize the foster mother's need for a vacation and make temporary arrangements for the care of the children
    B. remind the foster mother that she is receiving a special board rate which should be enough to provide her with babysitting relief
    C. find a new facility for the children since the foster mother's health is apparently failing as a result of taking care of the children
    D. try to determine if there is another reason for the foster mother's exhaustion

    3._____

4. In planning for 18-month-old twins, one who appears to be developing normally and one who is functioning below normal and has many physical problems, the child welfare worker should place the GREATEST emphasis on

    A. placing them in one foster home since research has shown that a symbiotic relationship exists between twins
    B. placing them separately since it would be psychologically harmful for the *normal* twin to live with his *abnormal* sibling

    4._____

C. finding an institution that has a specially trained staff for taking care of handicapped children but also accepts *normal* children so that the twins could remain together
D. finding an appropriate placement for each child according to his needs, realizing that meeting their individual needs is more important than their twin-ship

5. A mother has had all five of her children in placement since she was hospitalized for mental illness three years ago. The hospital has now discharged her, and she is receiving follow-up treatment in an after-care clinic where she receives her medication. She wants her children back, and the clinic approves. The private agency, however, feels that the mother is not ready and also reports that the children do not want to go home.
Of the following, the BEST course of action for you, as a supervisor, to take is to

   A. recommend that the children be returned to their mother as soon as possible since the clinic approves
   B. keep the children in placement until the private agency feels that the mother is ready to cope with them and that they want to go back to her
   C. refer the case to your psychiatric consultant and be guided by his recommendation
   D. confer with representatives of the private agency and the clinic to determine if and when the children should be returned, and how to prepare the mother and children for eventual reunion

5.____

6. A child welfare worker in one of your units reports that a mother with whom she is working claims that the school is discriminating against her children because she is a welfare recipient. Her children have a history of truancy and poor school achievement. The child welfare worker feels that the mother's assessment of the situation has some validity.
Of the following, the BEST course of action for you to suggest to your worker is to

   A. support the mother's defense of her children and report the alleged discrimination on the part of the school to the Board of Education
   B. inquire further into the reasons for the children's truancy and poor achievement with the children, the mother, and school officials
   C. explore with the mother her feelings about receiving public assistance and encourage her to find a job so she won't need assistance
   D. disengage herself from her close involvement in this case since she has stopped being objective

6.____

7. It is standard practice, in providing service to children in their own homes, for the child welfare worker to work directly with the child when

   A. it is determined that his parents have no emotional problem
   B. his problems are primarily in the school and community
   C. he needs help in coping with his living situation and in accepting parental limitations
   D. his parents do not speak English and the worker needs an interpreter

7.____

8. Which one of the following statements regarding the provision of services to children in their own homes is CORRECT?

   A. The caretaking parent is the primary client.
   B. Services for the child under six are generally provided through the parents.
   C. The way the home is kept is of primary importance in evaluating the case.
   D. The most pertinent service is the one given directly to the child.

8.____

9. Of the following, the MOST important problem in the development of group day care services for infants is that this service

   A. requires many safeguards to protect the child's physical health and emotional development
   B. costs too much for the parents or the community to support
   C. cannot be licensed by the Board of Health or State Department of Social Services
   D. is looked upon by the community with disfavor because people, in general, feel that mothers should stay home with infants

10. A child welfare worker should offer day care services

    A. to every mother on her caseload
    B. to mothers on her caseload who have the necessary motivation and strength to work but must provide for the care of their children during the day
    C. only to those mothers on her caseload who are already working and could take their children out of placement if day care services were available
    D. only to parents who have several children and are receiving supplementary assis-

11. The one of the following which is an important, although not the primary, function of a homemaker, from the point of view of the child welfare agency, is to

    tance which could be cut off if the mother went to work
    A. interpret foster care services to the family
    B. provide the family with counseling services, as needed, in relation to the problems the homemaker encounters in her work with the family
    C. provide the child welfare worker with additional information about the family which might not be obtained otherwise, and which could be used in further planning with the family
    D. help the mother to understand her feelings of inadequacy as a parent and to face reality

12. A mother who is legally married to someone not the father of her illegitimate child wants to surrender the child legally for adoption. Her husband does not know about the child. The child welfare worker should advise her that she may have difficulty in legally surrendering the child unless she

    A. signs a surrender and swears her husband is not the child's father
    B. informs her husband about the child and can obtain his written denial of paternity
    C. tells the court the child's real father abandoned her and the child
    D. can prove that she and her husband cannot care for the child properly

13. In planning for the placement of a ten-year-old child in foster care, it is standard practice for the child welfare worker to

    A. make the decision with the parents, without including the child in the planning
    B. enlist the child's participation to the fullest extent possible, depending on his level of maturity
    C. have the parents take responsibility for preparing the child for placement
    D. help the child to accept the agency's and his parents' decision since he cannot do anything about it

14. Of the following, the MOST important reason that child welfare agencies should place more emphasis upon early case finding is in order to

    A. help more families obtain needed public assistance
    B. offer families more extensive diagnostic evaluation
    C. prevent separation of children from their parents
    D. provide more extensive referral services

15. If a parent accused of child neglect refuses protective service, the caseworker should inform him that

    A. he does not have the right to refuse protective service since this service is mandatory
    B. the child will be removed from the home as soon as a foster home can be found
    C. the problem may be referred to the jurisdiction of the Family Court as the result of his refusal
    D. any further complaints of child neglect against him will be investigated by the agency and reported to the police if substantiated

16. As a supervisor, you are asked to work on a committee which is planning for the appropriate use of case aides in family and child welfare programs.
    Of the following, the one which would be the LEAST appropriate assignment for a case aide is

    A. determining, as a result of interviewing the client, the best solution to his family problems
    B. helping a parent to attend an important school meeting by caring for his children at home during the meeting
    C. finding and suggesting recipes to make a client's medically required diet more appetizing and palatable
    D. visiting an overburdened parent's home in order to suggest how to divide some of the home chores among the children

17. As a Supervisor II, you observe that the two case aides assigned to your area, who attend school parttime, are not given many work assignments. You discuss this situation with the Supervisors I, who state that it is too time-consuming to design appropriate tasks for the case aides since they are not available for a full day's work. The Supervisors I express their willingness to have the case aides do their school assignments in the office.
    Of the following, your BEST response would be that the

    A. Supervisors I should see to it that the case aides do not do homework in the office because it would give the clients a bad impression
    B. Supervisors I must assign appropriate tasks to case aides so that the agency and its clients may derive the maximum benefit from their time on the job
    C. agency has great confidence in the use of parapro-fessionals
    D. schools are able to adjust their schedules for case aides and that Supervisors I should be able to do the same

5 (#2)

18. As a supervisor, you are asked to help obtain assistance for a group of residents of your geographic area who have taken a number of unrelated children into their homes and are caring for them at their own expense.
Of the following, the MOST accurate information you can give this group is:

   A. There is no legal basis for meeting their requests
   B. Home Relief is not available as a means of providing for some of the cost of a child's care in a non-related home
   C. An ADC grant can be made for child care to friends of the child's parents who are now supporting the child
   D. They can apply to the Bureau of Child Welfare for certification as foster parents for these children and for payment of foster home boarding care rates

18.___

19. Mr. and Mrs. A are requesting the discharge from foster care of Mary, their eight-year-old daughter, who was placed voluntarily six weeks ago after the child told her teacher that Mr. A *bothered* her. Although Mary had given an elaborate account of this alleged sexual molestation, both parents denied that such an incident occurred, but requested placement as a way of relieving the tension in the home.
As the supervisor asked to participate in the decision about the parent's request for Mary's discharge from placement, your MAIN consideration should be

   A. the dynamics involved in differentiating between a child's fantasy and reality
   B. Mary's feelings about returning home to her family
   C. the factors that went into the earlier decision for placement
   D. that cases of alleged sexual molestation can be handled by court action only

19.___

20. As a supervisor on call for consultation on decisions to be made by the emergency night child welfare staff, you are asked to approve by telephone the discharge of a seven-year-old boy to his father. The boy had been admitted to a city children's shelter when his mother, who was separated from his father, died suddenly during surgery.
Of the following pieces of information supplied by the child welfare worker over the phone, which is the LEAST relevant to your decision? The

   A. father and child know each other
   B. child is in reasonably good health
   C. father has arranged with his mother to look after his son while he is at work
   D. father does not know whether the mother had initiated divorce proceedings

20.___

21. As a supervisor in the foster home program, you receive a request for a change of case worker from a foster mother who is caring for four adolescents. The mother complains that the case worker spends too much time with the children when he visits. In a conference with you, the Supervisor I, who had worked with this foster home until his recent promotion, states his belief that his positive relationship with the foster mother is more important than her relationship with the present case worker. He, therefore, wants to keep the foster home within his unit but assign it to a different case worker. He is concerned that any other course of action might result in the foster mother's request for removal of the children from her home.
Your conference with the Supervisor I on this situation should focus on the

   A. difficulty involved in securing homes for four adolescents
   B. rights of foster parents to request removal of foster children

21.___

C. rights of foster parents to request a different case worker
D. way in which the Supervisor I sees his enabling role

22. As the supervisor for the After Hours Emergency Child Care Services, you recognize, while reviewing the reports of the previous night's activities, the name of a five-year-old boy who had been reported as a runaway two weeks earlier. The current report again indicates that the police found the child wandering in the street at 3:00 A.M. about six blocks from his grandmother's house, where he has been living for the past six months. The current report also indicates that the grandmother arrived at the police station and took the boy home before any action was taken by the Emergency Child Care staff. Of the following, the LEAST valid focus for your next group conference with your staff in discussing this case would be to

    A. stress the advisability of placement of children referred for the second time in a two-week period
    B. discuss critical indices of potential difficulties that may be present when a five-year-old child is a chronic runaway
    C. review indices for referring emergency situations that are overtly resolved after hours to the regular unit the next day
    D. develop a workshop on how to interview children

23. As a Supervisor II in a Protective Services section, you are reviewing a case record forwarded to you by the Supervisor I of one of your units, to show you how promptly his case workers have been making field visits on new referrals. In this case, the case worker visited the home within an hour after receipt of an anonymous report of neglect of an infant. The record stated that the worker was impressed by the mother's politeness and the cleanliness of the home, that the allegation of neglect was false, and that no follow-up was indicated.
Of the following, your MAIN emphasis in reviewing this case material should be on

    A. determining how the case worker interpreted to the mother the reason for his visit
    B. finding out whether the baby was seen during the case worker's visit to the home
    C. planning to compliment the Supervisor I on having helped his caseworkers to make field visits promptly
    D. determining whether or not the record shows that the anonymous complaint was actually disproved

24. As a Supervisor II in an adoption program, you notice that the Supervisor I of one of your units presents about four times as many atypical situations for your review and approval as the Supervisor I of any other unit under your supervision.
Of the following, the BEST step for you take FIRST in order to evaluate the significance of this observation would be to

    A. recognize that, because many children are hard to place, no family that offers to adopt a child should be eliminated
    B. accept the fact that all atypical situations should be reviewed carefully because adoption policies are changing rapidly
    C. analyze the handling of all the studies initiated within this unit during a specific time span in order to determine if appropriate action has been taken in every case
    D. become aware that the supervisors of the other units are probably rejecting atypical situations without bringing them to your attention

25. As a supervisor, you read at night a newspaper report on a serious fire in an apartment building in your work area in which a number of children suffered from severe burns and smoke inhalation, and were admitted to X Hospital. The next morning, the MOST appropriate action for the district office to take would be to

    A. explore whether or not X Hospital sees evidence of abuse or neglect of any of the children hospitalized and, if so, whether the hospital plans to refer the children and families to the Bureau of Child Welfare
    B. initiate steps for referral for re-housing
    C. send a worker to the area to determine how or if he can be of help
    D. send a worker to the hospital to offer family and child welfare services

25.___

KEY (CORRECT ANSWERS)

1.	D	11.	C
2.	D	12.	B
3.	A	13.	B
4.	D	14.	C
5.	D	15.	C
6.	B	16.	A
7.	C	17.	B
8.	B	18.	D
9.	A	19.	C
10.	B	20.	D

21. D
22. A
23. D
24. C
25. A

TEST 3

DIRECTIONS: Each question or incomplete statement is followed by several suggested answers or completions. Select the one that BEST answers the question or completes the statement. *PRINT THE LETTER OF THE CORRECT ANSWER IN THE SPACE AT THE RIGHT.*

1. Of the following, the MOST important influence on the personality development of a child during the first year is the

    A. family as a whole
    B. mother
    C. way his siblings react to him
    D. relationship between the parents

    1._____

2. Of the following, the terms which is GENERALLY applied to the situation in which an infant in foster care has insufficient interaction with a substitute mother is

    A. maternal rejection
    B. mothering complex
    C. maternal deprivation
    D. interaction deficiency

    2._____

3. When a foster child exhibits nonconforming behavior, it is MOST important for the foster parents to be able to

    A. ignore this behavior since this is the child's way of expressing his emotional needs
    B. accept and condone this behavior as an expression of the child's insecurity
    C. use punishment and reward to force the child to conform
    D. accept this behavior without condoning it, while trying to meet the child's emotional needs

    3._____

4. Separation of the infant from his mother can be a traumatic experience.
The amount of emotional damage to the infant and the consequent effects on his personality depend MAINLY on the

    A. quality and consistency of the substitute mothering he receives
    B. reasons for and duration of the separation
    C. kind of preparation for separation the infant receives
    D. degree of the mother's acceptance of the placement

    4._____

5. Research studies of language development in young children have shown that

    A. the multiple mothering of children in a large family retards language development
    B. language retardation in otherwise normal children is usually related to inadequate language stimulation
    C. language retardation is always associated with slow motor development
    D. children are usually slow in learning to talk when more than one language is spoken in the home

    5._____

6. The two MOST important influences on the cultural development of a seven-year-old child are the

    A. home and peer group
    B. school and peer group
    C. home and school
    D. home and church

    6._____

7. In our culture, a child gains his sense of identity MAINLY from

   A. knowledge about and experience with his parents and extended family
   B. association with members of his own ethnic group
   C. a study of the historical and ethnic factors in this culture
   D. association with his peers

8. A child who has grown up in foster care may want to talk about his natural parents, although he has never known them.
   Of the following, the BEST way for a child welfare worker to deal with this situation is to

   A. help the child to forget that he is a foster child and to relate to his foster parents as though they were his natural parents
   B. encourage the child to express his feelings and fantasies about his natural parents so that the worker can help his understand these feelings and fantasies
   C. set up a psychiatric interview for the child to determine if he is making a satisfactory adjustment to his foster child status
   D. tell the child that he can look for his natural parents when he is older

9. Of the following, the MOST important reason that those responsible for the care of a child in placement should never depreciate the child's natural parents or the home from which he came is that the

   A. child's self-esteem depends on how he feels about his natural parents and his previous experiences
   B. natural parents may have been incapable of being adequate parents
   C. child may feel that the substitute parents are jealous of his natural parents
   D. child will be forced into the position of defending his natural parents and will resent the substitute parents

10. The Children's Apperception Test (CAT) is a commonly used protective test for preschool children in which the child

    A. has an opportunity to express his fantasies and moods through drawing and painting
    B. tells a story about pictures that are shown to him
    C. completes an unfinished story
    D. is given a variety of toys and is placed in a make-believe play situation

11. Sickle cell anemia is a blood disease MOST commonly found in children whose parents are

    A. Caucasian   B. interracial
    C. Black or Latin American   D. Oriental

12. Schizophrenia in children USUALLY becomes manifest

    A. during the latency period
    B. during adolescence only
    C. when the mother has a history of schizophrenia
    D. during early childhood or adolescence

13. Although day care was originally established mainly as a social service for working mothers, it has been found that

   A. day care can also be an educational experience for a child and help in the development of peer relationships
   B. most working mothers would prefer to leave their children with friends or relatives rather than at a day care center
   C. it would be economically feasible to make day care centers available to all mothers in the community
   D. working mothers of physically and mentally handicapped children do not benefit from day care facilities

14. In deciding on which day care center to recommend to a working mother, the MOST important of the following considerations is the

   A. educational background of the staff
   B. ratio of staff to children
   C. director of the center
   D. physical plant and recreational facilities

15. During the past few years, dramatic and serious incidents of child abuse have resulted in

   A. the passage of legislation in all states requiring medical and other designated personnel to report incidents of abuse
   B. the proliferation of child care agencies dealing with child abuse cases only
   C. a tightening of restrictions in most states on eligibility for public assistance of parents who abuse their children
   D. a slight decline in the number of child neglect cases reported to authorities and a slight increase in the number of child abuse cases reported

16. Of the following alternatives, the one which is LEAST available to the Black unwed mother in planning for her child is

   A. adoption
   B. temporary care in a small group home
   C. foster family care
   D. dependence upon her family

Questions 17-19.

DIRECTIONS: Questions 17 through 19 are to be answered by matching each of the persons listed in Column I with the field in which the person is an authority, as stated in Column II.

COLUMN I	COLUMN II
17. Lauretta Bender	A. Group work
	B. Homefinding
	C. Day care
18. Fritz Redl	D. Acting out, emotionally disturbed children and adolescents
19. Gisela Konopka	E. Childhood schizophrenia

4 (#3)

20. As a supervisor in the Division of Interagency Relationships, you become aware that a particular voluntary child-caring agency often reports discharges of children from foster care either on the date the discharge plan is to be implemented or shortly after the discharge has taken place. Your staff informs you that such late discharge reports are forwarded most frequently when the discharge plans indicate a need for intensive supportive help. The BEST approach for you to take would be to meet with

20.____

   A. your team and tell them to disapprove all such discharges in the future
   B. your team and tell them to take all appropriate clerical action as quickly as possible
   C. your immediate supervisor to inform him that a particular agency is making unsound discharges
   D. representatives of the voluntary child-caring agency to discuss the subject of discharge practice

21. As a supervisor, you are representing the Bureau of Child Welfare on a committee that meets bi-monthly to plan for the needs of retarded children. You note that the comments of the parents of retardates are warmly accepted at each session, but are never incorporated into the minutes or included in recommendations for follow-up action.
Of the following, the BEST approach for you to take would be to

21.____

   A. report this discrepancy to your immediate supervisor
   B. attempt to maneuver the group so that the parents of retardates will be encouraged to make more comments at committee meetings
   C. raise a question at the next regular meeting about the discrepancy you have found in the recording of participation by parents
   D. talk to several parents after the next meeting to find out if they object to the manner in which minutes are recorded

22. As a Supervisor II, you note that your staff appears to make minimal use of community resources to meet client needs. When you discuss this at a staff meeting, you meet a great deal of resistance from both the Supervisors I and the case workers, who say: *You are not out there.*
Of the following, your BEST response in this situation would be to

22.____

   A. refer to an article you have read about how workers can involve themselves in the community
   B. ask for volunteers for a committee to explore possible resources in the community they serve
   C. ask the group to give examples of their use of community resources
   D. ask the group to describe their experiences in seeking out community resources

23. As a supervisor, you are invited as an expert consultant to meet with a community group discussing child day care needs. At the meeting, one parent urges the establishment of group care for infants in her apartment building, where there are about ten infants between the ages of three and twelve months.
Of the following, the FIRST suggestion you should make concerning this proposal is that

23.____

   A. those parents in the building who are interested in infant care attend a meeting to discuss the specific needs of his own infant and what his expectations of group care are

B. the group invite an expert on infant development to its next meeting for the purpose of outlining a possible infant group care program
C. the community group insure that pediatric consultation would be available to the persons providing the infant group care
D. one parent contact the landlord of the apartment building to inquire about regulations or stipulations for use of an apartment or other building facility for an infant group care program

24. Of the following, the MOST desirable pattern to utilize in community planning of child welfare services is to

   A. leave each agency in the community free to develop those services which its constituency feels strongly about and wishes to support
   B. have each agency in the community assigned a particular function by the state licensing authority in line with community need
   C. consult a central planning body, representative of all agencies in the community, when any agency is considering developing a new service or dropping an old one
   D. merge all agencies in the community providing like services, in order to reduce administrative expenses

25. It is recognized that very young children should not remain in hospitals after the condition for which they were admitted is under control and can be managed outside the hospital setting.
Of the following, the BEST method for preventing well children from remaining in hospitals longer than necessary is for

   A. hospital policy to provide for referral of children to the Bureau of Child Welfare when the hospital staff believe parents may not be able to take their children home as soon as they are medically well
   B. hospital social service departments to prepare social histories on children hospitalized, focusing especially on children *at risk*
   C. the public child welfare agency to receive on a regular basis lists of children remaining in hospitals
   D. hospitals to send to child caring agencies lists of children not discharged, although medically well

KEY (CORRECT ANSWERS)

1.	B	11.	C
2.	C	12.	D
3.	D	13.	A
4.	A	14.	B
5.	B	15.	A
6.	C	16.	A
7.	A	17.	E
8.	B	18.	D
9.	A	19.	A
10.	B	20.	D

21. C
22. D
23. A
24. C
25. A

EXAMINATION SECTION
TEST 1

DIRECTIONS: Each question or incomplete statement is followed by several suggested answers or completions. Select the one that BEST answers the question or completes the statement. *PRINT THE LETTER OF THE CORRECT ANSWER IN THE SPACE AT THE RIGHT.*

1. The CHIEF aim of counseling in social casework is to

   A. enlist the cooperation of the client in dealing with his social problems and in making social adaptations
   B. instill in the client socially acceptable, meaningful, and constructive behavior patterns by the use of psychotherapeutically oriented discussions
   C. frankly point out to the client the real source of his difficulties and the weaknesses in his makeup which caused them
   D. present the client with the best solution to his social situation and persuade him to utilize it

2. To help others effectively demands respect for human personality and for a person's right to control his own life and pursue happiness and spiritual goals in his own way.
The BEST of the following ways for a social worker to apply this principle when dealing with a client who is living in a manner which is NOT socially acceptable is to

   A. assist the client toward rehabilitation by making concrete services and practical assistance to him contingent on his conforming to socially acceptable behavior
   B. give the client assistance as needed, without imposing on him goals, solutions, or standards of behavior
   C. help the client to become self-directing by insisting that he plan and execute his own solutions to his problems without assistance
   D. resist the desire to assist the client to change his way of living or to select goals that might provide a permanent solution to his problem

3. The one of the following which is the MOST important reason why many communities are considering greater use of homemaker service instead of foster-home care in cases where the mother of a family of several children is either absent or incapacitated is that homemaker

   A. personnel, being non-professional, are easier to obtain and train than skilled foster parents with adequate facilities for housing and caring for foster children
   B. service generally permits children to maintain affectionate ties with their own family in their own home
   C. personnel, being part of the casework team, are more likely to cooperate with the professional caseworker than are the foster parents in close observation of the children and execution of the caseworker's orders
   D. service provides more quickly foster parental care for the children on a temporary, as needed, basis

4. A caseworker deems it advisable to provide a certain family with homemaker service because of the long-term nature of the illness of the mother which is confining her to bed at home.
The caseworker should discuss with the family the proper use of homemaker service, prior to the assignment of a homemaker, CHIEFLY because

   A. the homemaker can prove of maximum help only when the family understands her role and agrees that this is the service they really desire
   B. they will understand clearly the duties which the homemaker is authorized to perform
   C. the homemaker will be more able to lessen the father's burden by skillfully resolving the family's daily emotional crises
   D. the caseworker will be more able to match the home-maker and the family on the basis of personality and background

5. The practice of retaining the same workers exclusively on intake instead of rotating them with field workers is generally considered

   A. *advisable;* having two or more workers, each with specialized skills, responsible for each case provides a greater range of professional opinion as to the proper action to take in any given situation
   B. *advisable;* allowing workers to perform the same functions exclusively helps them to perfect their interviewing skills and enables them to standardize their interviewing procedures
   C. *inadvisable;* this practice tends to develop stereotyped attitudes and procedures
   D. *inadvisable;* rotating the workers on a case assists in effecting a change of standards beneficial to the client

6. For the caseworker to understand the culture of a family is important CHIEFLY because the

   A. client tends to react to the casework situation largely in ways derived from attitudes learned at home
   B. needs of the entire family cannot be satisfied unless the individual needs of each member are satisfied first
   C. client can be treated more effectively when considered as a member of a cultural group rather than a separate individual
   D. family can be understood much more readily if the dominant individual motivating it is understood first

7. Emphasis in the practice of social casework has shifted from merely providing the client with a practical service to involving the client in using the service or treatment. This statement implies MOST nearly that, at present,

   A. social casework will attempt to help the client only when it is felt that he will profit from the service
   B. social casework is no longer deeply involved in assisting the client in a direct and realistic way
   C. the most important change in social casework today has been its shift from helping the client in a practical way to planning for him in a theoretical way
   D. the caseworker attempts to mobilize the client to active participation in decision-making

8. In all social casework practice, whether it be in an agency or in an institution, the properly prepared case history record is of great importance in the treatment of the client and his problem CHIEFLY because it

   A. gives the supervisory and administrative casework staff reviewing the case a keener understanding of the general sociological and psychological causes underlying dependency and other factors which make it necessary for clients to seek casework assistance
   B. furnishes the agency or institution involved in the case with a factual record as a basis for determining whether or not continuing treatment of the client is justified
   C. assists the caseworkers involved in the case by providing them, on a continuous basis, with a clear picture of the various factors underlying the client's problem and of what has been done to help resolve the situation
   D. provides the caseworker responsible for the case with the basic facts which will enable her to determine whether the client is really trying to help himself or whether he is passing his responsibility on to the caseworker

8._____

9. When comparing the narrative form with the summary, form of a casework recording, the narrative form is usually the BEST way to record

   A. objective material obtained from investigations of the client's statements, while the summary form is best to record worker's detailed observations of client's reactions to his present problem
   B. both social data and eligibility material, while the summary form is best to record material dealing with feelings, attitudes, and client-worker relationships
   C. material relating to prognosis, treatment given, and the results obtained, while the summary form is best to record a verbatim report of primary evidence obtained from personal worker-client contacts
   D. material dealing with feelings, attitudes, and client-worker relationships, while the summary form is best to record both social data and eligibility material

9._____

10. A problem in recording is to decide how much detail to have in a case record. The case history should generally include

    A. a more detailed description of the client's reaction to practical matters than to psychological conflicts
    B. a verbatim account of worker-client interaction in significant interviews and a detailed prescription of the client's feelings toward the treatment plan
    C. only as much data, whether it be sociological or psychological, as will enable the worker to understand the client, the problem to be solved, and the main factors, in its solution
    D. the full details of the client's personality development and emotional relationships regardless of the type or complexity of the problem

10._____

11. The mother of a child who is receiving foster care in a childcaring institution has gotten into the habit of coming in to the office of the Division of Foster Home Care whenever she is faced with a problem, no matter how trivial.
The social investigator assigned to this case could generally help this client MOST by

    A. insisting that in the future the client refrain from bringing all her problems to the social investigator

11._____

B. forming a basis in the client's attitudes to help her meet future problems
C. telling the client that she must learn to solve her simpler problems alone
D. solving the client's problems as quickly as possible

12. An obviously upset girl in her late teens comes in to the Bureau of Child Welfare with a personal problem. The girl begins to cry softly while being interviewed by a social investigator.
It would generally be BEST for the social investigator to

    A. give the girl an opportunity to release her emotions in telling her story
    B. suggest that the girl come back another day when she is in a calmer frame of mind
    C. ask the girl to speak calmly and quietly so that the entire office will not be annoyed
    D. terminate the interview as soon as the girl becomes emotional

13. In functional casework practice, agency function, rather than client need, becomes the pivot of the helping process. According to the above statement, the worker-client relationship is influenced by functional casework to the extent that the

    A. caseworker's responsibility must be to the agency and its function regardless of how it meets the client's needs
    B. client is given the responsibility of meeting the agency's requirements according to his own limitations
    C. function of the agency restricts the degree to which the caseworker can put herself at the disposal of the client
    D. caseworker's prime responsibility is in adjusting agency function to meet the needs of the client

14. There is general agreement among social caseworkers that one of the CHIEF ultimate goals of treatment in casework is to

    A. analyze the malfunctioning of the client in relation to his environment in order to determine its basic causes
    B. apply the knowledge of social resources, and skill in their use, in order to build a satisfactory worker-client relationship
    C. interpret agency policy and functions to the client so as to interest him in making greater use of its services
    D. stabilize or improve the functioning of the client in terms of his social adaptation or adjustment

15. When a caseworker encounters a situation in which a child is living in an unfavorable parental setting, the BEST action for the caseworker to take FIRST in an attempt to correct the situation is to

    A. approach the problem through the parent-child relationship and try to modify parental attitudes and behavior toward the child
    B. induce the child to behave better in order to influence the parent to lessen his parental pressures on the child
    C. place the child in an institution where he can avoid a close parental relationship by having to respond to several adults
    D. remove the child to a more favorable environment in a foster home where he can respond to a more satisfactory parental figure

16. In the case of a child who has both parents living but who has been placed in a foster-family home because of family problems, it is especially important that the foster parents be made to understand that they will not be taking the place of the child's own parents on a permanent basis CHIEFLY because it is inadvisable for them to

    A. have any emotional attachment for the child lest they find it too painful and difficult to relinquish custody of the child when it becomes necessary
    B. encourage the child's emotional dependency on them with resulting conflicting feelings about his relationships with them and with his own parents
    C. develop in the child a spirit of independence and self-reliance which may decrease the child's dependence on his own parents after his reunion with them
    D. support, reassure, and help the child to such an extent that he will feel indebted to them in later life when he is back with his own family

17. The currently prevailing point of view regarding foster home placement of children is that

    A. regardless of how poor the conditions are in a child's own home, it is generally better for him to remain in it than to be removed to a foster home
    B. regardless of the quality of care available in a foster family home, every possible alternative should be explored before a child is removed from his own home
    C. even when all indications are that a child will be harmed by prolonged residence in his own home, the child should not be moved to a foster home unless the change is fully acceptable to him
    D. when environmental conditions prevailing in a proposed foster home are far superior to those prevailing in the child's own home, it is generally advisable to remove him to the foster home and to do so as early in his life as possible

18. The one of the following which is the PRIMARY reason why institutional placement is NOT recommended for children from birth to school age is that children in this age group

    A. need such frequent attention to their physical wants that an institutional setting is relatively impractical
    B. derive little benefit from a group experience
    C. cannot find security in the known, monotonous daily routine of institutional living
    D. have a great need for attention and individualized care

19. The MOST frequent of the following reasons why foster parents are motivated to accept children for foster home care is the desire to

    A. fill the void in their childless home with a view to eventual adoption, if feasible
    B. find a suitable companion for an only child
    C. give a child who needs it a secure and meaningful experience in family living
    D. supplement their family income by means of child care fees

20. A child is being removed from his own home and placed in foster home care because of his misbehavior and the poor environment prevailing in his home.
    Of the following, the foster parents who are likely to provide the child with the MOST beneficial foster home experience are those who can

    A. accept his non-conforming behavior and can meet his needs so that he can become more secure and better adjusted
    B. be lenient with him and his shortcomings by allowing him to regulate his own activities as long as he keeps out of serious trouble

C. give him their full-time attention, changing his non-conforming behavior through firm discipline and a full daily program of organized activities
D. provide him with vigilant supervision and with the material needs and comforts, the lack of which in his own home contributed to his misbehavior

21. When a child is to be admitted to group day care for the first time, the investigator should enlist the active assistance of the parents in preparing the child CHIEFLY because the child

    A. will feel secure in the knowledge that his parents have arranged for the day care services
    B. does not generally respond to placement in group day care without some feelings of separation, loneliness, and bewilderment
    C. should be made to realize the importance of group day care for himself and his family
    D. must be carefully instructed in proper behavior in group situations lest he misbehave after being admitted to group day care

22. The one of the following situations in which it is generally LEAST advisable to recommend group day care for children is one in which the

    A. father is absent from the home and the mother's employment preserves a sense of self-sufficiency and family solidarity
    B. mother is ill or absent and the father hopes to avoid the necessity of placing his children in foster homes
    C. child lacks companionship with his peer group
    D. child shows definite signs of boredom with the play activities of his peers

23. In the light of present-day social work philosophy, the goals and objectives of a maternity home for unwed mothers should aim PRIMARILY at

    A. providing a comfortable, healthful, and private sanctuary for both mother and child until the out-of-wedlocked child's adoption, while keeping confidential the girl's offense and the child's status
    B. protecting mother and child before, during, and after confinement, and clarifying for the mother the spiritual implications of illegitimacy for both herself and her child
    C. meeting the girl's needs during pregnancy and confinement, the child's needs after birth, and providing a basis for the re-education and more constructive motivation of the mother
    D. sustaining the mother with needed shelter and medical care during pregnancy and confinement, and imparting to her an understanding of the sociological and psychological implications of her illicit behavior

24. In the past, before the advent of social work as a recognized profession, the general practice of child-placing agencies with regard to the placing for adoption of children born out-of-wedlock was more frequently geared to meeting the needs, desires, and inclinations of the adopting couple rather than the needs of the child, largely because at that time it was generally believed that

    A. the child could be easily molded to fit the environment in which his adoptive parents would raise him
    B. the child should be closely enough matched to the adoptive couple in race and appearance to be able to pass as their natural child

C. adoptive parents were taking a great risk, and, therefore, were available in sufficient numbers
D. the adoptive parents should know best which one of the several children offered could fit into their plans and meet their desires most completely

25. Professional child welfare workers handling the placement of children for adoption generally recognize and distinguish clearly between independent placements and agency placements. An agency placement may be described MOST accurately as one in which the

   A. child is relinquished by his parents to a licensed child placing agency which assumes responsibility for selecting the child's adoptive family and for placing him therein
   B. agency assumes responsibility for selecting the child's adoptive family but his own parents or their representatives must approve of the family and personally place the child therein
   C. child is placed in the adoptive home by his parents or by their representatives subject to the subsequent approval of a licensed child-placing agency
   D. child is voluntarily placed by his parents or by their representatives with one of several families previously approved by a licensed child-placing agency

26. In accordance with legal restrictions on the powers of the Children's Court to commit children as neglected or delinquent, children may be committed by order of this court

   A. if they have reached the age of sixteen and the neglect or delinquency responsible for their commitment occurred before their sixteenth birthday
   B. if they have reached the age of seventeen and the neglect or delinquency responsible for their commitment occurred before their seventeenth birthday
   C. if they are between the ages of sixteen and eighteen, and the neglect or delinquency responsible for their commitment occurred before the child's seventeenth birthday
   D. at any age during the child's legal minority, but only if the neglect or delinquency occurred before the child's eighteenth birthday

27. The laws governing the payment of public funds to charitable child-bearing institutions for the care of children committed by the Commissioner of Welfare, provide that an institution belonging to any particular religious faith may

   A. be paid public funds only if it agrees in advance to admit a stated proportion of children of other religions or races
   B. not be paid any public funds if it denies admission to children of other religions
   C. be paid public funds even if it restricts admission to children of the same race, color, and religious faith
   D. not be paid public funds if it limits the admission of children on the basis of race or color, but may be paid such funds if it refuses to admit children of other religions

28. An 11-year-old girl is to be committed by the Commissioner of Welfare as a dependent and neglected child. According to the rules and regulations governing such cases, it would be permissible to place this girl as a public charge in the same institution with delinquent children ONLY when the institution has requested and secured the written permission of the

A. Commissioner of Welfare
B. Director of the Bureau of Child Welfare
C. State Commissioner of Social Welfare
D. Presiding Justice of the Family Court

29. The one of the following set of conditions under which the Department of Welfare may place a child in foster care is if the child is born

    A. in wedlock, his parents are separated from each other, and the written consent of either parent is obtained
    B. out-of-wedlock, the parents are separated or living together, and the written consent of the acknowledged father is obtained
    C. in wedlock, his parents are living together, and the written consent of either one of the parents is obtained
    D. out-of-wedlock, his parents are separated or living together, and the written consent of the mother is obtained

30. According to the Social Welfare Law, if any person brings into this state a child who is a legal resident of another state, that person shall be responsible for the

    A. care and maintenance of the child until the child has resided in this state a sufficient period of time to gain legal residence in this state
    B. care and maintenance of the child until the child reaches adulthood and becomes self-supporting, unless the child is legally adopted by another person prior to reaching adulthood
    C. care and maintenance of the child until the public welfare district of which the child is a legal resident accepts responsibility for the child's care and maintenance
    D. cost of returning the child to the public welfare district of which the child is a legal resident

31. A woman comes into the Application Unit of the Bureau of Child Welfare to apply for foster care placement for her two children, age four and six, respectively. Based on the facts given by the mother, it is logical for the interviewer to presume that the children are in need of foster placement and that their parents can pay the full cost of such care. However, there is no emergency situation in this case to indicate the imperative need for immediate placement.
    The one of the following actions which would be MOST correct according to the Bureau's policies and procedures governing such situations is for the Bureau of Child Welfare to

    A. assign the case to a field unit in order to investigate and ascertain the applicant's actual eligibility for any form of child care at either public or private expense
    B. assign the case to a field unit for further investigation on the basis of which the Bureau can determine which child-caring agency best meets the children's needs
    C. attempt to have an appropriate child-caring agency accept the woman's application on a private basis
    D. notify the mother that because of her financial condition she must apply directly to a private child-caring agency of her own choice

32. The Bureau of Child Welfare separates foster care requests into the categories of temporary care, long-term care, interim care, and after care dependent upon the circumstances existing in each case.
A request for foster care should be assigned to the category of interim care in the case of a child who

    A. must be placed during his mother's hospitalization for confinement or surgery
    B. is awaiting acceptance for a long-term placement in a suitable agency
    C. is receiving institutional care while awaiting return to his own family
    D. is being institutionalized because of his behavior difficulties

32.____

33. There is need for foster care placement for babies born in the Training School for Girls or in a state institution for mental defectives. The Department of Welfare responds to requests for foster care placement when the mother is a city resident who was committed from the city. To obtain the consent of the mother for the baby's placement in such cases is

    A. essential in the case of all inmates of either institution who are capable of understanding specifically to what they are consenting
    B. essential only when the mother indicates her intention of assuming care of the child upon being discharged from the institution
    C. not essential for inmates of either type of institution when there are no relatives to give the baby adequate care
    D. not essential for inmates of the state institution for mental defectives, but is essential for inmates of state training schools for girls

33.____

34. When it has been determined that a child who is a member of a family receiving public assistance is presumptively in need of referral and admission to a voluntary child-caring agency, procedures governing such cases require the welfare center to

    A. furnish the voluntary child-caring agency with a case summary, insure the child's admission, and then obtain the approval of the Bureau of Child Welfare
    B. refer the child directly to the voluntary child-caring agency, concurrently notifying the Bureau of Child Welfare in writing of its action
    C. refer the child to the Bureau of Child Welfare, which has exclusive responsibility for the referral and admission of children to the voluntary child-caring agencies
    D. request the prior approval of the Bureau of Child Welfare and, upon obtaining it, refer the child to the voluntary child-caring agency

34.____

35. The procedure to be followed when an abandoned or deserted child is found late at night in urgent need of shelter is to make arrangements through the

    A. Children's Court for the child to be admitted on an emergency basis to either the city Foundling Hospital or the Children's Center
    B. Police Department for the child to be admitted on an emergency basis to either the Children's Center or the city Foundling Hospital
    C. nearest welfare center for the child to be admitted to the Children's Center only until an investigation can be made
    D. night receptionist at Central Office for the child to be admitted on an emergency basis to a shelter of the same religious faith as the child

35.____

36. In accordance with both the Social Welfare Law and the Public Health Law, the birth of a foundling must be registered by the preparation of a prescribed Health Department form by the

    A. police officer who prepared the police affidavit, and then routed to the Health Department by the office of the Commissioner of Welfare
    B. supervisor of the Allocation Unit of the Department of Welfare, and then routed to the Health Department by the office of the Commissioner of Welfare
    C. police officer who prepared the police affidavit, and then routed to the Health Department by the office of the Commissioner of Welfare
    D. supervisor of the Application Unit, and then routed to the Health Department by the office of the Director of the Bureau of Child Welfare

37. In the cases of blind or deaf children who are local charges but who are appointed under the Education Law as state pupils in special institutions for the instruction of the blind or deaf, the Bureau of Child Welfare investigation is directed PRIMARILY at determining the

    A. adequacy of the selected institution and its facilities for meeting the special needs of the individual child
    B. child's need for foster care at public expense during non-school periods and his family's ability to contribute to the cost of his care
    C. degree of disability of the child and his need for special training to enable him to live a socially useful life
    D. reason for the family's request for this type of special care and for their inability to place the child without the assistance of the bureau

38. The one of the following which is the MOST accurate statement regarding the financial responsibility of a family when the Bureau of Child Welfare places its children in foster care is:
    If the family income

    A. exceeds the allowed budget schedule, the family must make a minimum payment of the budget surplus
    B. exceeds the allowed budget schedule, the minimum payment the family must make is the full budget surplus plus 50% of any benefit the family receives for the child in placement
    C. is less than the allowed budget schedule, the family is not required to make any payment for any children in placement
    D. is less than the allowed budget schedule, the family must make a total payment of $1 weekly, regardless of the number of children in placement

39. When the father of an out-of-wedlock child is able but unwilling to contribute toward the cost of maintaining the child in a foster home, the Bureau of Child Welfare may, if the father lives in the city, refer the situation for adjudication to compel support, to the _____ the participation of the _____ .

    A. Family Court without; mother
    B. Court of Special Sessions with; mother
    C. Family Court with; father
    D. Court of Special Sessions without; mother

40. A child for whom the Bureau of Child Welfare has responsibility needs hospitalization. The child-caring agency through which the child is receiving foster care arranges to have him admitted to a hospital in the city, pays the hospital bill for his care, and presents the receipted bill to the city for reimbursement.
The agency

   A. can be reimbursed for the cost of hospitalization from the Charitable Institutions Budget if the child was treated in an approved voluntary hospital
   B. can be reimbursed by the Department of Health if the child is physically handicapped
   C. cannot in any case be reimbursed by any city department regardless of which hospital treated the child
   D. can only be reimbursed by the Department of Hospitals if the child was treated in a municipal hospital

41. There is general agreement among experts that squabbling and hair-pulling among nine- to-ten-year-old brothers and sisters is 9

   A. generally a danger sign indicating the need for child guidance, because it is caused by a deeper inner conflict smouldering below the surface
   B. often more salutary than harmful, because if the children bottled up their jealousy their parents might not be aware of it and be able to look for its cause
   C. perfectly natural, because it merely brings to the surface the deep-rooted, subconscious antagonism between the sexes that exists in normal persons
   D. usually an indication of the need for family counseling, because it signifies, in most cases, a poorly oriented home life and maladjusted parental relationships

42. An adolescent boy has acquired a socially undesirable habit. The MOST likely result of a social worker's endeavor to rid the boy of this habit by making him feel ashamed of it would be to

   A. assist the boy by inspiring him to make a conscious effort to rid himself of the habit permanently
   B. completely rid the boy of the habit without any detrimental side effects
   C. create in the boy the conscious and rebellious desire to engage in further anti-social actions of a more serious nature
   D. further complicate the problem by giving the boy a sense of guilt in addition to the habit itself

43. The one of the following which is the CHIEF reason why it is generally futile to attempt to eradicate habitual nail-biting in a ten-year-old girl by applying a bitter-tasting substance to her fingers is that this type of treatment

   A. does not remove the girl's inner tensions which are the actual cause of the habit
   B. fails to relax the girl because it prevents her from engaging in a pleasurable habit or activity
   C. generally results in the girl's dropping the nail-biting habit only temporarily and in substituting another socially disapproved habit for it
   D. actually strengthens the habit to a great extent by constantly calling the girl's attention to it

44. The CHIEF reason why it is important for a child to be raised by emotionally mature, accepting parents is that the resulting relationship between child and parents will generally

    A. give the child the deep sense of security, satisfaction, and mutual love needed for proper development
    B. develop in the child a sense of social security leading him, without disciplining, to socially acceptable behavior and goals
    C. slow the child's psychological development so that he will derive the full benefits of childhood play and behavior
    D. keep the child under the parental wing for a longer period by providing satisfying play involving parents and child

45. The one of the following which is generally the BEST method to employ in order to inculcate socially acceptable habits in children from 6 to 12 years of age is to

    A. advise them to form proper habits of behavior lest they be punished for improper conduct
    B. give them an incentive to behave properly by making their proper actions satisfying to them
    C. point out to them the proper conduct of the many famous people they learn about in school
    D. speak to them about how much adults appreciate proper behavior in children

46. An 8-year-old child has begun to form the habit of sulking when he fails to get his own way with his mother. For his mother to handle the situation solely by telling him firmly to stop sulking in such cases would be

    A. *advisable;* chiefly because it would instill in the child a respect for an authority stronger than his own
    B. *inadvisable;* chiefly because a child of that age should be permitted to express his opinions in order to develop his self-reliance and prevent over-dependency
    C. *advisable;* chiefly because it would cause the child to change his approach since it would seem obvious to him that his mother knew what was going on in his mind
    D. *inadvisable;* chiefly because it would increase his frustration and might increase his tendency to withdraw

47. An analysis of the basic need for love, acceptance, and emancipation of blind or otherwise physically handicapped children and of their basic reactions to their frustrations, rejection, and unhappiness shows that handicapped children generally

    A. demonstrate a less obvious basic need for attention and affection and show a more aggressive and hostile attitude toward frustration and unpleasantness than children without handicaps
    B. demonstrate a much greater basic need for security and react in a more docile and resigned manner to unpleasant situations than children without handicaps
    C. have the same basic needs and react to unpleasant situations in substantially the same manner as children without handicaps
    D. have the same basic needs as children without handicaps, but are unaffected by their handicaps only if their parents take great care to shield them from frustration and unpleasantness

48. It is generally felt by authorities in the field of special education that for a congenitally blind boy of pre-school age to be enrolled in a nursery school with sighted children is generally   48.____

    A. *advisable;* chiefly because the broader scope of the activities of the sighted children will enable the boy to become skilled in a broader range of activities
    B. *advisable;* chiefly because the group setting at school will give the boy no opportunity for peer relationships and for doing things without parental supervision
    C. *inadvisable;* chiefly because the boy will instinctively feel frustrated and punished by his impairment in the company of sighted children
    D. *inadvisable;* chiefly because the boy will be removed from parental affection and protection and will have to be idle during many of the activities of the sighted children

49. According to experts in the field today, the one of the following children MOST likely to become a delinquent is the one who   49.____

    A. behaves like a model child and is considered a good student in school, but is extremely difficult to handle at home
    B. feels that his parents are completely indifferent to him and his activities, and consequently feels that he is of no value to himself
    C. is punished by his mother for even slight misbehavior, and appears to be amused by such punishment
    D. is occasionally disciplined by severe spankings by his father for overt acts of misbehavior and is warned that such conduct borders on delinquency

50. Appropriate play and recreation is of immense value in the personality growth and development of a child CHIEFLY because it provides him with   50.____

    A. a group setting in which he can assert his desire to lead others as well as develop his leadership skills
    B. group experiences through which he learns to express his interests, his need for status and achievement, and his striving for independence and recognition
    C. healthful surroundings in which he can engage in supervised play under proper guidance
    D. the opportunity to learn new activities and skills, many of which will prove to be of great vocational value to him in later life

KEY (CORRECT ANSWERS)

1. A	11. B	21. B	31. C	41. B
2. B	12. A	22. D	32. B	42. D
3. B	13. C	23. C	33. C	43. A
4. A	14. D	24. A	34. C	44. A
5. C	15. A	25. A	35. B	45. B
6. A	16. B	26. A	36. D	46. D
7. D	17. B	27. D	37. B	47. C
8. C	18. D	28. C	38. D	48. A
9. D	19. C	29. D	39. B	49. B
10. C	20. A	30. B	40. C	50. B

EXAMINATION SECTION
TEST 1

DIRECTIONS: Each question or incomplete statement is followed by several suggested answers or completions. Select the one that BEST answers the question or completes the statement. *PRINT THE LETTER OF THE CORRECT ANSWER IN THE SPACE AT THE RIGHT.*

1. A person's behavior is both shaped and judged by the expectations he and his culture have invested in his status and the major social roles he carries. According to this principle, a caseworker can BEST make effective professional judgments and plan proper treatment if he recognizes that

    A. the client's problem may stem from role conflicts
    B. the client faces difficulties serenely once he knows what society expects of him
    C. cultural values have little to do with a client's status
    D. the status-seeking individual is not able to comprehend the function of cultural values in his life

2. The diagnostic approach in social casework, often called the Freudian School, has as its basic premise the

    A. investigation of past events of the client's life experiences and functioning in order to understand his present situation
    B. study of the subconscious mind of the client as to his present attitude and understanding about his situation
    C. examination of behavioral motivation of the client
    D. solution of the client's problem through aptitude testing and group therapy

3. There is implicit in casework an acceptance of a client's value system which may be different from that of the caseworker.
Of the following, the MOST valid conclusion to be derived from this statement is that

    A. clients do not have moral standards
    B. the caseworkers' standards are always stricter than the clients' standards
    C. cultural patterns have little effect on value systems of either clients or caseworkers
    D. a caseworker has no right to insist on conformity of a client's behavior with his own standards

4. The establishment and maintenance of a professional relationship with a client is stressed in casework. This relationship should be

    A. clear, business-like, and delimited by the agency function
    B. permissive, friendly, and kindly, with the pace determined by the client
    C. warm, enabling and consciously controlled by the caseworker
    D. variable and unpredictable because of the fluctuations in client need

5. There is great interest being shown currently in the possible merger of the child welfare and family casework fields, in private as well as public agencies.
The BEST argument in support of such a merger is that

A. families with child care problems would not be broken up through placement of children
B. the taxpayer's and the voluntary contributor's money would be saved
C. through intensive work with children, prevention of the development of behavior problems would be possible
D. new techniques in family casework treatment and the development of new community resources would probably result

6. Family casework involves working with parents and children about problems involving maintenance and survival.
Of the following types of problems, the MOST important one that a family caseworker has to handle generally involves

A. relationships with siblings
B. budgeting
C. psychotherapeutic problems
D. environmental deficiencies

7. The authoritative approach in casework, also known as aggressive casework, essentially involves

A. the break-up of families whose members no longer get along together
B. purposeful, persistent casework methods observing respect for the individual
C. direct supervision of a family until their problems are resolved
D. the application of techniques evolved by law enforcement agencies to social casework

8. The term *ambivalence,* as used in social casework, might BEST be illustrated by the

A. inability of the client to follow the recommendations of the caseworker due to his own unresolved conflicts
B. presentation to the client of more than one reasonable course of action for the client to follow
C. client's lack of any knowledge of how to solve his problem
D. client's fears for his future welfare

9. There is general agreement among experts in the field that, when dealing with a client or handling a case, a caseworker should

A. place emphasis on the objective aspects, directing her work primarily to the physical factors in the client that indicate need for change
B. place emphasis on the environmental factors, especially those surrounding the client which have caused him to be in his present state
C. give attention not only to the environmental factors and social experiences, but also to the client's feelings about, and reactions to, his experiences
D. consider each factor in the case as a separate unit after carefully distinguishing between the truly environmental and the truly emotional factors

10. In casework practice, the unit of attention is generally considered to be the family, although in some agencies the client or patient is often viewed as being outside of his family.
The trend in modern casework with respect to the family of a client is to

    A. involve the family wherever feasible in the total casework process
    B. scientifically determine wherein the family is harmful to the client and try to make plans for the client to leave his family
    C. educate the public so that families of clients will not interfere with agency plans
    D. refer every member of the family for casework help

11. John L., 15, was referred to a youth counseling agency by the principal of the high school he attends because he has been truanting for the past six months. He is of above average intelligence, is in his sophomore year, and is currently failing 4 out of 5 of his courses. His mother says that he frequently comes home after midnight and is friendly with two boys with court records. The family group consists of John and his mother, who supports then by working as a secretary. Two sisters, 19 and 21, are married and out of the home. Mr. L. deserted when John was 3. The principal told John he had to go to the youth counseling agency or be brought into court by the truant officer.
In beginning to work with John, the caseworker should FIRST

    A. recognize that since John did not come voluntarily he will refuse casework treatment
    B. establish himself as an adult who will keep John in line
    C. secure more facts about John and his situation in order to determine further case activity
    D. promise that the agency will keep John from being sent to juvenile court

12. A client tells the social worker that he is planning to leave his job as a junior executive trainee in a department store for a job as a laborer which will pay him a higher salary. After exploring the client's reasons for making this move, the caseworker feels the plan is unwise since the trainee position offers a considerably better future.
In this situation, it would be BEST for the caseworker to

    A. attempt to dissuade the client from making the job change, pointing out the reasons for the inadvisability of the move
    B. allow the client to change jobs, without attempting to dissuade or counsel him
    C. refuse to give the client permission to change jobs without an attempt to dissuade or counsel him
    D. try to dissuade the client from making the job change without giving the real reasons for thinking the move undesirable

13. Casework interviewing is always directed to the client and his situation.
The one of the following which is the MOST accurate statement with respect to the proper focus of an interview is that the

    A. caseworker limits the client to concentration on objective data
    B. client is generally permitted to talk about facts and feelings with no direction from the caseworker
    C. main focus in casework interviews is on feelings rather than facts
    D. caseworker is responsible for helping the client focus on any material which seems to be related to his problems or difficulties

14. Assume that you are conducting a training program for the caseworkers under your supervision. At one of the sessions, you discuss the problem of interviewing a dull and stupid client who gives a slow and disconnected case history.
The BEST of the following interviewing methods for you to recommend in such a case in order to ascertain the facts is for the caseworker to

    A. ask the client leading questions requiring *yes* or *no* answers
    B. request the client to limit his narration to the essential facts so that the interview can be kept as brief as possible
    C. review the story with the client, patiently asking simple questions
    D. tell the client that unless he is more cooperative he cannot be helped to solve his problem

15. A caseworker under your supervision has been assigned the task of interviewing a man who is applying for foster home placement for his two children. The caseworker seeks your advice as to how to question this man, stating that she finds the applicant to be a timid and self-conscious person who seems torn between the necessity of having to answer the worker's questions truthfully and the effect
he thinks his answers will have on his application. Of the following, the BEST method for the caseworker to use in order to determine the essential facts in this case is to

    A. assure the applicant that he need not worry since the majority of applications for foster home placement are approved
    B. delay the applicant's narration of the facts important to the case until his embarrassment and fears have been overcome
    C. ignore the statements made by the applicant and obtain all the required information from his friends and relatives
    D. inform the applicant that all statements made by him will be verified and are subject to the law governing perjury

16. A recent development in casework interviewing procedure, known as multiple-client interviewing, consists of interviews of the entire family at the same time. However, this may not be an effective casework method in certain situations.
Of the following, the situation in which the standard individual interview would be PREFERABLE is when

    A. family members derive consistent and major gratification from assisting each other in their destructive responses
    B. there is a crucial family conflict to which the members are reacting
    C. the family is overwhelmed by interpersonal anxieties which have not been explored
    D. the worker wants to determine the pattern of family interaction to further his diagnostic understanding

17. The one of the following which is the CHIEF value of verbatim recording of all or a portion of an important interview is the possibility it offers for

    A. careful study and clarification of psychological goals in treatment
    B. a prompt solution to the problem by preservation, in an orderly and concise fashion, of the full psychological and economic picture of the client's situation

C. quick determination of the more obvious social goals and offering of concrete services by presentation of the essential facts
D. supervision of experienced workers by showing the emotional overtones, subtle reactions, and intricate worker-client interchanges

18. Experts in the field of social casework recording generally agree that the kind of case material for which the narrative form of recording is MOST suitable is

    A. material that deals with feelings, attitudes, and client-worker relationships, because this style permits the use of primary evidence in the form of verbal material and behavior observed in the interview
    B. social data, including eligibility material and family background history, because it can then be presented in a chronological, orderly fashion to enable the worker to select the desired facts
    C. personal facts concerning the individual's personality patterns and their growth and development, because they can be seen in an orderly progression from primal immaturity until their ultimate stage of completion
    D. selectively chosen and documented material essential to a quicker and clearer understanding of the various ramifications of the case by a new worker, when responsibility for handling the client is reassigned

19. A case record includes relevant social and psychological facts about the client, the nature of his request, his feeling about his situation, his attitude towards the agency, and his use of and reaction to treatment.
    In addition, it should ALWAYS contain

    A. a routine history
    B. complete details of personality development and emotional relationships
    C. detailed process accounts of all contacts
    D. data necessary for understanding the problem and the factors important in arriving at a solution

20. The CHIEF basis for the inability of a troubled client to express his problem clearly to the caseworker is that the client

    A. sees his problem in complex terms and does not think it possible to give the caseworker the whole picture
    B. has erected defenses against emotions that seem to him inadmissible or intolerable
    C. cannot describe how he feels about his problem
    D. views the situation as unlikely to be solved and is blocked in self-expression

21. The one of the following statements which is MOST accurate with respect to the proper role of a social worker in giving casework service to medically ill clients is that she should

    A. understand the general aspects of medical treatment of the client's illness
    B. refrain from any involvement in the client's medical care or treatment routine
    C. be concerned only with problems directly relating to the client's illness
    D. consider problems of the client apart from the medical setting

22. Casework treatment of the ill involves various techniques. Of the following, the MOST important is one of

    A. imparting to the patient an understanding of the limits of his future vocational placement
    B. limiting the family's contact with the patient during the treatment regime
    C. instructing the patient in hospital routine
    D. dealing with the patient's feelings of dependency as part of his illness

23. Rehabilitation is an important part of the medical social worker's function.
    Of the following, the MAJOR limitation on the medical social worker's activity in rehabilitation may be caused by

    A. restrictive regulations imposed by the hospital
    B. deficiencies in professional medical supervision
    C. lack of any suitable after-care program
    D. the patient's financial problems

24. A medical social worker, newly assigned to a hospital medical service which had previously functioned without a social worker, is eager to develop a caseload of patients who can make the most appropriate use of her skills.
    After the initial step of interpreting the scope of the social worker's service to medical and other collaborative personnel, the BEST course for the social worker to take would be to

    A. accept all cases referred by medical and other personnel and quickly weed out those cases inappropriately referred
    B. accept for service all cases in which patients and relatives refer themselves and use these cases to reprove the medical personnel for their failure to refer
    C. reject all cases referred by medical and other collaborative personnel that are inappropriate and use these as illustrative material in interpreting her services
    D. accept all appropriate referrals from medical and other personnel and interpret her services to them using these specific cases as illustrative material

25. As a member of a team involved in the treatment of a patient, the psychiatric social worker has certain responsibilities.
    The one of the following which is the MOST accurate statement with respect to such responsibility is that she has

    A. primary responsibility for determining significant social factors
    B. major responsibility for establishing psychiatric diagnosis
    C. responsibility for working out a treatment regime
    D. sole responsibility for contact with the family

26. The MOST important of the following techniques in the treatment of the psychiatric patient by the social worker is

    A. intensive psychotherapy
    B. proving the irrationality of delusions
    C. modifying the patient's behavior so that he can live with his family successfully
    D. widening through education and support the area in which the patient functions

27. One of the contributions which a psychiatric social worker usually makes to the treatment of an individual under a mental hygiene program is

   A. the ability to make prognoses of the cases receiving treatment under the medical care program
   B. a recognition of the limitations of clinical medicine and of the futility of dispensing care that is not planned in relation to the client's social situation
   C. the determination of the extent to which a client's economic situation reflects his deep-seated emotional conflicts
   D. the mobilization, with the consent and participation of the individual, of resources in his home or community which may facilitate his recovery or adjustment

27.____

28. The one of the following factors which has had the GREATEST effect on the functioning of psychiatric social workers has been the

   A. decreasing trend in the number of identified cases of mental illness in the general population
   B. development of chemotherapy which cures psychiatric disorders
   C. expansion in community facilities for the care of psychiatric patients
   D. emergence of new successful forms of psychotherapy for psychiatric patients

28.____

29. In giving casework service, to a family, one or more of the members may require treatment.
   In giving such service,

   A. only one member of a family can be seen by the caseworker
   B. the decision as to the particular client selected for treatment will be based on the nature of the problem and the psychosocial diagnosis
   C. children are never selected for primary treatment focus
   D. all members of a family have to be seen by the caseworker at the same time

29.____

30. A 32-year-old wife and mother of two young children applies to a family counseling service because of her concern about the deterioration of her marriage of ten years' duration.
   In order to achieve optimum benefits from such counseling, it would be MOST desirable for the

   A. husband to be involved indirectly through counseling recommendations brought to him by his wife
   B. husband to participate directly in the counseling process along with his wife
   C. husband and the children to be involved directly in the counseling process
   D. wife only to receive counseling, without involving her husband

30.____

31. A child has been temporarily removed from his household and given foster home care because of continued neglect and mistreatment at home.
   The one of the following which is the CHIEF reason why it is important for casework therapy to be given to his parents is to

   A. bring them to a clearer realization of the undesirability of their conduct and the sad consequences to which their conduct had led

31.____

B. help them to effect a change during the child's stay in foster care so that he can return to a more secure and satisfying relationship with his own family
C. make them realize that it was their conduct alone which had made the child act in an anti-social manner and which had precipitated the action to remove him from the household
D. prevent them from degenerating further to a point where they too will become a more serious social problem and need possible institutionalization

32. When a decision has been reached that a wayward child's needs can best be met by foster home placement, the BEST of the following approaches for the caseworker assigned to the case to use in order to break the news to the child is to

   A. inform the child that, although he is being punished in this manner for his bad conduct, he is being separated from his family only temporarily until home conditions are good enough for him to return
   B. point out to the child that he is being placed in a fine home with foster parents who are more fit and interested in his welfare than his own parents and that as he grows older he will be thankful for this opportunity
   C. reassure the child that no punishment is involved in his separation from home and that efforts will be made to help him and his parents to achieve the needed changes which will enable him to return home
   D. tell the child in a friendly but frank manner that he is being removed from the home because of his parents' inability and lack of interest in helping him to become better adjusted

33. A child who has been placed in a foster home runs away to the home of his mother and stepfather. A decision to place him in the custody of another relative is being considered. To return the child to foster care while this change is under consideration would be

   A. *correct;* no change should be made until a careful consideration of all the facts in the case will point to a final decision
   B. *incorrect;* since the child ran away from a foster home, he was unhappy there, and his desires should be of prime importance
   C. *correct;* since the child had been placed in a foster home earlier, the home of his mother must have been a less desirable place for him
   D. *incorrect;* no matter how bad his own home may be, it is definitely better for a child to be with his own relatives than with strangers

34. In comparing the advantages of foster home over institutional placement, it is generally agreed that institutional care is LEAST advisable for children

   A. who cannot sustain the intimacy of foster family living because of their experiences with their own parents
   B. who are socially well-adjusted or have had considerable experience in living with a family
   C. who have need for special facilities for observation, diagnosis, and treatment
   D. whose natural parents find it difficult to accept the idea of foster home placement because of its close resemblance to adoption

35. The school can play a vital part in detecting the child who displays overt symptomatic behavior indicative of social maladjustment CHIEFLY because the teacher has the opportunity to

   A. assume a pseudo-parental role in regard to discipline and punishment, thereby limiting the extent of the maladjusted child's anti-social behavior
   B. observe how the child relates to the group and what reactions are stimulated in him by his peer relationships
   C. determine whether the adjustment difficulties displayed by the child were brought on by the teacher herself, or by the other students
   D. help the child's parents to resolve the difficulties in adjustment which are indicated by the child's reactions to the social pressures exerted by his peers

36. A 9-year-old boy is living at home with his remarried, widowed mother, his stepfather, and his 3-year-old half-sister. The boy is being neglected and often severely mistreated by his mother and stepfather. The stepfather resents the boy's presence in the home.
   After failing to correct the situation by discussions with the boy's mother and stepfather, the caseworker should recommend, for the boy's welfare,

   A. foster home placement in order to prevent his further mistreatment while corrective educational therapy is used on the parents
   B. permanent separation of the boy from his family as the best means of preventing his continued exposure to the unsatisfactory pressures in the household
   C. placement of the boy outside the household and a stern warning to the parents that similar action will be taken on behalf of the younger child should the situation warrant it
   D. temporary placement of the boy with a foster family until such time as the stepfather is no longer in the household

37. A deserted woman and her 13-year-old son have been receiving public assistance. The woman is drunk most of the time, is known to be consorting with men at all hours, and has been unresponsive to casework treatment. The son has been involved in a few minor incidents which have brought him to the attention of the authorities.
   The BEST action for the caseworker to take at this point in order to keep the son from becoming an outright delinquent is to recommend that

   A. the mother be arrested and jailed for contributing to the delinquency of a minor and the son be sent to a reformatory
   B. no action be taken against the mother because that will lower her status in the eyes of her son and will further weaken family controls
   C. the son be temporarily placed in a foster home and the mother be given treatment for alcoholism
   D. the son be committed to a corrective school where his bad habits can be corrected, since the mother is apparently too sick to assume her responsibilities toward her son

38. In treating juvenile delinquents, it has been found that there are some who make better social adjustment through group treatment than through an individual casework approach.
   In selecting delinquent boys for group treatment, the one of the following which is the MOST important consideration is that

A. the boys to be treated in one group be friends or from the same community
B. only boys who consent to group treatment be included in the group
C. the ages of the boys included in the group vary as much as possible
D. only boys who have not reacted to an individual casework approach be included in the group

39. Multi-problem families are generally characterized by various functional indicators. Of the following, the family which is MOST likely to be a multi-problem family is one which has

    A. unemployed adult family members
    B. parents with diagnosed character disorders
    C. children and parents with a series of difficulties in the community
    D. poor housekeeping standards

40. Multi-problem families generally have a complex history of intervention by a variety of social agencies.
    Of the following phases involved in planning for their treatment, the one which is MOST important to consider FIRST is the

    A. joint decision to limit any help to be given
    B. analysis of facts and definition of the problems involved
    C. determination of treatment priorities
    D. study of available community resources

41. The service given by the caseworker to the multi-problem family involves many approaches to this client group.
    Of the following, the MOST important task is

    A. referral to other agencies
    B. direct casework treatment of parents and children
    C. soliciting and sustaining agency service on a case basis
    D. intensive psychological treatment of the children

42. In the treatment of multi-problem families, the one of the following statements which should be accepted by the caseworker is:

    A. The existence of severe social pathology makes it impossible to deal with the psychiatric problems of the family members
    B. Multi-problem families tend to become known to social work agencies in neighborhoods with inadequate facilities to meet community needs
    C. Multi-problem families have not responded to the new approaches developed by social workers
    D. Full-time employment of family members will resolve the difficulties of multi-problem families

43. In aggressive casework, when a caseworker visits a multi-problem family, she should begin by

    A. arranging individual interviews with the children
    B. outlining the steps to be taken in the solution of their problems

C. inviting the family to visit the agency so that a normal casework situation may be created
D. explaining what points of risk or danger exist in their situation and inviting an expression of their feelings

44. In visiting a school attended by children of a *hard core* family under treatment by your agency, it would generally be ADVISABLE to

    A. keep the school visit a secret from the family so as not to embarrass the children
    B. encourage the parents to obtain all necessary information themselves
    C. inform the family only if you have secured positive information from the school
    D. have the family fully accept the purpose of the visit beforehand

45. In the process of *reaching out to* service multi-problem families, often many initial appointments are made with adolescents before their parents have received much sustained treatment.
    This practice is

    A. *undesirable;* adolescents are still subject to parental control and, therefore, the parents should be the focus of treatment
    B. *desirable;* juvenile delinquency is the chief cause of difficulty in multi-problem families
    C. *undesirable;* parental distrust of the worker is increased, thus negating the worker's efforts
    D. *desirable;* adolescents are individual clients and should be so treated

46. During several interviews with a child from a multi-problem family, you notice bruises on her upper arms, neck and face. Upon questioning, the child says she fell down the stairs.
    Of the following, the BEST procedure for you to follow is to

    A. call the police and have the parents arrested for child abuse
    B. assume the child is telling the truth
    C. have the child removed from the home pending an investigation
    D. refer the matter to child protective services

47. One of your clients, a 13-year-old girl, tells you she is pregnant.
    Of the following, your FIRST action should be to

    A. chastise the girl for her irresponsibility
    B. call the girl's parents
    C. discuss with her the options she has available
    D. suggest she have an abortion

48. Under state law, jurisdiction over cases involving the protection and treatment of persons under 16 years of age will be vested in the

    A. Family Court   B. Civil or District Court
    C. Supreme Court   D. County Court

49. Of the following, the condition which would concern you the LEAST during a visit to a client's home is   49.____

    A. no food in the refrigerator
    B. dirty dishes in the sink
    C. three naked children with bruises on their arms and backs
    D. many empty liquor bottles

50. A caseworker in a city agency is planning to refer one of her clients to a private agency in the community. The one of the following which is of GREATEST importance in insuring that the transfer will actually take place is that the   50.____

    A. agency is located within the client's proper district
    B. client will cooperate in bringing about such a transfer
    C. caseworker will assure the client that transfer does not mean rejection by the former
    D. agency does not require a fee in excess of what the client can afford

---

KEY (CORRECT ANSWERS)

1. A	11. C	21. A	31. B	41. C
2. A	12. A	22. D	32. C	42. B
3. D	13. D	23. C	33. A	43. D
4. C	14. C	24. D	34. B	44. D
5. D	15. B	25. A	35. B	45. C
6. D	16. A	26. D	36. A	46. D
7. B	17. A	27. D	37. C	47. C
8. A	18. A	28. C	38. B	48. A
9. C	19. D	29. B	39. C	49. B
10. A	20. B	30. B	40. B	50. B

INTERVIEWING

EXAMINATION SECTION

TEST 1

DIRECTIONS: Each question or incomplete statement is followed by several suggested answers or completions. Select the one that BEST answers the question or completes the statement. *PRINT THE LETTER OF THE CORRECT ANSWER IN THE SPACE AT THE RIGHT.*

1. Of the following, the MAIN advantage to the supervisor of using the indirect (or nondirective) interview, in which he asks only guiding questions and encourages the employee to do most of the talking, is that he can
   A. obtain a mass of information about the employee in a very short period of time
   B. easily get at facts which the employee wishes to conceal
   C. get answers which are not slanted or biased in order to win his favor
   D. effectively deal with an employee's serious emotional problems

2. An interviewer under your supervision routinely closes his interview with a reassuring remark such as, "I'm sure you soon will be well," or "Everything will soon be all right."
   This practice is USUALLY considered
   A. *advisable*, chiefly because the interviewer may make the patient feel better
   B. *inadvisable*, chiefly because it may cause a patient who is seriously ill to doubt the worker's understanding of the situation
   C. *advisable*, chiefly because the patient becomes more receptive if further interviews are needed
   D. *inadvisable*, chiefly because the interviewer should usually not show that he is emotionally involved

3. An interviewer has just ushered out a client he has interviewed. As the interviewer is preparing to leave, the client mentions a fact that seems to contradict the information he has given.
   Of the following, it would be BEST for the interviewer at this time to
   A. make no response but write the fact down in his report and plan to come back another day
   B. point out to the client that he has contradicted himself and ask for an explanation
   C. ask the client to elaborate on the comment and attempt to find out further information about the fact
   D. disregard the comment since the client was probably exhausted and not thinking clearly

2 (#1)

4. A client who is being interviewed insists on certain facts. The interviewer knows that these statements are incorrect.
   In regard to the rest of the client's statements, the interviewer is MOST justified to
   A. disregard any information the client gives which cannot be verified
   B. try to discover other misstatements by confronting the client with the discrepancy
   C. consider everything else which the client has said as the truth unless proved otherwise
   D. ask the client to prove his statements

5. Immediately after the interviewer identifies himself to a client, she says in a hysterical voice that he is not to be trusted.
   Of the following, the BEST course of action for the interviewer to follow would be to
   A. tell the woman sternly that if she does not stay calm, he will leave
   B. assure the woman that there is no cause to worry
   C. ignore the woman until she becomes quiet
   D. ask the woman to explain her problem

6. Assume that you are an interviewer and that one of your interviewees has asked you for advice on dealing with a personal problem.
   Of the following, the BEST action for you to take is to
   A. tell him about a similar problem which you know worked out well
   B. advise him not to worry
   C. explain that the problem is quite a usual one and that the situation will be brighter soon
   D. give no opinion and change the subject when practicable

7. All of the following are generally good approaches for an interviewer to use in order to improve his interviews EXCEPT
   A. developing a routine approach so that interviews can be standardized
   B. comparing his procedure with that of others engaged in similar work
   C. reviewing each interview critically, picking out one or two weak points to concentrate on improving
   D. comparing his own more successful and less successful interviews

8. Assume that a supervisor suggests at a staff meeting that digital recorders be provided for interviewers. Following are four arguments *against* the use of digital recorders that are raised by other members of the staff that might be valid:
   I. Recorded interviews provide too much unnecessary information
   II. Recorded interviews provide no record of manner or gestures
   III. Digital recorders are too cumbersome and difficult for the average supervisor to manage
   IV. Digital recorders may inhibit the interviewee

Which one of the following choices MOST accurately classifies the above into those which are generally *invalid* and those which are *not*?
- A. I and II are generally valid, but III and IV are not.
- B. IV is generally valid, but I, II, and III are not.
- C. I, II, and IV are generally valid, but III is not.
- D. I, II, III, and IV are generally valid.

9. During an interview, the PRIMARY advantage of the technique of using questions as opposed to allowing the interviewee to talk freely is that questioning
   - A. gives the interviewer greater control
   - B. provides a more complete picture
   - C. makes the interviewee more relaxed
   - D. decreases the opportunity for exaggeration

10. Assume that, in conducting an interview, an interviewer takes into consideration the age, sex, education, and background of the subject.
    This practice is GENERALLY considered
    - A. *undesirable*, mainly because an interviewer may be prejudiced by such factors
    - B. *desirable*, mainly because these are factors which might influence a person's response to certain questions
    - C. *undesirable*, mainly because these factors rarely have any bearing on the matter being investigated
    - D. *desirable*, mainly because certain categories of people answer certain questions in the same way

11. If a client should begin to tell his life story during an interview, the BEST course of action for an interviewer to take is to
    - A. interrupt immediately and insist that they return to business
    - B. listen attentively until the client finishes and then ask if they can return to the subject
    - C. pretend to have other business and come back later to see the client
    - D. interrupt politely at an appropriate point and direct the client's attention to the subject

12. An interviewer who is trying to discover the circumstances surrounding a client's accident would be MOST successful during an interview if he avoided questions which
    - A. lead the client to discuss the matter in detail
    - B. can easily be answered by either "yes" or "no"
    - C. ask for specific information
    - D. may be embarrassing or annoying to the client

13. A client being interviewed may develop an emotional reaction (positive or negative) toward the interviewer.
    The BEST attitude for the interviewer to take toward such feelings is that they are
    - A. *inevitable*; they should be accepted but kept under control
    - B. *unusual*; they should be treated impersonally

C. *obstructive*; they should be resisted at all costs
D. *abnormal*; they should be eliminated as soon as possible

14. Encouraging the client being interviewed to talk freely at first is a technique that is supported by all of the following reasons EXCEPT that it
    A. tends to counteract any preconceived ideas that the interviewer may have entertained about the client
    B. gives the interviewer a chance to learn the best method of approach to obtain additional information
    C. inhibits the client from looking to the interviewer for support and advice
    D. allows the client to reveal the answers to many questions before they are asked

14.____

15. Of the following, generally the MOST effective way for an interviewer to assure full cooperation from the client he is interviewing is to
    A. sympathize with the client's problems and assure him of concern
    B. tell a few jokes before beginning to ask questions
    C. convince the patient that the answers to the questions will help him as well as the interviewer
    D. arrange the interview when the client feels best

15.____

16. Since many elderly people are bewildered and helpless when interviewed, special consideration should be given to them.
    Of the following, the BEST way for an interviewer to *initially* approach elderly clients who express anxiety and fear is to
    A. assure them that they have nothing to worry about
    B. listen patiently and show interest in them
    C. point out the specific course of action that is best for them
    D. explain to them that many people have overcome much greater difficulties

16.____

17. Assume that, in planning an initial interview, an interviewer determines in advance what information is needed in order to fulfill the purpose of the interview.
    Of the following, this procedure usually does NOT
    A. reduce the number of additional interviews required
    B. expedite the processing of the case
    C. improve public opinion of the interviewer's agency
    D. assure the cooperation of the person interviewed

17.____

18. Sometimes an interviewer deliberately introduces his own personal interests and opinions into an interview with a client.
    In general, this practice should be considered
    A. *desirable*, primarily because the relationship between client and interviewer becomes social rather than businesslike
    B. *undesirable*, primarily because the client might complain to his supervisor
    C. *desirable*, primarily because the focus of attention is directed toward the client
    D. *undesirable*, primarily because an argument between client and interviewer could result

18.____

19. The one of the following types of interviewees who presents the LEAST difficult problem to handle is the person who
    A. answers with a great many qualifications
    B. talks at length about unrelated subjects so that the interviewer cannot ask questions
    C. has difficulty understanding the interviewer's vocabulary
    D. breaks into the middle of sentences and completes them with a meaning of his own

19._____

20. A man being interviewed is entitled to Medicaid, but he refuses to sign up for it because he says he cannot accept any form of welfare.
    Of the following, the BEST course of action for an interviewer to take FIRST is to
    A. try to discover the reason for his feeling this way
    B. tell him that he should be glad financial help is available
    C. explain that others cannot help him if he will not help himself
    D. suggest that he speak to someone who is already on Medicaid

20._____

21. Of the following, the outcome of an interview by an interviewer depend MOST heavily on the
    A. personality of the interviewee
    B. personality of the interviewer
    C. subject matter of the questions asked
    D. interaction between interviewer and interviewee

21._____

22. Some clients being interviewed by an interviewer are primarily interested in making a favorable impression.
    The interviewer should be aware of the fact that such clients are MORE likely than other clients to
    A. try to anticipate the answers the interviewer is looking for
    B. answer all questions openly and frankly
    C. try to assume the role of interviewer
    D. be anxious to get the interview over as quickly as possible

22._____

23. The type of interview which a hospital care interviewer usually conducts is *substantially different* from most interviewing situations in all of the following EXCEPT the
    A. setting   B. kinds of clients
    C. techniques employed   D. kinds of problems

23._____

24. During an interview, an interviewer uses a "leading question."
    This type of question is so-called because it *generally*
    A. starts a series of questions about one topic
    B. suggests the answer which the interviewer wants
    C. forms the basis for a following "trick" question
    D. sets, at the beginning, the tone of the interview

24._____

25. An interviewer may face various difficulties when he tries to obtain information from a client.
Of the following, the difficulty which is EASIEST for the interviewer to overcome occurs when a client
   A. is unwilling to reveal the information
   B. misunderstands what information is needed
   C. does not have the information available to him
   D. is unable to coherently give the information requested

KEY (CORRECT ANSWERS)

1.	C	11.	D
2.	B	12.	B
3.	C	13.	A
4.	C	14.	C
5.	D	15.	C
6.	D	16.	B
7.	A	17.	D
8.	C	18.	D
9.	A	19.	C
10.	B	20.	A

21.	D
22.	A
23.	C
24.	B
25.	B

TEST 2

DIRECTIONS: Each question or incomplete statement is followed by several suggested answers or completions. Select the one that BEST answers the question or completes the statement. *PRINT THE LETTER OF THE CORRECT ANSWER IN THE SPACE AT THE RIGHT.*

1. Of the following, the MOST appropriate manner for an interviewer to assume during an interview with a client is
   A. authoritarian   B. paternal   C. casual   D. businesslike

   1.____

2. The systematic study of interviewing theory, principles, and techniques by an interviewer will USUALLY
   A. aid him to act in a depersonalized manner
   B. turn his interviewees into stereotyped affairs
   C. make the people he interviews feel manipulated
   D. give him a basis for critically examining his own practice

   2.____

3. Compiling in advance a list of general questions to ask a client during an interview is a technique USUALLY considered
   A. *desirable*, chiefly because reference to the list will help keep the interview focused on the important issues
   B. *undesirable*, chiefly because use of such a list will discourage the client from speaking freely
   C. *desirable*, chiefly because the list will serve as a record of what questions were asked
   D. *undesirable*, chiefly because use of such a list will make the interview too mechanical and impersonal

   3.____

4. The one of the following which is usually of GREATEST importance in winning the cooperation of a person being interviewed and while achieving the purpose of the interview is the interviewer's ability to
   A. gain the confidence of the person being interviewed
   B. stick to the subject of the interview
   C. handle a person who is obviously lying
   D. prevent the person being interviewed from withholding information

   4.____

5. While interviewing clients, an interviewer should use the technique of interruption, beginning to speak when a client has temporarily paused at the end of a phrase or sentence, in order to
   A. limit the client's ability to voice his objections or complaints
   B. shorten, terminate or redirect a client's response
   C. assert authority when he feels that the client is too conceited
   D. demonstrate to the client that pauses in speech should be avoided

   5.____

6. An interviewer might gain background information about a client by being aware of the person's speech during an interview.
   Which one of the following patterns of speech would offer the LEAST accurate information about a client? The

   6.____

A. number of slang expressions and the level of vocabulary
B. presence and degree of an accent
C. rate of speech and the audibility level
D. presence of a physical speech defect

7. Suppose that you are interviewing a distressed client who claims that he was just laid off from his job and has no money to pay his rent.
Your FIRST action should be to
   A. ask if he has sought other employment or has other sources of income
   B. express your sympathy but explain that he must pay the rent on time
   C. inquire about the reasons he was laid off from work
   D. try to transfer him to a smaller apartment which he can afford

8. Suppose you have some background information on an applicant whom you are interviewing. During the interview, it appears that the applicant is giving you false information.
The BEST thing for you to do at that point is to
   A. pretend that you are not aware of the written facts and let him continue
   B. tell him what you already know and discuss the discrepancies with him
   C. terminate the interview and make a note that the applicant is untrustworthy
   D. tell him that, because he is making false statements, he will not be eligible for an apartment

9. A Spanish-speaking applicant may want to bring his bilingual child with him to an interview to act as an interpreter.
Which of the following would be LEAST likely to affect the value of an interview in which an applicant's child has act as interpreter?
   A. It may make it undesirable to ask certain questions.
   B. A child may do an inadequate job of interpretation.
   C. A child's answers may indicate his feelings toward his parents.
   D. The applicant may not want to reveal all information in front of his child.

10. Assume you are assigned to interview applicants.
Of the following, which is the BEST attitude for you to take in dealing with applicants?
    A. Assume they will enjoy being interviewed because they believe that you have the power of decision
    B. Expect that they have a history of anti-social behavior in the family, and probe deeply into the social development of family members
    C. Expect that they will try to control the interview, thus you should keep them on the defensive
    D. Assume that they will be polite and cooperative and attempt to secure the information you need in a business-like manner

11. If you are interviewing an applicant who is a minority group member in reference to his eligibility, it would be BEST for you to use language that is
    A. *informal*, using ethnic expressions known to the applicant
    B. *technical*, using the expressions commonly used in the agency

C. *simple*, using words and phrases which laymen understand
D. *formal* to remind the applicant that he is dealing with a government agency

12. When interviewing an applicant to determine his eligibility, it is MOST important to
    A. have a prior mental picture of the typical eligible applicant
    B. conduct the interview strictly according to a previously prepared script
    C. keep in mind the goal of the interview, which is to determine eligibility
    D. get an accurate and detailed account of the applicant's life history

13. The practice of trying to imagine yourself in the applicant's place during an interview is
    A. *good*, mainly because you will be able to evaluate his responses better
    B. *good*, mainly because it will enable you to treat him as a friend rather than as an applicant
    C. *poor*, mainly because it is important for the applicant to see you as an impartial person
    D. *poor*, mainly because it is too time-consuming to do this with each applicant

14. When dealing with clients from different ethnic backgrounds, you should be aware of certain tendencies toward prejudice.
    Which of the following statements is LEAST likely to be valid?
    A. Whites prejudiced against Blacks are more likely to be prejudiced against Hispanics than Whites not prejudiced against Blacks.
    B. The less a White is in competition with Blacks, the less likely he is to be prejudiced against them.
    C. Persons who have moved from one social group to another are likely to retain the attitudes and prejudices of their original social group.
    D. When there are few Blacks or Hispanics in a project, Whites are less likely to be prejudiced against them than when there are many.

15. Of the following, the one who is MOST likely to be a good interviewer of people seeking assistance, is one who
    A. tries to get applicants to apply to another agency instead
    B. believes that it is necessary to get as much pertinent information as possible in order to determine the applicant's real needs
    C. believes that people who seek assistance are likely to have persons with a history of irresponsible behavior in their households
    D. is convinced that there is no need for a request for assistance

KEY (CORRECT ANSWERS)

1.	D	6.	C	11.	C
2.	D	7.	A	12.	C
3.	A	8.	B	13.	A
4.	A	9.	C	14.	C
5.	B	10.	D	15.	B

PREPARING WRITTEN MATERIALS
EXAMINATION SECTION
TEST 1

DIRECTIONS: Each question consists of a sentence which may be classified appropriately under one of the following four categories:
- A. Incorrect because of faulty grammar or sentence structure.
- B. Incorrect because of faulty punctuation.
- C. Incorrect because of faulty spelling or capitalization.
- D. Correct

Examine each sentence carefully. Then, in the space at the right, print the capital letter preceding the option which is the BEST of the four suggested above. All incorrect sentences contain only one type of error. Consider a sentence correct if it contains none of the types of errors mentioned, although there may be other correct ways of expressing the same thought.

1. The fire apparently started in the storeroom, which is usually locked.   1._____

2. On approaching the victim two bruises were noticed by this officer.   2._____

3. The officer, who was there examined the report with great care.   3._____

4. Each employee in the office had a separate desk.   4._____

5. The suggested procedure is similar to the one now in use.   5._____

6. No one was more pleased with the new procedure than the chauffeur.   6._____

7. He tried to pursuade her to change the procedure.   7._____

8. The total of the expenses charged to petty cash were high.   8._____

9. An understanding between him and I was finally reached.   9._____

10. It was at the supervisor's request that the clerk agreed to postpone his vacation.   10._____

11. We do not believe that it is necessary for both he and the clerk to attend the conference.   11._____

12. All employees, who display perseverance, will be given adequate recognition.   12._____

13. He regrets that some of us employees are dissatisfied with our new assignments.   13._____

14. "Do you think that the raise was merited," asked the supervisor? 14._____

15. The new manual of procedure is a valuable supplament to our rules and regulation. 15._____

16. The typist admitted that she had attempted to pursuade the other employees to assist her in her work. 16._____

17. The supervisor asked that all amendments to the regulations be handled by you and I. 17._____

18. They told both he and I that the prisoner had escaped. 18._____

19. Any superior officer, who, disregards the just complaints of his subordinates, is remiss in the performance of his duty. 19._____

20. Only those members of the national organization who resided in the Middle west attended the conference in Chicago. 20._____

21. We told him to give the investigation assignment to whoever was available. 21._____

22. Please do not disappoint and embarass us by not appearing in court. 22._____

23. Despite the efforts of the Supervising mechanic, the elevator could not be started. 23._____

24. The U.S. Weather Bureau, weather record for the accident date was checked. 24._____

KEY (CORRECT ANSWERS)

1.	D	11.	A
2.	A	12.	B
3.	B	13.	D
4.	D	14.	B
5.	D	15.	C
6.	D	16.	C
7.	C	17.	A
8.	A	18.	A
9.	A	19.	B
10.	D	20.	C

21.	D
22.	C
23.	C
24.	B

TEST 2

DIRECTIONS: Each question consists of a sentence. Some of the sentences contain errors in English grammar or usage, punctuation, spelling, or capitalization. A sentence does not contain an error simply because it could be written in a different manner. Choose answer:
- A. If the sentence contains an error in English grammar or usage.
- B. if the sentence contains an error in punctuation.
- C. If the sentence contains an error in spelling or capitalization
- D. If the sentence does not contain any errors.

1. The severity of the sentence prescribed by contemporary statutes—including both the former and the revised New York Penal Laws—do not depend on what crime was intended by the offender.   1.____

2. It is generally recognized that two defects in the early law of attempt played a part in the birth of burglary: (1) immunity from prosecution for conduct short of the last act before completion of the crime, and (2) the relatively minor penalty imposed for an attempt (it being a common law misdemeanor) vis-à-vis the completed offense.   2.____

3. The first sentence of the statute is applicable to employees who enter their place of employment, invited guests, and all other persons who have an express or implied license or privilege to enter the premises.   3.____

4. Contemporary criminal codes in the United States generally divide burglary into various degrees, differentiating the categories according to place, time and other attendent circumstances.   4.____

5. The assignment was completed in record time but the payroll for it has not yet been prepaid.   5.____

6. The operator, on the other hand, is willing to learn me how to use the mimeograph.   6.____

7. She is the prettiest of the three sisters.   7.____

8. She doesn't know; if the mail has arrived.   8.____

9. The doorknob of the office door is broke.   9.____

10. Although the department's supply of scratch pads and stationery have diminished considerably, the allotment for our division has not been reduced.   10.____

11. You have not told us whom you wish to designate as your secretary.   11.____

12. Upon reading the minutes of the last meeting, the new proposal was taken up for consideration.   12.____

2 (#2)

13. Before beginning the discussion, we locked the door as a precautionery measure. 13.____

14. The supervisor remarked, "Only those clerks, who perform routine work, are permitted to take a rest period." 14.____

15. Not only will this duplicating machine make accurate copies, but it will also produce a quantity of work equal to fifteen transcribing typists. 15.____

16. "Mr. Jones," said the supervisor, "we regret our inability to grant you an extention of your leave of absence." 16.____

17. Although the employees find the work monotonous and fatigueing, they rarely complain. 17.____

18. We completed the tabulation of the receipts on time despite the fact that Miss Smith our fastest operator was absent for over a week. 18.____

19. The reaction of the employees who attended the meeting, as well as the reaction of those who did not attend, indicates clearly that the schedule is satisfactory to everyone concerned. 19.____

20. Of the two employees, the one in our office is the most efficient. 20.____

21. No one can apply or even understand, the new rules and regulations. 21.____

22. A large amount of supplies were stored in the empty office. 22.____

23. If an employee is occassionally asked to work overtime, he should do so willingly. 23.____

24. It is true that the new procedures are difficult to use but, we are certain that you will learn them quickly. 24.____

25. The office manager said that he did not know who would be given a large allotment under the new plan. 25.____

KEY (CORRECT ANSWERS)

1.	A	11.	D
2.	D	12.	A
3.	D	13.	C
4.	C	14.	B
5.	C	15.	A
6.	A	16.	C
7.	D	17.	C
8.	B	18.	B
9.	A	19.	D
10.	A	20.	A

21.	B
22.	A
23.	C
24.	B
25.	D

TEST 3

DIRECTIONS: Each of the following sentences may be classified MOST appropriately under one of the following categories:
   A. Faulty because of incorrect grammar
   B. Faulty because of incorrect punctuation
   C. Faulty because of incorrect capitalization
   D. Correct

Examine each sentence carefully. Then, in the space at the right, print the capital letter preceding the option which is the BEST of the four suggested above. All incorrect sentence contain but one type of error. Consider a sentence correct if it contains none of the types of errors mentioned, even though there may be other correct ways of expressing the same thought.

1. The desk, as well as the chairs, were moved out of the office.   1.____

2. The clerk whose production was greatest for the month won a day's vacation as first prize.   2.____

3. Upon entering the room, the employees were found hard at work at their desks.   3.____

4. John Smith our new employee always arrives at work on time.   4.____

5. Punish whoever is guilty of stealing the money.   5.____

6. Intelligent and persistent effort lead to success no matter what the job may be.   6.____

7. The secretary asked, "can you call again at three o'clock?"   7.____

8. He told us, that if the report was not accepted at the next meeting, it would have to be rewritten.   8.____

9. He would not have sent the letter if he had known that it would cause so much excitement.   9.____

10. We all looked forward to him coming to visit us.   10.____

11. If you find that you are unable to complete the assignment please notify me as soon as possible.   11.____

12. Every girl in the office went home on time but me; there was still some work for me to finish.   12.____

13. He wanted to know who the letter was addressed to, Mr. Brown or Mr. Smith.   13.____

14. "Mr. Jones, he said, please answer this letter as soon as possible."   14.____

143

15. The new clerk had an unusual accent inasmuch as he was born and educated in the south. 15.____

16. Although he is younger than her, he earns a higher salary. 16.____

17. Neither of the two administrators are going to attend the conference being held in Washington, D.C. 17.____

18. Since Miss Smith and Miss Jones have more experience than us, they have been given more responsible duties. 18.____

19. Mr. Shaw the supervisor of the stock room maintains an inventory of stationery and office supplies. 19.____

20. Inasmuch as this matter affects both you and I, we should take joint action. 20.____

21. Who do you think will be able to perform this highly technical work? 21.____

22. Of the two employees, John is considered the most competent. 22.____

23. He is not coming home on tuesday; we expect him next week. 23.____

24. Stenographers, as well as typists must be able to type rapidly and accurately. 24.____

25. Having been placed in the safe we were sure that the money would not be stolen. 25.____

KEY (CORRECT ANSWERS)

1. A
2. D
3. A
4. B
5. D

6. A
7. C
8. B
9. D
10. A

11. B
12. D
13. A
14. B
15. C

16. A
17. A
18. A
19. B
20. A

21. D
22. A
23. C
24. B
25. A

TEST 4

DIRECTIONS: Each of the following sentences consist of four sentences lettered A, B, C, and D. One of the sentences in each group contains an error in grammar or punctuation. Indicate the INCORRECT sentence in each group. *PRINT THE LETTER OF THE CORRECT ANSWER IN THE SPACE AT THE RIGHT.*

1. A. Give the message to whoever is on duty.
   B. The teacher who's pupil won first prize presented the award.
   C. Between you and me, I don't expect the program to succeed.
   D. His running to catch the bus caused the accident.

2. A. The process, which was patented only last year is already obsolete.
   B. His interest in science (which continues to the present) led him to convert his basement into a laboratory.
   C. He described the book as "verbose, repetitious, and bombastic".
   D. Our new director will need to possess three qualities: vision, patience, and fortitude.

3. A. The length of ladder trucks varies considerably.
   B. The probationary fireman reported to the officer to who he was assigned.
   C. The lecturer emphasized the need for we firemen to be punctual.
   D. Neither the officers nor the members of the company knew about the new procedure.

4. A. Ham and eggs is the specialty of the house.
   B. He is one of the students who are on probation.
   C. Do you think that either one of us have a chance to be nominated for president of the class?
   D. I assume that either he was to be in charge or you were.

5. A. Its a long road that has no turn.
   B. To run is more tiring than to walk.
   C. We have been assigned three new reports: namely, the statistical summary, the narrative summary, and the budgetary summary.
   D. Had the first payment been made in January, the second would be due in April.

6. A. Each employer has his own responsibilities.
   B. If a person speaks correctly, they make a good impression.
   C. Every one of the operators has had her vacation.
   D. Has anybody filed his report?

7. A. The manager, with all his salesmen, was obliged to go.
   B. Who besides them is to sign the agreement?
   C. One report without the others is incomplete.
   D. Several clerks, as well as the proprietor, was injured.

8. A. A suspension of these activities is expected.
    B. The machine is economical because first cost and upkeep are low.
    C. A knowledge of stenography and filing are required for this position.
    D. The condition in which the goods were received shows that the packing was not done properly.

9. A. There seems to be a great many reasons for disagreement.
    B. It does not seem possible that they could have failed.
    C. Have there always been too few applicants for these positions?
    D. There is no excuse for these errors.

10. A. We shall be pleased to answer your question.
    B. Shall we plan the meeting for Saturday?
    C. I will call you promptly at seven.
    D. Can I borrow your book after you have read it?

11. A. You are as capable as I.
    B. Everyone is willing to sign but him and me.
    C. As for he and his assistant, I cannot praise them too highly.
    D. Between you and me, I think he will be dismissed.

12. A. Our competitors bid above us last week.
    B. The survey which was began last year has not yet been completed.
    C. The operators had shown that they understood their instructions.
    D. We have never ridden over worse roads.

13. A. Who did they say was responsible?
    B. Whom did you suspect?
    C. Who do you suppose it was?
    D. Whom do you mean?

14. A. Of the two propositions, this is the worse.
    B. Which report do you consider the best—the one in January or the one in July?
    C. I believe this is the most practicable of the many plans submitted.
    D. He is the youngest employee in the organization.

15. A. The firm had but three orders last week.
    B. That doesn't really seem possible.
    C. After twenty years scarcely none of the old business remains.
    D. Has he done nothing about it?

KEY (CORRECT ANSWERS)

1.	B	6.	B	11.	C
2.	A	7.	D	12.	B
3.	C	8.	C	13.	A
4.	C	9.	A	14.	B
5.	A	10.	D	15.	C

PREPARING WRITTEN MATERIAL

PARAGRAPH REARRANGEMENT
COMMENTARY

The sentences that follow are in scrambled order. You are to rearrange them in proper order and indicate the letter choice containing the correct answer at the space at the right.

Each group of sentences in this section is actually a paragraph presented in scrambled order. Each sentence in the group has a place in that paragraph; no sentence is to be left out. You are to read each group of sentences and decide upon the best order in which to put the sentences so as to form a well-organized paragraph.

The questions in this section measure the ability to solve a problem when all the facts relevant to its solution are not given.

More specifically, certain positions of responsibility and authority require the employee to discover connection between events sometimes, apparently, unrelated. In order to do this, the employee will find it necessary to correctly infer that unspecified events have probably occurred or are likely to occur. This ability becomes especially important when action must be taken on incomplete information.

Accordingly, these questions require competitors to choose among several suggested alternatives, each of which presents a different sequential arrangement of the events. Competitors must choose the MOST logical of the suggested sequences.

In order to do so, they may be required to draw on general knowledge to infer missing concepts or events that are essential to sequencing the given events. Competitors should be careful to infer only what is essential to the sequence. The plausibility of the wrong alternatives will always require the inclusion of unlikely events or of additional chains of events which are NOT essential to sequencing the given events.

It's very important to remember that you are looking for the best of the four possible choices, and that the best choice of all may not even be one of the answers you're given to choose from.

There is no one right way to solve these problems. Many people have found it helpful to first write out the order of the sentences, as they would have arranged them, on their scrap paper before looking at the possible answers. If their optimum answer is there, this can save them some time. If it isn't, this method can still give insight into solving the problem. Others find it most helpful to just go through each of the possible choices, contrasting each as they go along. You should use whatever method feels comfortable and works for you.

While most of these types of questions are not that difficult, we've added a higher percentage of the difficult type, just to give you more practice. Usually there are only one or two questions on this section that contain such subtle distinctions that you're unable to answer confidently. And you then may find yourself stuck deciding between two possible choices, neither of which you're sure about.

EXAMINATION SECTION
TEST 1

DIRECTIONS: The sentences that follow are in scrambled order. You are to rearrange them in proper order and indicate the letter choice containing the correct answer. *PRINT THE LETTER OF THE CORRECT ANSWER IN THE SPACE AT THE RIGHT.*

1. Below are four statements labeled W, X, Y and Z.
    W. He was a strict and fanatic drillmaster.
    X. The word is always used in a derogatory sense and generally shows resentment and anger on the part of the user.
    Y. It is from the name of this Frenchman that we derive our English word, martinet.
    Z. Jean Martinet was the Inspector-General of Infantry during the reign of King Louis XIV.
    The PROPER order in which these sentences should be placed in a paragraph is:
    A. X, Z, W, Y   B. X, Z, Y, W   C. Z, W, Y, X   D. Z, Y, W, X

    1.____

2. In the following paragraph, the sentences, which are numbered, have been jumbled.
    I. Since then it has undergone changes.
    II. It was incorporated in 1955 under the laws of the State of New York.
    III. Its primary purposes, a cleaner city, has, however, remained the same.
    IV. The Citizens Committee works in cooperation with the Mayor's Inter-departmental Committee for a Clean City.
    The order in which these sentences should be arranged to form a well-organized paragraph is:
    A. II, IV, I, III   B. III, IV, I, II   C. IV, II, I, III   D. IV, III, II, I

    2.____

    3.____

Questions 3-5.

DIRECTIONS: The sentences listed below are part of a meaningful paragraph but they are not given in their proper order. You are to decide what would be the BEST order in which to put the sentences so as to form a well-organized paragraph. Each sentence has a place in the paragraph; there are no extra sentences. You are then to answer Questions 3 through 5 inclusive on the basis of your rearrangements of these scrambled sentences into a properly organized paragraph.

In 1887 some insurance companies organized an Inspection Department to advise their clients on all phases of fire prevention and protection. Probably this has been due to the smaller annual fire losses in Great Britain than in the United States. It tests various fire prevention devices and appliances and determines manufacturing hazards and their safeguards. Fire research began earlier in the United States and is more advanced than in Great Britain. Later they established a laboratory specializing in electrical, mechanical, hydraulic, and chemical fields.

151

3. When the five sentences are arranged in proper order, the paragraph starts with the sentence which begins
   A. "In 1887…"   B. "Probably this…"   C. "It tests…"
   D. "Fire research…"   E. "Later they…"

4. In the last sentence listed above, "they" refers to
   A. the insurance companies   B. the United States and Great Britain
   C. the Inspection Department   D. clients
   E. technicians

5. When the above paragraph is properly arranged, it ends with the words
   A. "…and protection."   B. "…the United States."
   C. "…their safeguards."   D. "…in Great Britain."
   E. "…chemical fields."

KEY (CORRECT ANSWERS)

1. C
2. C
3. D
4. A
5. C

TEST 2

DIRECTIONS: In each of the questions numbered I through V, several sentences are given. For each question, choose as your answer the group of number that represents the MOST logical order of these sentences if they were arranged in paragraph form. *PRINT THE LETTER OF THE CORRECT ANSWER IN THE SPACE AT THE RIGHT.*

1.
   I. It is established when one shows that the landlord has prevented the tenant's enjoyment of his interest in the property leased.
   II. Constructive eviction is the result of a breach of the covenant of quiet enjoyment implied in all leases.
   III. In some parts of the United States, it is not complete until the tenant vacates within a reasonable time.
   IV. Generally, the acts must be of such serious and permanent character as to deny the tenant the enjoyment of his possessing rights.
   V. In this event, upon abandonment of the premises, the tenant's liability for that ceases.
   The CORRECT answer is:
   A. II, I, IV, III, V
   B. V, II, III, I, IV
   C. IV, III, I, II, V
   D. I, III, V, IV, II

   1.____

2.
   I. The powerlessness before private and public authorities that is the typical experience of the slum tenant is reminiscent of the situation of blue-collar workers all through the nineteenth century.
   II. Similarly, in recent years, this chapter of history has been reopened by anti-poverty groups which have attempted to organize slum tenants to enable them to bargain collectively with their landlords about the conditions of their tenancies.
   III. It is familiar history that many of the worker remedied their condition by joining together and presenting their demands collectively.
   IV. Like the workers, tenants are forced by the conditions of modern life into substantial dependence on these who possess great political aid and economic power.
   V. What's more, the very fact of dependence coupled with an absence of education and self-confidence makes them hesitant and unable to stand up for what they need from those in power.
   The CORRECT answer is:
   A. V, IV, I, II, III
   B. II, III, I, V, IV
   C. III, I, V, IV, II
   D. I, IV, V, III, II

   2.____

3.
   I. A railroad, for example, when not acting as a common carrier may contract away responsibility for its own negligence.
   II. As to a landlord, however, no decision has been found relating to the legal effect of a clause shifting the statutory duty of repair to the tenant.
   III. The courts have not passed on the validity of clauses relieving the landlord of this duty and liability.
   IV. They have, however, upheld the validity of exculpatory clauses in other types of contracts.

   3.____

V. Housing regulations impose a duty upon the landlord to maintain leased premises in safe condition.
VI. As another example, a bailee may limit his liability except for gross negligence, willful acts, or fraud.

The CORRECT answer is:
A. II, I, VI, IV, III, V
B. I, III, IV, V, VI, II
C. III, V, I, IV, II, VI
D. V, III, IV, I, VI, II

4.
I. Since there are only samples in the building, retail or consumer sales are generally eschewed by mart occupants, and in some instances, rigid controls are maintained to limit entrance to the mart only to those persons engaged in retailing.
II. Since World War I, in many larger cities, there has developed a new type of property, called the mart building.
III. It can, therefore, be used by wholesalers and jobbers for the display of sample merchandise.
IV. This type of building is most frequently a multi-storied, finished interior property which is a cross between a retail arcade and a loft building.
V. This limitation enables the mart occupants to ship the orders from another location after the retailer or dealer makes his selection from the samples.

The CORRECT answer is:
A. II, IV, III, I, V
B. IV, III, V, I, II
C. I, III, II, IV, V
D. I, IV, II, III, V

5.
I. In general, staff-line friction reduces the distinctive contribution of staff personnel.
II. The conflicts, however, introduce an uncontrolled element into the managerial system.
III. On the other hand, the natural resistance of the line to staff innovations probably usefully restrains over-eager efforts to apply untested procedures on a large scale.
IV. Under such conditions, it is difficult to know when valuable ideas are being sacrificed.
V. The relatively weak position of staff, requiring accommodation to the line, tends to restrict their ability to engage in free, experimental innovation.

The CORRECT answer is:
A. IV, II, III, I, V
B. I, V, III, II, IV
C. V, III, I, II, IV
D. II, I, IV, V, III

KEY (CORRECT ANSWERS)

1. A
2. D
3. D
4. A
5. B

TEST 3

DIRECTIONS: Questions 1 through 4 consist of six sentences which can be arranged in a logical sequence. For each question, select the choice which places the numbered sentences in the MOST logical sequent. *PRINT THE LETTER OF THE CORRECT ANSWER IN THE SPACE AT THE RIGHT.*

1. I. The burden of proof as to each issue is determined before trial and remains upon the same party throughout the trial.
    II. The jury is at liberty to believe one witness' testimony as against a number of contradictory witnesses.
    III. In a civil case, the party bearing the burden of proof is required to prove his contention by a fair preponderance of the evidence.
    IV. However, it must be noted that a fair preponderance of evidence does not necessarily mean a greater number of witnesses.
    V. The burden of proof is the burden which rests upon one of the parties to an action to persuade the trier of the facts, generally the jury, that a proposition he asserts is true.
    VI. If the evidence is equally balanced, or if it leaves the jury in such doubt as to be unable to decide the controversy either way, judgment must be given against the party upon whom the burden of proof rests.
    The CORRECT answer is:
    A. III, II, V, IV, I, VI
    B. I, II, VI, V, III, IV
    C. III, IV, V, I, II, VI
    D. V, I, III, VI, IV, II

    1.____

2. I. If a parent is without assets and is unemployed, he cannot be convicted of the crime of non-support of a child.
    II. The term "sufficient ability" has been held to mean sufficient financial ability.
    III. It does not matter if his unemployment is by choice or unavoidable circumstances.
    IV. If he fails to take any steps at all, he may be liable to prosecution for endangering the welfare of a child.
    V. Under the penal law, a parent is responsible for the support of his minor child only if the parent is "of sufficient ability."
    VI. An indigent parent may meet his obligation by borrowing money or by seeking aid under the provisions of the Social Welfare Law.
    The CORRECT answer is:
    A. VI, I, V, III, II, IV
    B. I, III, V, II, IV, VI
    C. V, II, I, III, VI, IV
    D. I, VI, IV, V, II, III

    2.____

3. I. Consider, for example, the case of a rabble rouser who urges a group of twenty people to go out and break the windows of a nearby factory.
    II. Therefore, the law fills the indicated gap with the crime of inciting to riot.
    III. A person is considered guilty of inciting to riot when he urges ten or more persons to engage in tumultuous and violent conduct of a kind likely to create public alarm.
    IV. However, if he has not obtained the cooperation of at least four people, he cannot be charged with unlawful assembly.

    3.____

155

2 (#3)

    V. The charge of inciting to riot was added to the law to cover types of conduct which cannot be classified as either the crime of "riot" or the crime of "unlawful assembly."
    VI. If he acquires the acquiescence of at least four of them, he is guilty of unlawful assembly even if the project does not materialize.
    The CORRECT answer is:
      A. III, V, I, VI, IV, II
      B. V, I, IV, VI, II, III
      C. III, IV, I, V, II, VI
      D. V, I, IV, VI, III, II

4.
    I. If, however, the rebuttal evidence presents an issue of credibility, it is for the jury to determine whether the presumption has, in fact, been destroyed.
    II. Once sufficient evidence to the contrary is introduced, the presumption disappears from the trial.
    III. The effect of a presumption is to place the burden upon the adversary to come forward with evidence to rebut the presumption.
    IV. When a presumption is overcome and ceases to exist in the case, the fact or facts which gave rise to the presumption still remain.
    V. Whether a presumption has been overcome is ordinarily a question for the court.
    VI. Such information may furnish a basis for a logical inference.
    The CORRECT answer is:
      A. IV, VI, II, V, I, III
      B. III, II, V, I, IV, VI
      C. V, III, VI, IV, II, I
      D. V, IV, I, II, VI, III

KEY (CORRECT ANSWERS)

1. D
2. C
3. A
4. B

PHILOSOPHY, PRINCIPLES, PRACTICES, AND TECHNICS
OF
SUPERVISION, ADMINISTRATION, MANAGEMENT, AND ORGANIZATION

TABLE OF CONTENTS

	Page
MEANING OF SUPERVISION	1
THE OLD AND THE NEW SUPERVISION	1
THE EIGHT (8) BASIC PRINCIPLES OF THE NEW SUPERVISION	1
I. Principle of Responsibility	1
II. Principle of Authority	2
III. Principle of Self-Growth	2
IV. Principle of Individual Worth	2
V. Principle of Creative Leadership	2
VI. Principle of Success and Failure	2
VII. Principle of Science	3
VIII. Principle of Cooperation	3
WHAT IS ADMINISTRATION?	3
I. Practices Commonly Classed as "Supervisory"	3
II. Practices Commonly Classed as "Administrative"	3
III. Practices Commonly Classed as Both "Supervisory" and "Administrative"	4
RESPONSIBILITIES OF THE SUPERVISOR	4
COMPETENCIES OF THE SUPERVISOR	4
THE PROFESSIONAL SUPERVISOR-EMPLOYEE RELATIONSHIP	4
MINI-TEXT IN SUPERVISION, ADMINISTRATION, MANAGEMENT, AND ORGANIZATION	5
I. Brief Highlights	5
A. Levels of Management	6
B. What the Supervisor Must Learn	6
C. A Definition of Supervision	6
D. Elements of the Team Concept	6
E. Principles of Organization	6
F. The Four Important Parts of Every Job	7
G. Principles of Delegation	7
H. Principles of Effective Communications	7
I. Principles of Work Improvement	7
J. Areas of Job Improvement	7
K. Seven Key Points in Making Improvements	8

	L.	Corrective Techniques for Job Improvement	8
	M.	A Planning Checklist	8
	N.	Five Characteristics of Good Directions	9
	O.	Types of Directions	9
	P.	Controls	9
	Q.	Orienting the New Employee	9
	R.	Checklist for Orienting New Employees	9
	S.	Principles of Learning	10
	T.	Causes of Poor Performance	10
	U.	Four Major Steps in On-the-Job Instructions	10
	V.	Employees Want Five Things	10
	W.	Some Don'ts in Regard to Praise	11
	X.	How to Gain Your Workers' Confidence	11
	Y.	Sources of Employee Problems	11
	Z.	The Supervisor's Key to Discipline	11
	AA.	Five Important Processes of Management	12
	BB.	When the Supervisor Fails to Plan	12
	CC.	Fourteen General Principles of Management	12
	DD.	Change	12
II.	Brief Topical Summaries		13
	A.	Who/What is the Supervisor?	13
	B.	The Sociology of Work	13
	C.	Principles and Practices of Supervision	14
	D.	Dynamic Leadership	14
	E.	Processes for Solving Problems	15
	F.	Training for Results	15
	G.	Health, Safety, and Accident Prevention	16
	H.	Equal Employment Opportunity	16
	I.	Improving Communications	16
	J.	Self-Development	17
	K.	Teaching and Training	17
		1. The Teaching Process	17
		a. Preparation	17
		b. Presentation	18
		c. Summary	18
		d. Application	18
		e. Evaluation	18
		2. Teaching Methods	18
		a. Lecture	18
		b. Discussion	18
		c. Demonstration	19
		d. Performance	19
		e. Which Method to Use	19

PHILOSOPHY, PRINCIPLES, PRACTICES, AND TECHNICS
OF
SUPERVISION, ADMINISTRATION, MANAGEMENT, AND ORGANIZATION

MEANING OF SUPERVISION

The extension of the democratic philosophy has been accompanied by an extension in the scope of supervision. Modern leaders and supervisors no longer think of supervision in the narrow sense of being confined chiefly to visiting employees, supplying materials, or rating the staff. They regard supervision as being intimately related to all the concerned agencies of society, they speak of the supervisor's function in terms of "growth," rather than the "improvement" of employees.

This modern concept of supervision may be defined as follows: Supervision is leadership and the development of leadership within groups which are cooperatively engaged in inspection, research, training, guidance, and evaluation.

THE OLD AND THE NEW SUPERVISION

TRADITIONAL
1. Inspection
2. Focused on the employee
3. Visitation
4. Random and haphazard
5. Imposed and authoritarian
6. One person usually

MODERN
1. Study and analysis
2. Focused on aims, materials, methods, supervisors, employees, environment
3. Demonstrations, intervisitation, workshops, directed reading, bulletins, etc.
4. Definitely organized and planned (scientific)
5. Cooperative and democratic
6. Many persons involved (creative)

THE EIGHT (8) BASIC PRINCIPLES OF THE NEW SUPERVISION

I. Principle of Responsibility
   Authority to act and responsibility for acting must be joined.
   A. If you give responsibility, give authority.
   B. Define employee duties clearly.
   C. Protect employees from criticism by others.
   D. Recognize the rights as well as obligations of employees.
   E. Achieve the aims of a democratic society insofar as it is possible within the area of your work.
   F. Establish a situation favorable to training and learning.
   G. Accept ultimate responsibility for everything done in your section, unit, office, division, department.
   H. Good administration and good supervision are inseparable.

II. Principle of Authority
The success of the supervisor is measured by the extent to which the power of authority is not used.
- A. Exercise simplicity and informality in supervision
- B. Use the simplest machinery of supervision
- C. If it is good for the organization as a whole, it is probably justified.
- D. Seldom be arbitrary or authoritative.
- E. Do not base your work on the power of position or of personality.
- F. Permit and encourage the free expression of opinions.

III. Principle of Self-Growth
The success of the supervisor is measured by the extent to which, and the speed with which, he is no longer needed.
- A. Base criticism on principles, not on specifics.
- B. Point out higher activities to employees.
- C. Train for self-thinking by employees to meet new situations.
- D. Stimulate initiative, self-reliance, and individual responsibility
- E. Concentrate on stimulating the growth of employees rather than on removing defects.

IV. Principle of Individual Worth
Respect for the individual is a paramount consideration in supervision.
- A. Be human and sympathetic in dealing with employees.
- B. Don't nag about things to be done.
- C. Recognize the individual differences among employees and seek opportunities to permit best expression of each personality.

V. Principle of Creative Leadership
The best supervision is that which is not apparent to the employee.
- A. Stimulate, don't drive employees to creative action.
- B. Emphasize doing good things.
- C. Encourage employees to do what they do best.
- D. Do not be too greatly concerned with details of subject or method.
- E. Do not be concerned exclusively with immediate problems and activities.
- F. Reveal higher activities and make them both desired and maximally possible.
- G. Determine procedures in the light of each situation but see that these are derived from a sound basic philosophy.
- H. Aid, inspire, and lead so as to liberate the creative spirit latent in all good employees.

VI. Principle of Success and Failure
There are no unsuccessful employees, only unsuccessful supervisors who have failed to give proper leadership.
- A. Adapt suggestions to the capacities, attitudes, and prejudices of employees.
- B. Be gradual, be progressive, be persistent.
- C. Help the employee find the general principle; have the employee apply his own problem to the general principle.
- D. Give adequate appreciation for good work and honest effort.
- E. Anticipate employee difficulties and help to prevent them.
- F. Encourage employees to do the desirable things they will do anyway.
- G. Judge your supervision by the results it secures.

VII. Principle of Science
Successful supervision is scientific, objective, and experimental. It is based on facts, not on prejudices.
   A. Be cumulative in results.
   B. Never divorce your suggestions from the goals of training.
   C. Don't be impatient of results.
   D. Keep all matters on a professional, not a personal, level.
   E. Do not be concerned exclusively with immediate problems and activities.
   F. Use objective means of determining achievement and rating where possible.

VIII. Principle of Cooperation
Supervision is a cooperative enterprise between supervisor and employee.
   A. Begin with conditions as they are.
   B. Ask opinions of all involved when formulating policies.
   C. Organization is as good as its weakest link.
   D. Let employees help to determine policies and department programs.
   E. Be approachable and accessible—physically and mentally.
   F. Develop pleasant social relationships.

WHAT IS ADMINISTRATION

Administration is concerned with providing the environment, the material facilities, and the operational procedures that will promote the maximum growth and development of supervisors and employees. (Organization is an aspect and a concomitant of administration.)

There is no sharp line of demarcation between supervision and administration; these functions are intimately interrelated and, often, overlapping. They are complementary activities.

I. Practices Commonly Classed as "Supervisory"
   A. Conducting employees' conferences
   B. Visiting sections, units, offices, divisions, departments
   C. Arranging for demonstrations
   D. Examining plans
   E. Suggesting professional reading
   F. Interpreting bulletins
   G. Recommending in-service training courses
   H. Encouraging experimentation
   I. Appraising employee morale
   J. Providing for intervisitation

II. Practices Commonly Classified as "Administrative"
   A. Management of the office
   B. Arrangement of schedules for extra duties
   C. Assignment of rooms or areas
   D. Distribution of supplies
   E. Keeping records and reports
   F. Care of audio-visual materials
   G. Keeping inventory records
   H. Checking record cards and books

      I.   Programming special activities
      J.   Checking on the attendance and punctuality of employees

III.   Practices Commonly Classified as Both "Supervisory" and "Administrative"
      A.   Program construction
      B.   Testing or evaluating outcomes
      C.   Personnel accounting
      D.   Ordering instructional materials

RESPONSIBILITIES OF THE SUPERVISOR

A person employed in a supervisory capacity must constantly be able to improve his own efficiency and ability. He represent the employer to the employees and only continuous self-examination can make him a capable supervisor.

Leadership and training are the supervisor's responsibility. An efficient working unit is one in which the employees work with the supervisor. It is his job to bring out the best in his employees. He must always be relaxed, courteous, and calm in his association with his employees. Their feelings are important, and a harsh attitude does not develop the most efficient employees.

COMPETENCES OF THE SUPERVISOR

      I.   Complete knowledge of the duties and responsibilities of his position.
      II.   To be able to organize a job, plan ahead, and carry through.
      III. To have self-confidence and initiative.
      IV. To be able to handle the unexpected situation and make quick decisions.
      V.   To be able to properly train subordinates in the positions they are best suited for.
      VI. To be able to keep good human relations among his subordinates.
      VII. To be able to keep good human relations between his subordinates and himself and to earn their respect and trust.

THE PROFESSIONAL SUPERVISOR-EMPLOYEE RELATIONSHIP

There are two kinds of efficiency: one kind is only apparent and is produced in organizations through the exercise of mere discipline; this is but a simulation of the second, or true, efficiency which springs from spontaneous cooperation. If you are a manager, no matter how great or small your responsibility, it is your job, in the final analysis, to create and develop this involuntary cooperation among the people whom you supervise. For, no matter how powerful a combination of money, machines, and materials a company may have, this is a dead and sterile thing without a team of willing, thinking, and articulate people to guide it.

The following 21 points are presented as indicative of the exemplary basic relationship that should exist between supervisor and employee:

1. Each person wants to be liked and respected by his fellow employee and wants to be treated with consideration and respect by his superior.
2. The most competent employee will make an error. However, in a unit where good relations exist between the supervisor and his employees, tenseness and fear do not exist. Thus, errors are not hidden or covered up, and the efficiency of a unit is not impaired.

3. Subordinates resent rules, regulations, or orders that are unreasonable or unexplained.
4. Subordinates are quick to resent unfairness, harshness, injustices, and favoritism.
5. An employee will accept responsibility if he knows that he will be complimented for a job well done, and not too harshly chastised for failure; that his supervisor will check the cause of the failure, and, if it was the supervisor's fault, he will assume the blame therefore. If it was the employee's fault, his supervisor will explain the correct method or means of handling the responsibility.
6. An employee wants to receive credit for a suggestion he has made, that is used. If a suggestion cannot be used, the employee is entitled to an explanation. The supervisor should not say "no" and close the subject.
7. Fear and worry slow up a worker's ability. Poor working environment can impair his physical and mental health. A good supervisor avoids forceful methods, threats, and arguments to get a job done.
8. A forceful supervisor is able to train his employees individually and as a team, and is able to motivate them in the proper channels.
9. A mature supervisor is able to properly evaluate his subordinates and to keep them happy and satisfied.
10. A sensitive supervisor will never patronize his subordinates.
11. A worthy supervisor will respect his employees' confidences.
12. Definite and clear-cut responsibilities should be assigned to each executive.
13. Responsibility should always be coupled with corresponding authority.
14. No change should be made in the scope or responsibilities of a position without a definite understanding to that effect on the part of all persons concerned.
15. No executive or employee, occupying a single position in the organization, should be subject to definite orders from more than one source.
16. Orders should never be given to subordinates over the head of a responsible executive. Rather than do this, the officer in question should be supplanted.
17. Criticisms of subordinates should, whoever possible, be made privately, and in no case should a subordinate be criticized in the presence of executives or employees of equal or lower rank.
18. No dispute or difference between executives or employees as to authority or responsibilities should be considered too trivial for prompt and careful adjudication.
19. Promotions, wage changes, and disciplinary action should always be approved by the executive immediately superior to the one directly responsible.
20. No executive or employee should ever be required, or expected, to be at the same time an assistant to, and critic of, another.
21. Any executive whose work is subject to regular inspection should, wherever practicable, be given the assistance and facilities necessary to enable him to maintain an independent check of the quality of his work.

MINI-TEXT IN SUPERVISION, ADMINISTRATION, MANAGEMENT, AND ORGANIZATION

I. Brief Highlights

Listed concisely and sequentially are major headings and important data in the field for quick recall and review.

A. Levels of Management

Any organization of some size has several levels of management. In terms of a ladder, the levels are:

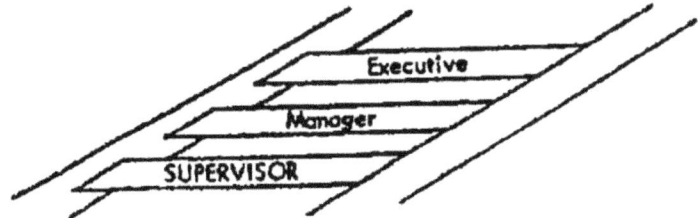

The first level is very important because it is the beginning point of management leadership.

B. What the Supervisor Must Learn

A supervisor must learn to:
1. Deal with people and their differences
2. Get the job done through people
3. Recognize the problems when they exist
4. Overcome obstacles to good performance
5. Evaluate the performance of people
6. Check his own performance in terms of accomplishment

C. A Definition of Supervisor

The term supervisor means any individual having authority, in the interests of the employer, to hire, transfer, suspend, lay-off, recall, promote, discharge, assign, reward, or discipline other employees or responsibility to direct them, or to adjust their grievances, or effectively to recommend such action, if, in connection with the foregoing, exercise of such authority is not of a merely routine or clerical nature but requires the use of independent judgment.

D. Elements of the Team Concept

What is involved in teamwork? The component parts are:
1. Members
2. A leader
3. Goals
4. Plans
5. Cooperation
6. Spirit

E. Principles of Organization
1. A team member must know what his job is.
2. Be sure that the nature and scope of a job are understood.
3. Authority and responsibility should be carefully spelled out.
4. A supervisor should be permitted to make the maximum number of decisions affecting his employees.
5. Employees should report to only one supervisor.
6. A supervisor should direct only as many employees as he can handle effectively.
7. An organization plan should be flexible.

8. Inspection and performance of work should be separate.
9. Organizational problems should receive immediate attention.
10. Assign work in line with ability and experience.

F. The Four Important Parts of Every Job
1. Inherent in every job is the *accountability* for results.
2. A second set of factors in every job is *responsibilities*.
3. Along with duties and responsibilities one must have the *authority* to act within certain limits without obtaining permission to proceed.
4. No job exists in a vacuum. The supervisor is surrounded by key *relationships*.

G. Principles of Delegation
Where work is delegated for the first time, the supervisor should think in terms of these questions:
1. Who is best qualified to do this?
2. Can an employee improve his abilities by doing this?
3. How long should an employee spend on this?
4. Are there any special problems for which he will need guidance?
5. How broad a delegation can I make?

H. Principles of Effective Communications
1. Determine the media.
2. To whom directed?
3. Identification and source authority.
4. Is communication understood?

I. Principles of Work Improvement
1. Most people usually do only the work which is assigned to them.
2. Workers are likely to fit assigned work into the time available to perform it.
3. A good workload usually stimulates output.
4. People usually do their best work when they know that results will be reviewed or inspected.
5. Employees usually feel that someone else is responsible for conditions of work, workplace layout, job methods, type of tools/equipment, and other such factors.
6. Employees are usually defensive about their job security.
7. Employees have natural resistance to change.
8. Employees can support or destroy a supervisor.
9. A supervisor usually earns the respect of his people through his personal example of diligence and efficiency.

J. Areas of Job Improvement
The areas of job improvement are quite numerous, but the most common ones which a supervisor can identify and utilize are:
1. Departmental layout
2. Flow of work
3. Workplace layout
4. Utilization of manpower
5. Work methods
6. Materials handling

      7. Utilization
      8. Motion economy

K. Seven Key Points in Making Improvements
1. Select the job to be improved
2. Study how it is being done now
3. Question the present method
4. Determine actions to be taken
5. Chart proposed method
6. Get approval and apply
7. Solicit worker participation

l. Corrective Techniques of Job Improvement
Specific Problems
1. Size of workload
2. Inability to meet schedules
3. Strain and fatigue
4. Improper use of men and skills
5. Waste, poor quality, unsafe conditions
6. Bottleneck conditions that hinder output
7. Poor utilization of equipment and machine
8. Efficiency and productivity of labor

General Improvement
1. Departmental layout
2. Flow of work
3. Work plan layout
4. Utilization of manpower
5. Work methods
6. Materials handling
7. Utilization of equipment
8. Motion economy

Corrective Techniques
1. Study with scale model
2. Flow chart study
3. Motion analysis
4. Comparison of units produced to standard allowance
5. Methods analysis
6. Flow chart and equipment study
7. Down time vs. running time
8. Motion analysis

M. A Planning Checklist
1. Objectives
2. Controls
3. Delegations
4. Communications
5. Resources
6. Manpower

7. Equipment
8. Supplies and materials
9. Utilization of time
10. Safety
11. Money
12. Work
13. Timing of improvements

N. Five Characteristics of Good Directions
In order to get results, directions must be:
1. Possible of accomplishment
2. Agreeable with worker interests
3. Related to mission
4. Planned and complete
5. Unmistakably clear

O. Types of Directions
1. Demands or direct orders
2. Requests
3. Suggestion or implication
4. volunteering

P. Controls
A typical listing of the overall areas in which the supervisor should establish controls might be:
1. Manpower
2. Materials
3. Quality of work
4. Quantity of work
5. Time
6. Space
7. Money
8. Methods

Q. Orienting the New Employee
1. Prepare for him
2. Welcome the new employee
3. Orientation for the job
4. Follow-up

R. Checklist for Orienting New Employees   Yes   No
1. Do you appreciate the feelings of new employees
   when they first report for work?   ___   ___
2. Are you aware of the fact that the new employee must
   make a big adjustment to his job?   ___   ___
3. Have you given him good reasons for liking the job and
   the organization?   ___   ___
4. Have you prepared for his first day on the job?   ___   ___
5. Did you welcome him cordially and make him feel needed?   ___   ___

		Yes	No
6.	Did you establish rapport with him so that he feels free to talk and discuss matters with you?	___	___
7.	Did you explain his job to him and his relationship to you?	___	___
8.	Does he know that his work will be evaluated periodically on a basis that is fair and objective?	___	___
9.	Did you introduce him to his fellow workers in such a way that they are likely to accept him?	___	___
10.	Does he know what employee benefits he will receive?	___	___
11.	Does he understand the importance of being on the job and what to do if he must leave his duty station?	___	___
12.	Has he been impressed with the importance of accident prevention and safe practice?	___	___
13.	Does he generally know his way around the department?	___	___
14.	Is he under the guidance of a sponsor who will teach the right way of doing things?	___	___
15.	Do you plan to follow-up so that he will continue to adjust successfully to his job?	___	___

S. Principles of Learning
1. Motivation
2. Demonstration or explanation
3. Practice

T. Causes of Poor Performance
1. Improper training for job
2. Wrong tools
3. Inadequate directions
4. Lack of supervisory follow-up
5. Poor communications
6. Lack of standards of performance
7. Wrong work habits
8. Low morale
9. Other

U. Four Major Steps in On-The-Job Instruction
1. Prepare the worker
2. Present the operation
3. Tryout performance
4. Follow-up

V. Employees Want Five Things
1. Security
2. Opportunity
3. Recognition
4. Inclusion
5. Expression

W. Some Don'ts in Regard to Praise
1. Don't praise a person for something he hasn't done.
2. Don't praise a person unless you can be sincere.
3. Don't be sparing in praise just because your superior withholds it from you.
4. Don't let too much time elapse between good performance and recognition of it

X. How to Gain Your Workers' Confidence
Methods of developing confidence include such things as:
1. Knowing the interests, habits, hobbies of employees
2. Admitting your own inadequacies
3. Sharing and telling of confidence in others
4. Supporting people when they are in trouble
5. Delegating matters that can be well handled
6. Being frank and straightforward about problems and working conditions
7. Encouraging others to bring their problems to you
8. Taking action on problems which impede worker progress

Y. Sources of Employee Problems
On-the-job causes might be such things as:
1. A feeling that favoritism is exercised in assignments
2. Assignment of overtime
3. An undue amount of supervision
4. Changing methods or systems
5. Stealing of ideas or trade secrets
6. Lack of interest in job
7. Threat of reduction in force
8. Ignorance or lack of communications
9. Poor equipment
10. Lack of knowing how supervisor feels toward employee
11. Shift assignments

Off-the-job problems might have to do with:
1. Health
2. Finances
3. Housing
4. Family

Z. The Supervisor's Key to Discipline
There are several key points about discipline which the supervisor should keep in mind:
1. Job discipline is one of the disciplines of life and is directed by the supervisor.
2. It is more important to correct an employee fault than to fix blame for it.
3. Employee performance is affected by problems both on the job and off.
4. Sudden or abrupt changes in behavior can be indications of important employee problems.
5. Problems should be dealt with as soon as possible after they are identified.
6. The attitude of the supervisor may have more to do with solving problems than the techniques of problem solving.
7. Correction of employee behavior should be resorted to only after the supervisor is sure that training or counseling will not be helpful.

8. Be sure to document your disciplinary actions.
9. Make sure that you are disciplining on the basis of facts rather than personal feelings.
10. Take each disciplinary step in order, being careful not to make snap judgments, or decisions based on impatience.

AA. Five Important Processes of Management
1. Planning
2. Organizing
3. Scheduling
4. Controlling
5. Motivating

BB. When the Supervisor Fails to Plan
1. Supervisor creates impression of not knowing his job
2. May lead to excessive overtime
3. Job runs itself—supervisor lacks control
4. Deadlines and appointments missed
5. Parts of the work go undone
6. Work interrupted by emergencies
7. Sets a bad example
8. Uneven workload creates peaks and valleys
9. Too much time on minor details at expense of more important tasks

CC. Fourteen General Principles of Management
1. Division of work
2. Authority and responsibility
3. Discipline
4. Unity of command
5. Unity of direction
6. Subordination of individual interest to general interest
7. Remuneration of personnel
8. Centralization
9. Scalar chain
10. Order
11. Equity
12. Stability of tenure of personnel
13. Initiative
14. Esprit de corps

DD. Change

Bringing about change is perhaps attempted more often, and yet less well understood, than anything else the supervisor does. How do people generally react to change? (People tend to resist change that is imposed upon them by other individuals or circumstances.

Change is characteristic of every situation. It is a part of every real endeavor where the efforts of people are concerned.

1. Why do people resist change?
   People may resist change because of:
   a. Fear of the unknown
   b. Implied criticism
   c. Unpleasant experiences in the past
   d. Fear of loss of status
   e. Threat to the ego
   f. Fear of loss of economic stability

2. How can we best overcome the resistance to change?
   In initiating change, take these steps:
   a. Get ready to sell
   b. Identify sources of help
   c. Anticipate objections
   d. Sell benefits
   e. Listen in depth
   f. Follow up

II. Brief Topical Summaries

   A. Who/What is the Supervisor?
      1. The supervisor is often called the "highest level employee and the lowest level manager."
      2. A supervisor is a member of both management and the work group. He acts as a bridge between the two.
      3. Most problems in supervision are in the area of human relations, or people problems.
      4. Employees expect: Respect, opportunity to learn and to advance, and a sense of belonging, and so forth.
      5. Supervisors are responsible for directing people and organizing work. Planning is of paramount importance.
      6. A position description is a set of duties and responsibilities inherent to a given position.
      7. It is important to keep the position description up-to-date and to provide each employee with his own copy.

   B. The Sociology of Work
      1. People are alike in many ways; however, each individual is unique.
      2. The supervisor is challenged in getting to know employee differences. Acquiring skills in evaluating individuals is an asset.
      3. Maintaining meaningful working relationships in the organization is of great importance.
      4. The supervisor has an obligation to help individuals to develop to their fullest potential.
      5. Job rotation on a planned basis helps to build versatility and to maintain interest and enthusiasm in work groups.
      6. Cross training (job rotation) provides backup skills.

14

7. The supervisor can help reduce tension by maintaining a sense of humor, providing guidance to employees, and by making reasonable and timely decisions. Employees respond favorably to working under reasonably predictable circumstances.
8. Change is characteristic of all managerial behavior. The supervisor must adjust to changes in procedures, new methods, technological changes, and to a number of new and sometimes challenging situations.
9. To overcome the natural tendency for people to resist change, the supervisor should become more skillful in initiating change.

C. Principles and Practices of Supervision
1. Employees should be required to answer to only one superior.
2. A supervisor can effectively direct only a limited number of employees, depending upon the complexity, variety, and proximity of the jobs involved.
3. The organizational chart presents the organization in graphic form. It reflects lines of authority and responsibility as well as interrelationships of units within the organization.
4. Distribution of work can be improved through an analysis using the "Work Distribution Chart."
5. The "Work Distribution Chart" reflects the division of work within a unit in understandable form.
6. When related tasks are given to an employee, he has a better chance of increasing his skills through training.
7. The individual who is given the responsibility for tasks must also be given the appropriate authority to insure adequate results.
8. The supervisor should delegate repetitive, routine work. Preparation of recurring reports, maintaining leave and attendance records are some examples.
9. Good discipline is essential to good task performance. Discipline is reflected in the actions of employees on the job in the absence of supervision.
10. Disciplinary action may have to be taken when the positive aspects of discipline have failed. Reprimand, warning, and suspension are examples of disciplinary action.
11. If a situation calls for a reprimand, be sure it is deserved and remember it is to be done in private.

D. Dynamic Leadership
1. A style is a personal method or manner of exerting influence.
2. Authoritarian leaders often see themselves as the source of power and authority.
3. The democratic leader often perceives the group as the source of authority and power.
4. Supervisors tend to do better when using the pattern of leadership that is most natural for them.
5. Social scientists suggest that the effective supervisor use the leadership style that best fits the problem or circumstances involved.
6. All four styles—telling, selling, consulting, joining—have their place. Using one does not preclude using the other at another time.

7. The theory X point of view assumes that the average person dislikes work, will avoid it whenever possible, and must be coerced to achieve organizational objectives.
8. The theory Y point of view assumes that the average person considers work to be a natural as play, and, when the individual is committed, he requires little supervision or direction to accomplish desired objectives.
9. The leader's basic assumptions concerning human behavior and human nature affect his actions, decisions, and other managerial practices.
10. Dissatisfaction among employees is often present, but difficult to isolate. The supervisor should seek to weaken dissatisfaction by keeping promises, being sincere and considerate, keeping employees informed, and so forth.
11. Constructive suggestions should be encouraged during the natural progress of the work.

E. Processes for Solving Problems
1. People find their daily tasks more meaningful and satisfying when they can improve them.
2. The causes of problems, or the key factors, are often hidden in the background. Ability to solve problems often involves the ability to isolate them from their backgrounds. There is some substance to the cliché that some persons "can't see the forest for the trees."
3. New procedures are often developed from old ones. Problems should be broken down into manageable parts. New ideas can be adapted from old one.
4. People think differently in problem-solving situations. Using a logical, patterned approach is often useful. One approach found to be useful includes these steps:
    a. Define the problem
    b. Establish objectives
    c. Get the facts
    d. Weigh and decide
    e. Take action
    f. Evaluate action

F. Training for Results
1. Participants respond best when they feel training is important to them.
2. The supervisor has responsibility for the training and development of those who report to him.
3. When training is delegated to others, great care must be exercised to insure the trainer has knowledge, aptitude, and interest for his work as a trainer.
4. Training (learning) of some type goes on continually. The most successful supervisor makes certain the learning contributes in a productive manner to operational goals.
5. New employees are particularly susceptible to training. Older employees facing new job situations require specific training, as well as having need for development and growth opportunities.
6. Training needs require continuous monitoring.
7. The training officer of an agency is a professional with a responsibility to assist supervisors in solving training problems.

8. Many of the self-development steps important to the supervisor's own growth are equally important to the development of peers and subordinates. Knowledge of these is important when the supervisor consults with others on development and growth opportunities.

G. Health, Safety, and Accident Prevention
1. Management-minded supervisors take appropriate measures to assist employees in maintaining health and in assuring safe practices in the work environment.
2. Effective safety training and practices help to avoid injury and accidents.
3. Safety should be a management goal. All infractions of safety which are observed should be corrected without exception.
4. Employees' safety attitude, training and instruction, provision of safe tools and equipment, supervision, and leadership are considered highly important factors which contribute to safety and which can be influenced directly by supervisors.
5. When accidents do occur, they should be investigated promptly for very important reasons, including the fact that information which is gained can be used to prevent accidents in the future.

H. Equal Employment Opportunity
1. The supervisor should endeavor to treat all employees fairly, without regard to religion, race, sex, or national origin.
2. Groups tend to reflect the attitude of the leader. Prejudice can be detected even in very subtle form. Supervisors must strive to create a feeling of mutual respect and confidence in every employee.
3. Complete utilization of all human resources is a national goal. Equitable consideration should be accorded women in the work force, minority-group members, the physically and mentally handicapped, and the older employee. The important question is: "Who can do the job?"
4. Training opportunities, recognition for performance, overtime assignments, promotional opportunities, and all other personnel actions are to be handled on an equitable basis.

I. Improving Communications
1. Communications is achieving understanding between the sender and the receiver of a message. It also means sharing information—the creation of understanding.
2. Communication is basic to all human activity. Words are means of conveying meanings; however, real meanings are in people.
3. There are very practical differences in the effectiveness of one-way, impersonal, and two-way communications. Words spoken face-to-face are better understood. Telephone conversations are effective, but lack the rapport of person-to-person exchanges. The whole person communicates.
4. Cooperation and communication in an organization go hand in hand. When there is a mutual respect between people, spelling out rules and procedures for communicating is unnecessary.
5. There are several barriers to effective communications. These include failure to listen with respect and understanding, lack of skill in feedback, and misinterpreting the meanings of words used by the speaker. It is also common

practice to listen to what we want to hear, and tune out things we do not want to hear.
6. Communication is management's chief problem. The supervisor should accept the challenge to communicate more effectively and to improve interagency and intra-agency communications.
7. The supervisor may often plan for and conduct meetings. The planning phase is critical and may determine the success or the failure of a meeting.
8. Speaking before groups usually requires extra effort. Stage fright may never disappear completely, but it can be controlled.

J. Self-Development
1. Every employee is responsible for his own self-development.
2. Toastmaster and toastmistress clubs offer opportunities to improve skills in oral communications.
3. Planning for one's own self-development is of vital importance. Supervisors know their own strengths and limitations better than anyone else.
4. Many opportunities are open to aid the supervisor in his developmental efforts, including job assignments; training opportunities, both governmental and non-governmental—to include universities and professional conferences and seminars.
5. Programmed instruction offers a means of studying at one's own rate.
6. Where difficulties may arise from a supervisor's being away from his work for training, he may participate in televised home study or correspondence courses to meet his self-development needs.

K. Teaching and Training
1. The Teaching Process
Teaching is encouraging and guiding the learning activities of students toward established goals. In most cases this process consists of five steps: preparation, presentation, summarization, evaluation, and application.

   a. Preparation
   Preparation is two-fold in nature; that of the supervisor and the employee. Preparation by the supervisor is absolutely essential to success. He must know what, when, where, how, and whom he will teach. Some of the factors that should be considered are:
   1) The objectives
   2) The materials needed
   3) The methods to be used
   4) Employee participation
   5) Employee interest
   6) Training aids
   7) Evaluation
   8) Summarization

   Employee preparation consists in preparing the employee to receive the material. Probably the most important single factor in the preparation of the employee is arousing and maintaining his interest. He must know the objectives of the training, why he is there, how the material can be used, and its importance to him.

b. Presentation
In presentation, have a carefully designed plan and follow it. The plan should be accurate and complete, yet flexible enough to meet situations as they arise. The method of presentation will be determined by the particular situation and objectives.

c. Summary
A summary should be made at the end of every training unit and program. In addition, there may be internal summaries depending on the nature of the material being taught. The important thing is that the trainee must always be able to understand how each part of the new material relates to the whole.

d. Application
The supervisor must arrange work so the employee will be given a chance to apply new knowledge or skills while the material is still clear in his mind and interest is high. The trainee does not really know whether he has learned the material until he has been given a chance to apply it. If the material is not applied, it loses most of its value.

e. Evaluation
The purpose of all training is to promote learning. To determine whether the training has been a success or failure, the supervisor must evaluate this learning.
In the broadest sense, evaluation includes all the devices, methods, skills, and techniques used by the supervisor to keep himself and the employees informed as to their progress toward the objectives they are pursuing. The extent to which the employee has mastered the knowledge, skills, and abilities, or changed his attitudes, as determined by the program objectives, is the extent to which instruction has succeeded or failed.
Evaluation should not be confined to the end of the lesson, day, or program but should be used continuously. We shall note later the way this relates to the rest of the teaching process.

2. Teaching Methods
A teaching method is a pattern of identifiable student and instructor activity used in presenting training material.
All supervisors are faced with the problem of deciding which method should be used at a given time.

a. Lecture
The lecture is direct oral presentation of material by the supervisor. The present trend is to place less emphasis on the trainer's activity and more on that of the trainee.

b. Discussion
Teaching by discussion or conference involves using questions and other techniques to arouse interest and focus attention upon certain areas, and by doing so creating a learning situation. This can be one of the most

valuable methods because it gives the employees an opportunity to express their ideas and pool their knowledge.

    c. Demonstration
The demonstration is used to teach how something works or how to do something. It can be used to show a principle or what the results of a series of actions will be. A well-staged demonstration is particularly effective because it shows proper methods of performance in a realistic manner.

    d. Performance
Performance is one of the most fundamental of all learning techniques or teaching methods. The trainee may be able to tell how a specific operation should be performed but he cannot be sure he knows how to perform the operation until he has done so.
As with all methods, there are certain advantages and disadvantages to each method.

    e. Which Method to Use
Moreover, there are other methods and techniques of teaching. It is difficult to use any method without other methods entering into it. In any learning situation, a combination of methods is usually more effective than any one method alone.

Finally, evaluation must be integrated into the other aspects of the teaching-learning process.

It must be used in the motivation of the trainees; it must be used to assist in developing understanding during the training; and it must be related to employee application of the results of training.

This is distinctly the role of the supervisor.

GLOSSARY OF LEGAL, MEDICAL, SOCIAL WORK TERMS

TABLE OF CONTENTS

	Page
Abandonment ... Advocacy	1
Affidavit ... Annual Review of Dependency Cases	2
Anomie ... Battery	3
Best Interests of the Child ... Caretaker	4
Cartilage ... Child Abuse	5
Child Abuse and Neglect	6
Child Abuse Prevention and Treatment Act ... Child Health Visitor	7
Child in Need of Supervision ... Child Welfare League of America	8
Child Welfare Resource Information Exchange ... Circumstantial Evidence	9
Civil Proceeding ... Community Organization	10
Community Support Systems	11
Compliance ... Corporal Punishment	12
Cortex ... Custody	13
Custody Hearing ... Denver Model	14
Dependency ... Discipline	15
Dislocation ... Due Process	16
Duodenum ... Evidence	17
Exhibit ... Expungement	18
Extravasated Blood ... Family Dynamics	19
Family Dysfunction ... Family Violence	20
Federal Regulations ... Fracture	21
Frontal ... Helpline	22
Hematemesis ... Hypovitaminosis	23
Identification of Child Abuse and Neglect ... Incest	24
Incidence ... Infanticide	25
Institutional Child Abuse and Neglect ... Juvenile Judge	27
Labeling ... Legal Rights of Persons Identified in Reports	28
Lesion ... Local Authority	29
Long Bone ... Maternal Characteristics Scale	30
Maternal-Infant Bonding ... Model Child Protection Act	31
Mondale Act ... National Center for the Prevention and Treatment of Child Abuse and Neglect	32
National Center on Child Abuse and Neglect ... National Committee for the Prevention of Child Abuse	33
National Register ... Nurturance	34
Occipital ... Parent Effectiveness Training	35
Parental Stress Services ... Pathognomonic	36
Perinatal ... Pre-trial Diversion	37

TABLE OF CONTENTS
(Continued)

Prevention of Child Abuse and Neglect ... Probation	38
Program Coordination ... Public Defender	39
Public Law 93-247 ... Regional Resource Center	40
Registry ... Res Ipsa Loquitor	41
Retina ... Self-Incrimination	42
Sentencing ... Social Assessment	43
Social History ... Societal Child Abuse and Neglect	44
Special Child ... State Authority	45
Status Offense ... Subdural Hematoma	46
Subpoena ... Surrogate Parent	47
Suspected Child Abuse and Neglect ... Trauma	48
Trauma X ... Vascular	49
Venereal Disease ... Willful	50
Witness ... X-Rays	51
ACRONYMS	52

GLOSSARY OF
Legal, Medical, Social Work Terms

ABANDONMENT
Act of a parent or caretaker leaving a child without adequate supervision or provision for his/her needs for an excessive period of time. State laws vary in defining adequacy of supervision and the length of time a child may be left alone or in the care of another before abandonment is determined. The age of the child also is an important factor. In legal terminology, "abandonment cases" are suits calling for the termination of parental rights.

ABDOMINAL DISTENTION
Swelling of the stomach area. The distention may be caused by internal injury or obstruction or by malnutrition.

ABRASION
Wound in which an area of the body surface is scraped of skin or mucous membrane.

ABUSE (See CHILD ABUSE AND NEGLECT)

ABUSED CHILD (See INDICATORS OF CHILD ABUSE AND NEGLECT)

ABUSED PARENT
Parent who has been abused as a child and who therefore may be more likely to abuse his/her own child.

ABUSER, PASSIVE (See PASSIVE ABUSER)

ACADEMY OF CERTIFIED SOCIAL WORKERS (ACSW)
Professional category identifying experienced social workers. Eligibility is determined by written examination following two years' full-time or 3,000 hours part-time paid post-Master's degree experience and continuous National Association of Social Workers (NASW) membership.

ACTING OUT
1) Behavior of an abusive parent who may be unconsciously and indirectly expressing anger toward his/her own parents or other significant person.
2) Aggressive or sexual behavior explained by some psychoanalytic theorists as carrying out fantasies or expressing unconscious feelings and conflicts.
3) Children's play or play therapy activities used as a means of expressing hitherto repressed feelings.

ACUTE CARE CAPACITY
Capacity of a community to respond quickly and responsibly to a report of a child abuse or neglect. It involves receiving the report and providing a diagnostic assessment including both a medical assessment and an evaluation of family dynamics. It also involves rapid intervention, including immediate protection of the child when needed and referral for long term care or service to the child and his/her family.

ADJUDICATION HEARING
Court hearing in which it is decided whether or not charges against a parent or caretaker are substantiated by admissible evidence. Also known as jurisdictional or evidentiary hearing.

ADMISSIBLE EVIDENCE
Evidence which may be legally and properly used in court. (See also EVIDENCE, EVIDENTIARY STANDARDS, EXPERT TESTIMONY)

ADVOCACY
Interventive strategy in which a helping person assumes an active role in assisting or supporting a specific child and/or family or a cause on behalf of children and/or families. This could involve finding and facilitating services for specific cases or developing new

services or promoting program coordination. The advocate uses his/her power to meet client needs or to promote causes.

AFFIDAVIT
Written statement signed in the presence of a Notary Public who "swears in" the signer. The contents of the affidavit are stated under penalty of perjury. Affidavits are frequently used in the initiation of juvenile court cases and are, at times, presented to the court as evidence.

AGAINST MEDICAL ADVICE (AMA)
Going against the orders of a physician. In cases of child abuse or neglect, this usually means the removal of a child from a hospital without the physician's consent.

AID TO FAMILIES WITH DEPENDENT CHILDREN (AFDC) (See SOCIAL SECURITY ACT)

ALLEGATION
An assertion, declaration, or statement of a party to a legal action, which sets out what he or she expects to prove. In a child abuse or neglect case, the allegation forms the basis of the petition or accusation containing charges of specific acts of maltreatment which the petitioner hopes to prove at the trial.

ALOPECIA
Absence of hair from skin areas where it normally appears; baldness.

AMERICAN ACADEMY OF PEDIATRICS (AAP)
P.O. Box 1034
Evanston, Illinois 60204
AAP is the pan-American association of physicians certified in the care of infants, children, and adolescents. It was founded in 1930 for the primary purpose of ensuring "the attainment of all children of the Americas of their full potential for physical, emotional, and social health." Services and activities of AAP include standards-setting for pediatric residencies, scholarships, continuing education, standards-setting for child health care, community health services, consultation, publications, and research.

AMERICAN HUMANE ASSOCIATION, CHILDREN'S DIVISION (AHA)
5351 S. Roslyn St.
Englewood, Colorado 80110
National association of individuals and agencies working to prevent neglect, abuse, and exploitation of children. Its objectives are to inform the public of the problem, to promote understanding of its causes, to advise on the identification and protection of abused and neglected children, and to assist in organizing new and improving existing child protection programs and services. Some of the programs and services of CDAHA include research, consultation and surveys, legislative guidance, staff development training and workshops, and publications. AHA includes an Animal Division in addition to the Children's Division.

AMERICAN PUBLIC WELFARE ASSOCIATION (APWA)
1125 Fifteenth St. N.W. Suite 300
Washington, D.C. 20005
APWA was founded in 1930 and has, from its inception, been a voluntary membership organization composed of individuals and agencies interested in issues of public welfare. National in scope, its dual purpose is to: 1) exert a positive influence on the shaping of national social policy, and 2) promote professional development of persons working in the area of public welfare. APWA sponsors an extensive program of policy analysis and research, testimony and consultation, publications, conferences, and workshops. It works for policies which are more equitable, less complex, and easier to administer in order that public welfare personnel can respond efficiently and effectively to the needs of persons they serve.

ANNUAL REVIEW OF DEPENDENCY CASES
Annual or other periodic reviews of dependency cases to determine whether continued

child placement or court supervision of a child is necessary. Increasingly required by state law, such reviews by the court also provide some judicial supervision of probation or casework services.

ANOMIE
A state of anomie is characterized by attitudes of aimlessness, futility, and lack of motivation and results from the breakdown or failure of standards, rules, norms, and values that ordinarily bind people together in some socially organized way.

ANOREXIA
Lack or loss of appetite for food.

APATHY-FUTILITY SYNDROME
Immature personality type often associated with child neglect and characterized by an inability to feel and to find any significant meaning in life. This syndrome, often arising from early deprivations in childhood, is frequently perpetuated from generation to generation within a family system. (Polansky)

APPEAL
Resort to a higher court in an attempt to have a decision or ruling of the lower court corrected or reversed because of some claimed error or injustice. Appeals follow several different formats. Occasionally, appeals will result in a rehearing of the entire case. Usually, however, appeals are limited to consideration of questions of whether the lower court judge correctly applied the law to the facts of the case.

ASSESSMENT
1) Determination of the validity of a reported case of suspected child abuse or neglect through investigatory interviews with persons involved. This could include interviews with the family, the child, school, and neighbors, as well as with other professionals and paraprofessionals having direct contact with the child or family.
2) Determination of the treatment potential and treatment plan for confirmed cases.

ASSAULT
Intentional or reckless threat of physical injury to a person. Aggravated assault is committed with the intention of carrying out the threat or other crimes. Simple assault is committed without the intention of carrying out the threat or if the attempt at injury is not completed. (See also BATTERY, SEXUAL ASSAULT)

ATROPHY
Wasting away of flesh, tissue, cell, or organ.

AVITAMINOSIS
Condition due to complete lack of one or more essential vitamins. (See also HYPOVITAMINOSIS)

BATTERED CHILD SYNDROME
Term introduced in 1962 by C. Henry Kempe, M.D., in the *Journal of the American Medical Association* in an article describing a combination of physical and other signs indicating that a child's internal and/or external injuries result from acts committed by a parent or caretaker. In some states, the battered child syndrome has been judicially recognized as an accepted medical diagnosis. Frequently this term is misused or misunderstood as the only type of child abuse and neglect. (See also CHILD ABUSE AND NEGLECT)

BATTERED WOMEN
Women who are victims of non-accidental physical and/or psychological injury inflected by a spouse or mate. There seems to be a relationship between child abuse and battered women, with both often occurring in the same family. (See also SPOUSE ABUSE)

BATTERY
Offensive contact or physical violence with a person without his/her consent, and which may or may not be preceded by a threat of assault. Because a minor cannot legally give consent, any such contact or violence against a child is considered battery. The action may be aggravated, meaning intentional, or it may be simple, meaning that the action was not intentional or did not cause

severe harm. Assault is occasionally used to mean attempted battery. (See also ASSAULT)

BEST INTERESTS OF THE CHILD
Standard for deciding among alternative plans for abused or neglected children. This is also known as the least detrimental alternative principle. Usually it is assumed that it is in the child's best interest and least detrimental if the child remains in the home, provided that the parents can respond to treatment. However, the parents' potential for treatment may be difficult to assess and it may not be known whether the necessary resources are available. A few authorities believe that except where the child's life is in danger, it is always in the child's best interest to remain in the home. This view reflects the position that in evaluating the least detrimental alternative and the child's best interest, the child's psychological as well as physical well-being must be considered. In developing a plan, the best interest of the child may not be served because of parents' legal rights or because agency policy and practice focuses on foster care. The best interest of the child and least detrimental alternative principles were articulated as a reaction to the overuse of child placement in cases of abuse and neglect. Whereas "best interest of the child" suggests that some placement may be justified, "least detrimental alternative" is stronger in suggesting that any placement or alternative can have some negative consequences and should be monitored.

BEYOND A REASONABLE DOUBT (See EVIDENTIARY STANDARDS)

BONDING
The psychological attachment of mother to child which develops during and immediately following childbirth. Bonding, which appears to be crucial to the development of a health parent/child relationship, may be studied during and immediately following delivery to help identify potential families-at-risk. Bonding is normally a natural occurrence but it may be disrupted by separation of mother and baby or by situational or psychological factors causing the mother to reject the baby at birth.

BRUISE (See INTRADERMAL HEMORRHAGE)

BURDEN OF PROOF
The duty, usually falling on the state as petitioner in a child maltreatment case, of producing evidence at a trial so as to establish the truth of the allegations against the parent. At the commencement of a trial, it is always up to the petitioner to first present evidence which proves their case. (See also EVIDENCE, EVIDENTIARY STANDARDS)

BURN
Wound resulting from the application of too much heat. Burns are classified by the degree of damage caused.
    1st degree: Scorching or painful redness of the skin.
    2nd degree: Formation of blisters.
    3rd degree: Destruction of outer layers of the skin.

BURN OUT (See staff burn out.)

CALCIFICATION
Formation of bone. The amount of calcium deposited can indicate via X-ray the degree of healing of a broken bone or the location of previous fractures which have healed prior to the X-ray.

CALLUS
New bone formed during the healing process of a fracture.

CALVARIUM
Dome-like portion of the skull.

CARETAKER
A person responsible for a child's health or welfare, including the child's parent, guardian, or other person within the child's own home; or a person responsible for a child's health or welfare in a relative's home, foster care home, or residential institution. A caretaker is responsible for meeting a child's

basic physical and psychological needs and for providing protection and supervision.

CARTILAGE
The hard connective tissue that is not bone but, in the unborn and growing child, may be the forerunner of bone before calcium is deposited in it.

CASE MANAGEMENT
Coordination of the multiplicity of services required by a child abuse and neglect client. Some of these services may be purchased from an agency other than the mandated agency. In general, the role of the case manager is not the provision of direct services but the monitoring of those services to assure that they are relevant to the client, delivered in a useful way, and appropriately used by the client. To do this, a case manager assumes the following responsibilities.
1) Ascertains that all mandated reports have been properly filed.
2) Informs all professionals involved with the family that reports of suspected child abuse or neglect have been made.
3) Keeps all involved workers apprised of new information.
4) Calls and chairs the intial case conference for assessment, disposition, and treatment plans; conference may include parents, physician, probation worker, police, public health nurse, private therapist, parent aide, protective service and welfare workers, or others.
5) Coordinates interagency follow-up.
6) Calls further case conferences as needed. (See also PURCHASE OF SERVICE)

CASEWORK
A method of social work intervention which helps an individual or family improve their functioning in society by changing both internal attitudes and feelings and external circumstances directly affecting the individual or family. This contrasts with community organization and other methods of social work intervention which focuses on changing institutions or society. Social casework relies on a relationship between the worker and client as the primary tool for effecting change.

CATEGORICAL AID
Government financial assistance given to individuals who are aged or disabled or to families with dependent children. The eligibility requirements and financial assistance vary for different categories of persons, according to the guidelines of the Social Security Act. (See also SOCIAL SECURITY ACT)

CENTRAL REGISTER
Records of child abuse reports collected centrally from various agencies under state law or voluntary agreement. Agencies receiving reports of suspected abuse check with the central register to determine whether prior reports have been received by other agencies concerning the same child or parents. The purposes of central registers may be to alert authorities to families with a prior history of abuse, to assist agencies in planning for abusive families, and to provide data for statistical analysis of child abuse. Due to variance in state laws for reporting child abuse and neglect, there are diverse methods of compiling these records and of access to them. Although access to register records is usually restricted, critics warn of confidentiality problems and the importance of expunging unverified reports. (See also EXPUNGEMENT)

CHILD
A person, also known as minor, from birth to legal age of maturity for whom a parent and/or caretaker, foster parent, public or private home, institution, or agency is legally responsible. The 1974 Child Abuse Prevention and Treatment Act defines a child as a person under 18. In some states, a person of any age with a developmental disability is defined as a child.

CHILD ABUSE (See CHILD ABUSE AND NEGLECT)

CHILD ABUSE AND NEGLECT (CAN)
All-inclusive term, as defined in the Child Abuse Prevention and Treatment Act, for "the physical or mental injury, sexual abuse, negligent treatment or maltreatment of a child under the age of eighteen by a person who is responsible for the child's welfare. There is agreement that some parental care and supervision is essential, there is disagreement as to how much is necessary for a minimally acceptable environment.

Child Abuse refers specifically to an act of commission by a parent or caretaker which is not accidental and harms or threatens to harm a child's physical or mental health or welfare. All 50 States have a child abuse reporting law with varying definitions of child abuse and varying provisions as to who must and may report, penalties for not reporting, and required agency action following the report. Factors such as the age of the child and the severity of injury are important in determining abuse.

Physical Abuse
Child abuse which results in physical injury, including fractures, burns, bruises, welts, cuts, and/or internal injuries. Physical abuse often occurs in the name of discipline or punishment, and ranges from a slap of the hand to use of objects such as straps, belts, kitchen utensils, pipes, etc. (See also BATTERED CHILD SYNDROME)

Psychological/Emotional Abuse
Child abuse which results in impaired psychological growth and development. Frequently occurs as verbal abuse or excessive demands on a child's performance and results in a negative self-image on the part of the child and disturbed child behavior. May occur with or without physical abuse.

Sexual Abuse
Child abuse which results in any act of a sexual nature upon or with a child. Most states define any sexual involvement of a parent or caretaker with a child as a sexual act and therefore abuse. The most common form is incest between fathers and daughters.

Verbal Abuse
A particular form of psychological/emotional abuse characterized by constant verbal harassment and denigration of a child. Many persons abused as children report feeling more permanently damaged by verbal abuse than by isolated or repeated experiences of physical abuse.

Child Neglect refers to an act of omission, specifically the failure of a parent or other person legally responsible for a child's welfare to provide for the child's basic needs and proper level of care with respect to food, clothing, shelter, hygiene, medical attention, or supervision. Most states have neglect and/or dependency statutes; however, not all states require the reporting of neglect. While there is agreement that some parental care and supervision is essential, there is disagreement as to how much is necessary for a minimally acceptable environment. Severe neglect sometimes occurs because a parent is apathetic, impulse-ridden, mentally retarded, depressed, or psychotic.

Educational Neglect
Failure to provide for a child's cognitive development. This may include failure to conform to state legal requirements regarding school attendance.

Medical Neglect
Failure to seek medical or dental treatment for a health problem or condition which, if untreated, could become severe enough to represent a danger to the child. Except among religious sects prohibiting medical treatment, medical neglect is usually only one part of a larger family problem.

Moral Neglect
Failure to give a child adequate guidance in developing positive social values, such as parents who allow or teach their children to steal.

Physical Neglect
Failure to provide for a child's basic survival needs, such as food, clothing, shelter, and supervision, to the extent that the failure represents a hazard to the child's health or safety. Determining neglect for lack of supervision depends upon the child's age and competence, the amount of unsupervised time, the time of day when the child is unsupervised, and the degree of parental planning for the unsupervised period. For a particular kind of physical neglect involving failure to feed a baby or small child sufficiently, see FAILURE TO THRIVE SYNDROME.

Psychological /Emotional Neglect
Failure to provide the psychological nurturance necessary for a child's psychological growth and development. It is usually very difficult to prove the cause and effect relationship between the parent's unresponsiveness and lack of nurturance and the child's symptoms, and many states do not include psychological or emotional neglect in their reporting laws.

CHILD ABUSE PREVENTION AND TREATMENT ACT (PUBLIC LAW 93-247)
Act introduced and promoted in Congress by then U.S. Senator Walter Mondale and signed into law on January 31, 1974. The act established the National Center on Child Abuse and Neglect in the HEW Children's Bureau and authorized annual appropriations of between $15 million and $25 million through Fiscal Year 1977, but it is anticipated that Congress will extend the act for several years. Actual appropriations have been less than authorized. The purpose of the National Center is to conduct and compile research, provide an information clearinghouse, compile and publish training materials, provide technical assistance, investigate national incidence, and fund demonstration projects related to prevention, identification, and treatment of child abuse and neglect. In the 1974 act, not more than 20% of the appropriated funds may be used for direct assistance to states, which must be in compliance with specific legislative requirements including, among others, reporting and investigation of suspected neglect as well as abuse, provision of multidisciplinary programs, and appointment of a *guardian ad litem* to represent the child in all judicial proceedings. The act emphasizes multidisciplinary approaches. It also provides for funding for parent self-help projects.

Many persons do not understand that this act is primarily to support research and demonstration projects. Much larger amounts of funding for the ongoing provisions of child abuse and neglect services are provided to states through Title IV-B and Title XX of the Social Security Act.

CHILD DEVELOPMENT
Pattern of sequential stages of interrelated physical, psychological, and social development in the process of maturation from infancy and total dependence to adulthood and relative independence. Parents need to understand the level of maturity consistent with each stage of development and should not expect a child to display a level of maturity of which the child is incapable at a particular stage. Abusive or neglectful parents frequently impair a child's healthy growth and development because they do not understand child development or are otherwise unable to meet the child's physical, social, and psychological needs at a given stage or stages of development.

CHILD HEALTH VISITOR
Professional or paraprofessional who visits a home shortly after the birth of a baby and periodically thereafter to identify current and potential child health and development and family stress problems and to facilitate use of needed community services. While currently operating in many European countries, child health visitor programs are rare in the U.S. because they are perceived as contrary to the right to privacy and parental rights. A universal mandatory child health visitor program has, however, been recommended by several

authorities as the most effective way to assure children's rights and prevent child abuse and neglect. Also known as Home Health Visitor.

CHILD IN NEED OF SUPERVISION
Juvenile who has committed a delinquent act and has been found by a children's court judge to require further court supervision, such as 1) probation, or 2) the transfer of custody of the child to a relative or public or private welfare agency for a period of time, usually not to exceed one year. Also known as Person in Need of Supervision (PINS) or Minor in Need of Supervision (MINS).

CHILD NEGLECT (See CHILD ABUSE AND NEGLECT)

CHILD PORNOGRAPHY
The obscene or pornographic photography, filming, or depiction of children for commercial purposes. Recent campaigns have begun to increase public awareness of this problem. Also as a result of public pressure against these materials, the federal government and some states are currently implementing special legislation to outlaw the sale and interstate transportation of pornographic materials that portray children engaged in explicit sexual acts.

CHILD PROSTITUTION
Legislation prohibiting the use of children as prostitutes is currently being implemented by the federal government and many states. The use of or participation by children in sexual acts with adults for reward or financial gain when no force is present.

CHILD PROTECTIVE SERVICES or CHILD PROTECTION SERVICES (CPS)
A specialized child welfare service, usually part of a county department of public welfare, legally responsible in most states for investigating suspected cases of child abuse and neglect and intervening in confirmed cases. Qualifications of CPS workers vary, with some counties employing CPS workers without prior human services training and others requiring at least a , Bachelor's degree in social work. With over 3,000 counties in the U.S., there are many kinds of CPS programs of varying quality. Common to most is the problem of insufficient staff overburdened with excessive caseloads. This plus the pressure of CPS work creates stress for many CPS staff. (See also STAFF BURNOUT, STAFF FLIGHT, and STAFF SATISFACTION)

CHILD WELFARE AGENCY
A public or voluntary agency providing service to children in their own homes and/or in day care, and which may be licensed to place children in foster homes, group homes, or institutions or into permanent adoptive homes. The number of children served annually by child welfare agencies in the U.S. is estimated to be over one million, the majority being served by public agencies. Payments for foster care represent well over half the total of child welfare agencies' expenditures.

Child welfare agencies which meet certain standards, including Standards for Protective Services, are accredited by the Child Welfare League of America. It is estimated that the majority of social workers employed by these accredited agencies hold a Master's degree. In public child welfare agencies, Master's degree social workers are a minority, with specific educational requirements varying from state to state. However, unlike many other fields of social work which share responsibility with other professions, child welfare is a domain for which social work has been accorded major responsibility. Believing that child protection is a public child welfare agency responsibility, few private agencies provide it.

CHILD WELFARE LEAGUE OF AMERICA (CWLA)
67 Irving Place
New York,
N.Y. 10003
Founded in 1920, the Child Welfare League of America is a privately supported, non-sectarian organization which is dedicated to the improvement of care and services for

deprived, neglected, and dependent children and their families. Its program is directed toward helping agencies and communities in the U.S. and Canada to provide essential social services to promote the well-being of children. CWLA is an advocate for children and families, a clearinghouse and forum for knowledge and experience of persons in the field, and a coordinating facility through which all concerned with child welfare can share their efforts. Programs of the League and its membership of over 300 affiliated public and private agencies include: accreditation of agencies, adoption services, conferences, consultation, training, library/information services, publications, personnel services, public affairs and legislative programs, standards development, and surveys.

CHILD WELFARE RESOURCE INFORMATION EXCHANGE
A project of the Children's Bureau of the Administration for Children, Youth and Families, HEW. It is a source for materials on exemplary programs, curricula, technologies, and methods which ahve brought more effective and efficient services to children. Its purpose is to improve the delivery of child welfare services by identifying successful programs, methods, research, and materials, and by assisting agencies in adapting them for their own use. The Exchange disseminates information it has gathered through abstracts, a bimonthly bulletin, regional workshops, and colloquia.

CHILDHOOD LEVEL OF LIVING SCALE (CLL)
Instrument used to measure the level of physical and emotional/cognitive care a child is receiving in his/her home. Rated are adequacy of food, clothing, furniture, etc., as well as evidence of affection, type of discipline, and cultural stimulation. The scale is designed to be used as a guide to assessing nurturance levels rather than as objective evidence of neglect.

CHILDREN-AT-RISK
May refer to the possibility that children in the custody of a state or county will get lost in a series of placements or for other reasons not be returned to their natural homes when these homes are no longer threatening to the children's welfare. May also refer to children in potentially abusive institutions, but usually refer to children in families-at-risk. (See also FAMILIES-AT-RISK)

CHILDREN'S DEFENSE FUND (CDF) 1520 New Hampshire Ave., N.W. Washington, D.C. 20036
A non-profit organization founded in 1973. Staff includes researchers, lawyers, and others dedicated to long-range and systematic advocacy on behalf of children. CDF works at federal, state, and local levels to reform policies and practices which harmfully affect large numbers of children. Activities include investigation and public information, litigation, monitoring of federal agencies, and technical assistance to local organizations. Program priorities are to assure the rights of children to proper education, adequate health care, comprehensive child care and family support services, fair and humane treatment in the juvenile justice system, and the avoidance of institutionalization.

CHILDREN'S RIGHTS
Rights of children as individuals to the protections provided in the Constitution as well as to the care and protection necessary for normal growth and development. Children's rights are actually exercised through adult representatives and advocates. The extent to which children's rights are protected varies according to the individual state laws providing for the identification and treatment of child abuse and neglect. An unresolved issue is the conflict between children's rights and parents' rights or rights to privacy. (See also PARENTS' RIGHTS)

CHIP FRACTURE (See FRACTURE)

CIRCUMSTANTIAL EVIDENCE (See EVIDENCE)

CIVIL PROCEEDING
Any lawsuit other than criminal prosecutions. Juvenile and family court cases are civil proceedings. Also called a civil action.

CLEAR AND CONVINCING EVIDENCE
(See EVIDENTIARY STANDARDS)

CLOTTING FACTOR
Material in the blood that causes it to coagulate. Deficiencies in clotting factors can cause profuse internal or external bleeding and/or bruising, as in the disease hemophilia. Bruises or bleeding caused by such a disease may be mistaken as resulting from abuse.

COLON
The large intestine.

COMMINUTED FRACTURE (See FRACTURE)

COMMISSION, ACTS OF
Overt acts by a parent or caretaker toward a child resulting in physical or mental injury, including but not limited to beatings, excessive disciplining, or exploitation. (See also CHILD ABUSE AND NEGLECT)

COMMISSIONER (See HEARING OFFICER)

COMMUNITY AWARENESS
A community's level of understanding of child abuse and neglect. Ideally, this should include knowledge about the extent and nature of the problem and how to use the local resources. In reality, community awareness tends to focus on reporting rather than treatment and prevention.

COMMUNITY COUNCIL FOR CHILD ABUSE AND NEGLECT
Community group, including both professionals and citizens, which attempts to develop and coordinate resources and/or legislation for the prevention, identification, and treatment of child abuse and neglect. It is often the name given to the program coordination component of the community team (see COMMUNITY TEAM).

COMMUNITY EDUCATION
Developed for public audiences, this type of local level education provides understanding about a problem or issue of community and/or societal relevance, and information about appropriate community resources and services available to deal with the problem or issue. Sponsored by a professional agency or citizens' group, community education is usually provided through an ongoing speaker's bureau, through periodic lecture and discussion meetings open to the general public or offered to special groups, and/or through the local media and other publicity devices.

With reference to child abuse and neglect, it is important to combine community education with public awareness. Generally, public awareness is geared only to reporting child abuse and neglect, and may communicate a punitive image toward parents who abuse or neglect their children without communicating an understanding of the problem.

COMMUNITY NEGLECT
Failure of a community to provide adequate support and social services for families and children, or lack of community control over illegal or discriminatory activities with respect to families and children.

COMMUNITY ORGANIZATION
A social work method of achieving change in human service organizations or service delivery and utilization through social planning and/or social action. This kind of intervention rests explicitly or implicitly on understanding the nature of the community or service system which is the target of change and on organizing members of the community or system to participate in the change process. Professional community organizers assist, but do not direct, community groups in developing community organization strategies of confrontation, collaboration, coalition,

etc. Since child abuse and neglect is a multidisciplinary, multiagency problem, community organization for coordination of services is imperative.

COMMUNITY SUPPORT SYSTEMS

Community resources such as schools, public health services, day care centers, welfare advocacy, whose utilization can aid in preventing family dysfunction and child abuse and neglect, and aid in treating identified cases of abuse and neglect.

COMMUNITY TEAM

Often used incorrectly to refer to a multidisciplinary professional group which only diagnoses and plans treatment for specific cases of child abuse and neglect. More accurately, a community team separates the diagnosis and treatment functions and provides a third component for education, training, and public relations. The community tream also includes a community task force or council, including citizens as well as professionals from various disciplines, which coordinates the three community team components and advocates for resources and legislation. Citizens on the community team also monitor the professionals and agency participants. For effective child abuse and neglect management, a community team should be established for every geographic area of 400,000 to 500,000 population, and should consist of the following components:

Identification/Diagnostic Team Component
The identification/diagnostic team component has primary responsibility for diagnosing actual cases of child abuse and neglect among those which are reported or otherwise come to their attention, providing acute care or crisis intervention for the child in immediate danger, and developing long-term treatment recommendations. This team should be multidisciplinary and should probably include a public health nurse, pediatrician, psychologist or psychiatrist, lawyer, law enforcement person, case aides, and a number of child protective services workers. The protective services workers on the diagnostic team undergo unusual physical and emotional fatigue, and they should have a two or three week break from this activity every several months. However, to further relieve this stress, the diagnostic team, and not the protective services workers alone, should make and be accountable for all decisions. To function effectively, this team must establish protocol, define roles of each team member, establish policies and procedures, and establish a network of coordination with acute care service agencies.

Long Term Treatment Component
The long term treatment component has responsibility to review treatment needs and progress of specific cases periodically, to establish treatment goals, to coordinate existing treatment services, and to develop new treatment programs. This component should include supervisors and workers from supportive and advocacy services as well as from adult, children, and family treatment programs. The community team must assure provision and use of this component.

Education, Training, and Public Relations Component
The education, training, and public relations component has responsibility for community and professional awareness and education. Professional education includes implementation and/or evaluation of ongoing training programs for professionals and paraprofessionals.

The interrelationship among these various components is diagrammed below:

A - Identification and Diagnosis	1 - Case Coordination
B - Long-Term Treatment	2 - Professional Training and Recruitment
C - Education, Training, Public Relations	3 - Public and Professional ducation, Professional Training
	4 - Program Coordination

COMPLIANCE

1) The behavior of children who readily yield to demands in an attempt to please abusive or neglectful parents or caretakers.
2) A state child abuse and neglect law which conforms to requirements outlined in the Child Abuse Prevention and Treatment Act and further HEW regulations, and which therefore permits funding under this act for child abuse and neglect activities in the state. (See also CHILD ABUSE PREVENTION AND TREATMENT ACT)

COMPLAINT

1) An oral statement, usually made to the police, charging criminal, abusive, or neglectful conduct.
2) A district attorney's document which starts a criminal prosecution.
3) A petitioner's document which starts a civil proceeding. In juvenile or family court, the complaint is usually called a petition.
4) In some states, term used for a report of suspected abuse or neglect.

COMPOUND FRACTURE (See FRACTURE)

COMPREHENSIVE EMERGENCY SERVICES (CES)

A community system of coordinated services available on a 24-hour basis to meet emergency needs of children and/or families in crisis. Components of a CES system can include 24-hour protective services, homemaker services, crisis nurseries, family shelters, emergency foster care, outreach, and follow-up services.

CONCILIATION COURT (See COURTS)

CONCUSSION

An injury of a soft structure resulting from violent shaking or jarring; usually refers to a brain concussion.

CONFIDENTIALITY

Professional practice of not sharing with others information entrusted by a client or patient. Sometimes communications from parent to physician or social worker are made with this expectation but are later used in court, and many physicians and social workers are torn between legal vs. professional obligations. Confidentiality which is protected by statute is known as privileged communications. Confidentiality need not obstruct information sharing with a multidisciplinary team provided that the client is advised of the sharing and the team has articulated its own policy and guidelines on confidentiality. (See also PRIVILEGED COMMUNICATIONS)

CONGENITAL

Refers to any physical condition present at birth, regardless of its cause.

CONJUNCTIVA

Transparent lining covering the white of the eye and eyelids. Bleeding beneath the conjunctiva can occur spontaneously or from accidental or non-accidental injury.

CONTRAINDICATION

Reason for not giving a particular drug or prescribing a particular treatment, as it may do more harm than good.

CONTUSION

A wound producing injury to soft tissue without a break in the skin, causing bleeding into surrounding tissues.

CORPORAL PUNISHMENT

Physical punishment inflected directly upon the body. Some abusive parents mistakenly believe that corporal punishment is the only way to discipline children, and some child development specialists believe that almost all parents must occasionally resort to corporal punishment to discipline or train children. Other professionals believe that corporal punishment is never advisable. In a Supreme Court ruling (Ingraham vs. Wright, April 19, 1977), corporal punishment in the schools was upheld. The Supreme Court ruled that the cruel and unusual punishment clause of the Eighth Amendment does not apply to corporal punishment in the schools. (See also DISCIPLINE).

CORTEX
Outer layer of an organ or other body structure.

COURTS
Places where judicial proceedings occur. There is an array of courts involved with child abuse and neglect cases, partly because different states divide responsibility for certain proceedings among different courts, and also because tradition has established a variety of names for courts which perform similar functions. Child abuse reports can result in proceedings in any of the following courts:

Criminal Court
Usually divided into superior court, which handles felony cases, and municipal court, which handles misdemeanors and the beginning stages of most felony cases.

Domestic Relations Court
A civil court in which divorces and divorce custody hearings are held.

Family Court
A civil court which, in some states, combines the functions of domestic relations, juvenile, and probate courts. Establishment of family courts is often urged to reform the presently wasteful and poorly-coordinated civil court system. Under some proposals, family courts would also deal with criminal cases involving family relations, thus improving coordination in child abuse litigation.

Court of Conciliation
A branch of domestic relations courts in some states, usually staffed by counselors and social workers rather than by lawyers or judges, and designed to explore and promote reconciliation in divorce cases.

Juvenile Court
Juvenile court, which has jurisdiction over minors, usually handles cases of suspected delinquency as well as cases of suspected abuse or neglect. In many states, terminations of parental rights occur in juvenile court proceedings, but that is generally the limit of juvenile court's power over adults.

Probate Court
Probate court may handle cases of guardianship and adoption in addition to estates of deceased persons.

CRANIUM
The skull.

CRIMINAL PROSECUTION
The process involving the filing of charges of a crime, followed by arraignment and trial of the defendant. Criminal prosecution may result in fines, imprisonment, and/or probation. Criminal defendants are entitled to acquittal unless charges against them are proven beyond a reasonable doubt. Technical rules of evidence exclude many kinds of proof in criminal trials, even though that proof might be admissible in civil proceedings. Criminal defendants are entitled to a jury trial; in many civil proceedings concerning children, there is no right to a jury trial.

CRISIS INTERVENTION
Action to relieve a specific stressful situation or series of problems which are immediately threatening to a child's health and/or welfare. This involves alleviation of parental stress through provision of emergency services in the home and/or removal of the child from the home. (See also EMERGENCY SERVICES and COMPREHENSIVE EMERGENCY SERVICES)

CRISIS NURSERY
Facility offering short-term relief of several hours to several days' duration to parents temporarily unable or unwilling to care for their children. The primary purpose are child protection, stabilization of the home, and prevention of child abuse and neglect.

CUSTODY
The right to care and control of a child and the duty to provide food, clothing, shelter, ordinary medical care, education, and discipline for a child. Permanent legal custody

may be taken from a parent or given up by a parent by a court action (see TERMINATION OF PARENTAL RIGHTS). Temporary custody of a child may be granted for a limited time only, usually pending further action or review by the court. Temporary custody may be granted for a period of months or, in the case of protective or emergency custody, for a period of hours or several days.

Emergency Custody
The ability of a law enforcement officer, pursuant to the criminal code, to take temporary custody of a child who is in immediate danger and place him/her in the control of child protective services. A custody hearing must usually be held within 48 hours of such action. Also known as police custody.

Protective Custody
Emergency measure taken to detain a child, often in a hospital, until a written detention request can be filed. In some states, telephone communication with a judge is required to authorize protective custody. In other states, police, social workers, or doctors have statutory authority to detain minors who are in imminent danger. (See also DETENTION)

CUSTODY HEARING
Hearing, usually held in children's court, to determine who has the rights of legal custody of a minor. It may involve one parent against the other or the parents vs. a social service agency.

CYCLE OF CHILD ABUSE OR NEGLECT
(See
WORLD OF ABNORMAL REARING)

DAUGHTERS UNITED
Organization name sometimes used for self-help groups of daughters who have been sexually abused. Daughters United is one component of a model Child Sexual Abuse Treatment Program in Santa Clara County, California. (See also PARENTS UNITED)

DAY CARE
A structured, supervised place for children to go more or less regularly while parents work or attend school. Experts believe that family stress can be relieved by more extensive provision of day care services, and day care providers are increasingly concerned with identification and prevention of child abuse and neglect.

DAY TREATMENT
1) Program providing treatment as well as structured supervision for children with identified behavioral problems, including abused and neglected children, while they remain in their own, foster, or group homes. Day treatment services usually include counseling with families or caretakers with whom the children reside.
2) Treatment and structured activities for parents or entire families in a treatment setting from which they return to their own homes evenings and weekends.

DELINQUENCY
Behavior of a minor which would, in the case of an adult, constitute criminal conduct. In some states, delinquency also includes "waywardness" or disobedient behavior on the part of the child. In contrast to dependency cases, where the parent(s) rather than the minor is assumed responsible, delinquency cases assume that the minor has some responsibility for his/her behavior.

DENVER MODEL
A multidisciplinary hospital-community coalition which originated in Denver, Colorado, and which has become a model replicated by many other programs. The following diagram outlines the components:

TIME	PLACE	FUNCTION
	Community	Child is identified as suspected abuse or neglect.
24 hours	Hospital	Child is admitted to hospital.
	Hospital	Telephone report is made to protective services.
	Community	Home is evaluated by protective services.
72 hours	Both	Dispositional conference is held.
	Community	Court is involved if needed.
2 weeks	Both	Implement dispositional plan.
6-9 months	Community	Maintain case.
	Both	Long-term Treatment program is followed.
	Both	Child is returned home when home has been made safe.

DEPENDENCY
A child's need for care and supervision from a parent or caretaker. Often a legal term referring to cases of children whose natural parent(s) cannot or will not properly care for them or supervise them so that the state must assume this responsibility. Many states distinguish findings of dependency, for which the juvenile is assumed to have little or no responsibility, from findings of delinquency, in which the juvenile is deemed to be at least partially responsible for his/her behavior.

DETENTION
The temporary confinement of a person by a public authority. In a case of child abuse or neglect, a child may be detained pending a trial when a detention hearing indicates that it is unsafe for the child to remain in his/her own home. This is often called protective custody or emergency custody. The child may be detained in a foster home, group home, hospital, or other facility.

DETENTION HEARING
A court hearing held to determine whether a child should be kept away from his/her parents until a full trial of neglect, abuse, or delinquency allegations can take place. Detention hearings must usually be held within 24 hours of the filing of a detention request. (See also CUSTODY)

DETENTION REQUEST
A document filed by a probation officer, social worker, or prosecutor with the clerk of a juvenile or family court, asking that a detention hearing be held, and that a child be detained until the detention hearing has taken place. Detention requests must usually be filed within 48 hours of the time protective custody of the child begins. (See also CUSTODY)

DIAGNOSTIC TEAM (See COMMUNITY TEAM)

DIAPHYSIS
The shaft of a long bone.

DIFFERENTIAL DIAGNOSIS
The determination of which of two or more diseases or conditions a patient may be suffering from by systematically comparing and contrasting the clinical findings.

DIRECT EVIDENCE (See EVIDENCE)

DIRECT SERVICE PROVIDERS
Those groups and individuals who directly interact with clients and patients in the delivery of health, education, and welfare services, or those agencies which employs them. It includes, among others, policemen, social workers, physicians, psychiatrists, and clinical psychologists who see clients or patients.

DISCIPLINE
1) A branch of knowledge or learning or a particular profession, such as law, medicine, or social work.
2) Training that develops self-control, self-sufficiency, orderly conduct. Discipline is

often confused with punishment, particularly by abusive parents who resort to corporal punishment. Although interpretations of both "discipline" and "punishment" tend to be vague and often overlapping, there is some consensus that discipline has positive connotations and punishment is considered negatively. Some general comparisons between the terms are:

a) Discipline can occur before, during, and/or after an event; punishment occurs only after an event.
b) Discipline is based on respect for a child and his/her capabilities; punishment is based on behavior or events precipitating behavior.
c) Discipline implies that there is an authority figure; punishment implies power and dominance vs. submissiveness.
d) The purpose of discipline is educational and rational; the purpose of punishment is to inflict pain, often in an attempt to vent frustration or anger.
e) Discipline focuses on deterring future behavior by encouraging development of internal controls; punishment is a method of external control which may or may not alter future behavior.
f) Discipline can lead to extrapolation and generalized learning patterns; punishment may relate only to a specific event.
g) Discipline can strengthen interpersonal bonds and recognizes individual means and worth; punishment usually causes deterioration of relationships and is usually a dehumanizing experience.
h) Both discipline and punishment behavior patterns may be transmitted to the next generation.

According to legal definitions applying to most schools and school districts, to accomplish the purposes of education, a schoolteacher stands in the place of a parent and may exercise powers of control, restraint, discipline, and correction as necessary, provided that the discipline is reasonable. The Supreme Court has ruled that under certain circumstances, the schools may also employ corporal punishment. (See also CORPORAL PUNISHMENT)

DISLOCATION
The displacement of a bone, usually disrupting a joint, which may accompany a fracture or may occur alone.

DISPOSITION
The order of a juvenile or family court issued at a dispositional hearing which determines whether a minor, already found to be a dependent or delinquent child, should continue in or return to the parental home, and under what kind of supervision, or whether the minor should be placed out-of-home, and in what kind of setting: a relative's home, foster home, or institution. Disposition in a civil case parallels sentencing in a criminal case.

DISPOSITIONAL CONFERENCE
A conference, preferably multidisciplinary, in which the child, parent, family, and home diagnostic assessments are evaluated and decisions are made as to court involvement, steps needed to protect the child, and type of long-term treatment. This conference should be held within the first 72 hours after hospital admission or reporting of the case.

DISPOSITIONAL HEARING (See DISPOSITION)

DISTAL
Far; farther from any point of reference. Opposite of proximal.

DOMESTIC RELATIONS COURT (See COURTS)

DUE PROCESS
The rights of persons involved in legal proceedings to be treated with fairness. These rights include the right to adequate notice in advance of hearings, the right to notice of allegations of misconduct, the right to assis-

tance of a lawyer, the right to confront and cross-examine witnesses, and the right to refuse to give self-incriminating testimony. In child abuse or neglect cases, courts are granting more and more due process to parents in recognition of the fact that loss of parental rights, temporarily or permanently, is as serious as loss of liberty. However, jury trials and presumptions of innocence are still afforded in very few juvenile or family court cases.

DUODENUM
The first portion of the small intestine which connects it to the stomach.

EARLY AND PERIODIC SCREENING, DIAGNOSIS, AND TREATMENT (EPSDT)
Program enacted in 1967 under Medicaid (Title 19 of the Social Security Act), with early detection of potentially crippling or disabling conditions among poor children as its goal. The establishment of EPSDT was a result of studies indicating that physical and mental defects were high among poor children and that early detection of the problems and prompt receipt of health care could reduce the consequences and the need for remedial services in later life. Although a recent study by the Children's Defense Fund has indicated that existing health systems are not adequate to facilitate the goals of EPSDT, the program has uncovered many previously undetected or untreated health problems among those children whom it has been able to reach.

EARLY INTERVENTION
Programs and services focusing on prevention by relieving family stress before child abuse and neglect occur; for example, helplines, Head Start, home health visitors, EPSDT, crisis nurseries.

ECCHYMOSIS (See INTRADERMAL HEMORRHAGE)

EDEMA
Swelling caused by an excessive amount of fluid in body tissue. It often follows a bump or bruise but may also be caused by allergy, malnutrition, or disease.

EMERGENCY CUSTODY (See CUSTODY)

EMERGENCY SERVICES
The focus of these services is protection of a child and prevention of further maltreatment through availability of a reporting mechanism on a 24-hour basis and immediate intervention. This intervention could include hospitalization of the child, assistance in the home including homemakers, or removal of the child from the home to a shelter or foster home. (See also COMPREHENSIVE EMERGENCY SERVICES)

EMOTIONAL ABUSE (See CHILD ABUSE AND NEGLECT)

EMOTIONAL NEGLECT (See CHILD ABUSE AND NEGLECT)

ENCOPRESIS
Involuntary passage of feces.

ENURESIS
Involuntary passage of urine.

EPIPHYSIS
Growth center near the end of a long bone.

EVIDENCE
Any sort of proof submitted to the court for the purpose of influencing the court's decision. Some special kinds of evidence are:

Circumstantial
Proof of circumstances which may imply another fact. For example, proof that a parent kept a broken appliance cord may connect the parent to infliction of unique marks on a child's body.

Direct
Generally consisting of testimony of the type such as a neighbor stating that he/she saw the parent strike the child with an appliance cord.

Hearsay
Second-hand evidence, generally consisting of testimony of the type such as, "I heard him say. . . ." Except in certain cases, such evidence is usually excluded because it is considered unreliable and because the person making the original statement cannot be cross-examined.

Opinion
Although witnesses are ordinarily not permitted to testify to their beliefs or opinions, being restricted instead to reporting what they actually saw or heard, when a witness can be qualified as an expert on a given subject, he/she can report his/her conclusions, for example, "Based upon these marks, it is my opinion as a doctor that the child must have been struck with a flexible instrument very much like this appliance cord." Lawyers are sometimes allowed to ask qualified experts "hypothetical questions," in which the witness is asked to assume the truth of certain facts and to express an opinion based on those "facts." (See also EXPERT TESTIMONY)

Physical
Any tangible piece of proof such as a document, X-ray, photograph, or weapon used to inflict an injury. Physical evidence must usually be authenticated by a witness who testifies to the connection of the evidence (also called an exhibit) with other facts in the case.

Evidentiary Standards
State laws differ in the quantum of evidence which is considered necessary to prove a case of child maltreatment. Three of the most commonly used standards are:

Beyond a Reasonable Doubt (the standard required in all criminal court proceedings). Evidence which is entirely convincing or satisfying to a moral certainty. This is the strictest standard of all.

Clear and Convincing Evidence. Less evidence than is required to prove a case beyond a reasonable doubt, but still an amount which would make one confident of the truth of the allegations.

Preponderance of the Evident (the standard in most civil court proceedings). Merely presenting a greater weight of credible evidence than that presented by the opposing party. This is the easiest standard of proof of all.

EXHIBIT
Physical evidence used in court. In a child abuse case, an exhibit may consist of X-rays, photographs of the child's injuries, or the actual materials presumably used to inflict the injuries. (See also EVIDENCE)

EXPERT TESTIMONY
Witnesses with various types of expertise may testify in child abuse or neglect cases; usually these expert witnesses are physicians or radiologists. Experts are usually questioned in court about their education or experience which qualifies them to give professional opinions about the matter in question. Only after the hearing officer determines that the witness is, in fact, sufficiently expert in the subject matter may that witness proceed to state his/her opinions. (See also EVIDENCE)

EXPERT WITNESS (See EXPERT TESTIMONY)

EXPLOITATION OF CHILDREN
1) Involving a child in illegal or immoral activities for the benefit of a parent or caretaker. This could include child pornography, child prostitution, sexual abuse, or forcing a child to steal.
2) Forcing workloads on a child in or outside the home so as to interfere with the health, education, and well-being of the child.

EXPUNGEMENT

Destruction of records. Expungement may be ordered by the court after a specified number of years or when the juvenile, parent, or defendant applies for expungement and shows that his/her conduct has improved. Expungement also applies to the removal of an unverified report of abuse or neglect that has been made to a central registry. (See also CENTRAL REGISTRY)

EXTRAVASATED BLOOD
Discharge or escape of blood into tissue.

FAILURE TO THRIVE SYNDROME (FTT)
A serious medical condition most often seen in children under one year of age. An FTT child's height, weight, and motor development fall significantly short of the average growth rates of normal children. In about 10% of FTT cases, there is an organic cause such as serious heart, kidney, or intestinal disease, a genetic error of metabolisin, or brain damage. All other cases are a result of a disturbed parent-child relationship manifested in severe physical and emotional neglect of the child. In diagnosing FTT as child neglect, certain criteria should be considered:
1) The child's weight is below the third percentile, but substantial weight gain occurs when the child is properly nurtured, such as when hospitalized.
2) The child exhibits developmental retardation which decreases when there is adequate feeding and appropriate stimulation.
3) Medical investigation provides no evidence that disease or medical abnormality is causing the symptoms.
4) The child exhibits clinical signs of deprivation which decrease in a more nurturing environment.
5) There appears to be a significant environmental psychosocial disruption in the child's family.

FAMILIES ANONYMOUS
1) Name used by the National Center for the Prevention and Treatment of Child Abuse and Neglect at Denver for self-help groups for abusive parents. These groups operate in much the same way as the more widely-known Parents Anonymous. (See also PARENTS ANONYMOUS)
2) Self-help groups for families of drug abusers.

FAMILIES-AT-RISK
May refer to families evidencing high potential for child abuse or neglect because of a conspicuous, severe parental problem, such as criminal behavior, substance abuse, mental retardation, or psychosis. More often refers to families evidencing high potential for abuse or neglect because of risk factors which may be less conspicuous but multiple. These include: 1) environmental stress such as unemployment or work dissatisfaction; social isolation; anomie; lack of child care resources; I and/or 2) family stress such as marital discord; chronically and/or emotionally immature parent with a history of abuse or neglect as a child; unwanted pregnancy; colicky, hyperactive, or handicapped baby or child; siblings a year or less apart; sudden changes in family due to illness, separation, or death; parentla ignorance of child care and child development. Increasingly, the maternal-infant bonding process at childbirth is evaluated and used as one means to identify families-at-risk. Families thus identified should be offered immediate and periodic assistance.

FAMILY
Two or more persons related by blood, marriage, or mutual agreement who interact and provide one another with mutual physical, emotional, social, and/or economic care. Families can be described as "extended," with more than one generation in a household; or "nuclear," with only parent(s) and child(ren). Families can also be described as "mixed" or "multiracial"; "multi-parent," as in a commune or collective; or "single-parent." These types are not mutually exclusive.

FAMILY COURT (See COURTS)

FAMILY DYNAMICS
Interrelationships between and among individual family members. The evaluation of family dynamics is an important factor in the

identification, diagnosis, and treatment of child abuse and neglect.

FAMILY DYSFUNCTION
Ineffective functioning of the family as a unit or of individual family members in their family role because of physical, mental, or situational problems of one or more family members. A family which does not have or use internal or external resources to cope with its problems or fulfill its responsibilities to children may be described as dysfunctional. Child abuse and neglect is evidence of family dysfunction.

FAMILY IMPACT STATEMENT
Report which assesses the effect of existing and proposed legislation, policies, regulations, and practices on family life. The purpose is to promote legislation and policies which work for, not against, healthy family life. At the federal level, this activity is being developed by the Family Impact Seminar, George Washington University Institute for Educational Leadership (1001 Connecticut Ave., N.W., Suite 732, Washington, D.C. 20036).

FAMILY LIFE EDUCATION
Programs focusing on educating, enlightening, and supporting individuals and families regarding aspects of family life; for example, child development classes, communication skills workshops, sex education courses, or money management courses. Family life education might well be part of every child abuse and neglect prevention program, and may be part of the treatment program for abusive or neglectful parents who lack this information.

FAMILY PLANNING
Information and counseling provided to assist in controlling family size and spacing of children, including referrals to various agencies such as Planned Parenthood.

As a condition of receiving federal funding for AFDC (see SOCIAL SECURITY ACT), states are required to offer family planning services to applicants designated as "appropriate." Family planning should be part of a child abuse and neglect prevention program.

FAMILY POLICY
Generally refers to public social and economic policies that centrally affect families. There is considerable confusion about the term, with some persons believing that family policy should mean more direct policies affecting families, such as family planning policies. There is much more agreement that we should look at the impact of numerous policies on families, and that these should include a wide range of governmental policies. (See also FAMILY IMPACT STATEMENT)

FAMILY SHELTER
A 24-hour residential care facility for entire families. The setting offers around-the-clock care, and often provides diagnosis and comprehensive treatment on a short-term basis. In child abuse and neglect, a family shelter is used primarily for crisis intervention.

FAMILY SYSTEM
The concept that families operate as an interacting whole and are an open system, so that many factors in the environment affect the functioning of family members and the interaction among members. It is also conceptualized that the behavior of the family as an interacting unit has an effect on a number of factors in the outer environment.

FAMILY VIOLENCE
Abusive or aggressive behavior between parents, known as wife battering or spouse abuse; between children, known as sibling abuse; and/or between parents and children within a family, usually child abuse. This behavior is related to factors within the structure of a family system and/or society; for example, poverty, models of violent behavior displayed via mass media, stress due to excessive numbers of children, values of dominance and submissiveness, and attitudes toward discipline and punishment. It may also occur as a result of alcoholism or other substance abuse.

The terms family violence and domestic violence are sometimes used interchangeably but some persons exclude child abuse from the definition of domestic violence and limit it to violence between adult mates or spouses.

FEDERAL REGULATIONS
Guidelines and regulations developed by departments or agencies of the federal government to govern programs administered or funded by those agencies. Regulations specify policies and procedures outlined in a more general way in public laws or acts. Proposed federal regulations, or changes in existing regulations, are usually published in the *Federal Register* for public review and comment. They are subsequently published in the final form adopted by the governing agency.

FEDERAL STANDARDS (See STANDARDS)

FELONY
A serious crime for which the punishment may be imprisonment for longer than a year and/or a fine greater than $1,000. Distinguished from misdemeanor or infraction, both of lesser degree.

FIFTH AMENDMENT
The Fifth Amendment to the U.S. Constitution guarantees a defendant that he/she cannot be compelled to present self-incriminating testimony.

FONTANEL
The soft spots on a baby's skull where the bones of the skull have not yet grown together.

FORENSIC MEDICINE
That branch of the medical profession concerned with establishing evidence for legal proceedings.

FOSTER CARE
A form of substitute care for children who need to be removed from their own homes. Usually this is a temporary placement in which a child lives with a licensed foster family or caretaker until he/she can return to his/her own home or until reaching the age of majority. Foster care all too often becomes a permanent method of treatment for abused or neglected children. Effective foster care ideally includes service to the child, service to the natural parents, service to the foster parents, and periodic review of the placement.

FOSTER GRANDPARENTS
Retired persons or senior citizens who provide nurturance and support for children to whom they are not related, including abused and neglected children, by babysitting or taking them for recreational outings. This enables parents to have some respite and allows retired or older persons an opportunity to become involved in community activities. Sometimes foster grandparents are volunteers and sometimes they are paid by an agency program.

FOUNDED REPORT
Any report of suspected child abuse or neglect made to the mandated agency which is confirmed or verified. Founded reports outnumber unfounded reports.

FRACTURE
A broken bone, which is one of the most common injuries found among battered children. The fracture may occur in several ways:

Chip Fracture
A small piece of bone is flaked from the major part of the bone.

Comminuted Fracture
Bone is crushed or broken into a number of pieces.

Compound Fracture
Fragment(s) of broken bone protrudes through the skin, causing a wound.

Simple Fracture
Bone breaks without wounding the surrounding tissue.

Spiral Fracture

Twisting causes the line of the fracture to encircle the bone like a spiral staircase.

Torus Fracture
A folding, bulging, or buckling fracture. See diagram on next page for names and locations of the major bones of the human skeleton.

FRONTAL
Referring to the front of the head; the forehead.

FUNDASCOPIC EXAM
Opthalmic examination to determine if irregularities or internal injuries to the eye exist.

GATEKEEPERS
Professionals and the agencies which employ them who are in frequent or periodic contact with families or children and who are therefore in an advantageous position to spot individual and family problems, including child abuse and neglect, and make appropriate referrals for early intervention or treatment.

GLUTEAL
Related to the buttocks, which are made up of the large gluteus maximus muscles.

GONORRHEA (See VENEREAL DISEASE)

GRAND ROUNDS
Hospital staff meetings for presentation and discussion of a particular case or medical problem.

GUARDIAN
Adult charged lawfully with the responsibility for a child. A guardian has almost all the rights and powers of a natural parent, but the relationship is subject to termination or change. A guardian may or may not also have custody and therefore actual care and supervision of the child.

GUARDIAN AD LITEM (GAL)
Adult appointed by the court to represent the child in a judicial proceeding. The *guardian ad litem* may be, but is not necessarily, an attorney. Under the Child Abuse Prevention and Treatment Act, a state cannot qualify for federal assistance unless it provides by statute "that in every case involving an abused or neglected child which results in a judicial proceeding a *guardian ad litem* shall be appointed to represent the child in such proceedings." Some states have begun to allow a GAL for children in divorce cases.

HEAD START
A nationwide comprehensive program for disadvantaged preschool children, funded by the HEW Administration for Children, Youth and Families to meet the educational, nutritional, and health needs of the children and to encourage parent participation in their children's development.

Through federal policy instructions (see *Federal Register,* January 26, 1977), all Head Start staff are mandated to report suspected cases of child abuse and neglect. These policy instructions supersede individual child abuse and neglect reporting laws in states which do not include Head Start staff as mandated reporters.

HEARING
Judicial proceeding where issues of fact or law are tried and in which both parties have a right to be heard. A hearing is synonymous with a trial.

HEARING OFFICER
A judge or other individual who presides at a judicial proceeding. The role of judge is performed in some juvenile court hearings by referees or commissioners, whose orders are issued in the name of the supervising judge. Acts of a referee or commissioner may be undone after the supervising judge has conducted a rehearing in the case.

HELPLINE
Usually a telephone counseling, information, and referral service characterized by caller anonymity, late hour availability, and the use

of trained volunteers as staff. The goal is usually early intervention in any kind of family stress, as well as crisis intervention in child abuse and neglect. Helplines relieve social isolation and offer ways of ventilating stress which are not destructive. Unlike hotlines, helplines generally cannot report cases of child abuse and neglect since they do not know the caller's name. Instead, the helpline attempts to have the caller himself/herself seek professional assistance and/or maintain a regular calling relationship for support and as an alternative to violent behavior. Helplines appear to be very cost effective in the preventive of child abuse and neglect. Major disadvantages are lack of visual cues to problems and limited opportunity for follow-up services. (See also HOTLINE)

HEMATEMESIS
Vomiting of blood from the stomach, often resulting from internal injuries.

HEMATOMA
A swelling caused by a collection of blood in an enclosed space, such as under the skin or the skull.

HEMATUREA
Blood in the urine.

HEMOPHILIA
Hereditary blood clotting disorder characterized by spontaneous or traumatic internal and external bleeding and bruising.

HEMOPTYSIS
Spitting or coughing blood from the windpipe or lungs.

HEMORRHAGE
The escape of blood from the vessels; bleeding.

HOME HEALTH VISITOR (See CHILD HEALTH VISITOR)

HOME START
A nationwide home-based program funded by the HEW Administration for Children, Youth and Families to strengthen parents as educators of their own children.

HOMEMAKER SERVICES
Provision of assistance, support, and relief for parents who may be unable or unwilling to fulfill parenting functions because of illness or being overwhelmed with parenting responsibilities. A homemaker is placed in a home on an hourly or weekly basis and assists with housekeeping and child care while demonstrating parenting skills and providing some degree of nurturance for parents and children.

HOSPITAL HOLD
Hospitalization for further observation and protection of a child suspected of being abused or neglected. This usually occurs when a suspected case is discovered in an emergency room. In most cases, holding the child is against the wishes of the parent or caretaker. (See also CUSTODY)

HOTLINE
Twenty-four hour statewide or local answering service for reporting child abuse or neglect and initiating investigation by a local agency. This is often confused with a helpline. (See also HELPLINE)

HYPERACTIVE
More active than is considered normal.

HYPERTHERMIA
Condition of high body temperature.

HYPHEMA
Hemorrhage within the anterior chamber of the eye, often appearing as a bloodshot eye. The cause could be a blow to the head or violent shaking.

HYPOACTIVE
Less active than is considered normal.

HYPOTHERMIA
Condition of low body temperature.

HYPOVITAMINOSIS

Condition due to the deficiency of one or more essential vitamins. (See also AVITAMINOSIS)

IDENTIFICATION OF CHILD ABUSE AND NEGLECT

Diagnosis or verification of child abuse and neglect cases by mandated agency workers or a diagnostic team following investigation of suspected child abuse and neglect (see INDICATORS OF CHILD ABUSE AND NEGLECT). Identification of child abuse and neglect therefore depends not only on professional diagnostic skill but also on the extent to which the public and professionals report suspected cases. Public awareness campaigns are important to effect identification, but at the same time it is important to have sufficient staff in the mandated agency to handle all the reports a public awareness campaign may generate (see COMMUNITY AWARENESS and COMMUNITY EDUCATION). More reporting and therefore identification will also occur as states strengthen their reporting laws so as to extend the number of persons who must report and penalize them more heavily if they don't. It is generally agreed that to date the identification of child abuse and neglect represents only a small proportion of the actual incidence of the problem. It is also generally agreed that a greater degree of identification occurs in minority and low income groups because these persons are more visible to agencies and professionals required to report. The incidence is probably as high in upper socio-economic groups, but identification is more difficult, particularly because private physicians generally dislike to report.

ILEUM

Final portion of the small intestine which connects with the colon.

IMMUNITY, LEGAL

Legal protection from civil or criminal liability.
1) Child abuse and neglect reporting statutes often confer immunity upon persons mandated to report, giving them an absolute defense to libel, slander, invasion of privacy, false arrest, and other lawsuits which the person accused of the act might file. Some grants of immunity are limited only to those persons who report in good faith and without malicious intent.
2) Immunity from criminal liability is sometimes conferred upon a witness in order to obtain vital testimony. Thereafter, the witness cannot be prosecuted with the use of information he/she disclosed in his/her testimony. If an immunized witness refuses to testify, he/she can be imprisoned for contempt of court.

IMPETIGO

A highly contagious, rapidly spreading skin disorder which occurs principally in infants and young children. The disease, characterized by red blisters, may be an indicator of neglect and poor living conditions.

IMPULSE-RIDDEN MOTHER

Term often used to describe one kind of neglectful parent who demonstrates restlessness, aggressiveness, inability to tolerate stress, manipulativeness, and craving for excitement or change. This parent may have a lesser degree of early deprivation than the apathetic-futile parent, but lacks self-control over strong impulses and/or has not learned limit-setting.

IN CAMERA

Any closed hearing before a judge in his chambers is said to be *in camera*.

IN LOCO PARENTIS

"In the place of a parent." Refers to actions of a guardian or other non-parental custodian.

INCEST

Sexual intercourse between persons who are closely related. Some state laws recognize incest only as sexual intercourse among consaguineous, or blood, relations; other states recognize incest as sexual relations between a variety of family members related by blood and/or law. In the U.S., the prohibition against incest is specified by many states' laws as well as by cultural tradition, with state laws usually defining incest as marriage or sexual relationships between relatives who are closer than second, or sometimes even more distant, cousins. While incest and sexual abuse are sometimes thought to be synonymous, it should be realized that incest is only one aspect of sexual abuse. Incest can occur within families between members of the same sex, but the most common form of incest is between father and daughters. It is generally agreed that incest is much more common than the number of reported cases indicates. Also, because society has not until the present done much about this problem, professionals have generally not had adequate training to deal with it, and the way the problem is handled may prove more traumatic for a child victim of incest than the incest experience itself. It should be noted that sexual relations between relatives may be defined as incest, but that in cest is not considered child sexual abuse unless a minor is involved. (See also CHILD ABUSE AND NEGLECT, SEXUAL ABUSE, SEXUAL MISUSE)

INCIDENCE

The extent to which a problem occurs in a given population. No accurate or complete data is available on the actual incidence of child abuse and neglect in the U.S. because major studies have not been able to obtain data from some states or have found the data not to be comparable. For continuing efforts to solve this problem, see NATIONAL STUDY ON CHILD ABUSE AND NEGLECT REPORTING. Informed estimates of incidence range from 600,000 to one million cases of child abuse and neglect per year in this country. It is generally agreed that child neglect is four to five or more times more common than child abuse. Incidence of actual child abuse and neglect should not be confused with the number of reported cases in a central registry, since the latter include reports of suspected but unconfirmed cases. On the other hand, it is generally agreed that because of insufficient reporting, the number of actual cases coming to the attention of local agencies is but a small proportion of the actual number of cases in the population. (See also CENTRAL REGISTRY and IDENTIFICATION OF CHILD ABUSE AND NEGLECT)

INDICATED CHILD ABUSE AND NEGLECT

1) In some state statutes, "indicated" child abuse and neglect means a confirmed or verified case.
2) Medically, "indicated" means a probable case.

INDICATORS OF CHILD ABUSE AND NEGLECT

Signs or symptoms which, when found in various combinations, point to possible abuse or neglect. See chart on next page for common indicators of child abuse and neglect.

INDICTMENT

The report of a grand jury charging an adult with criminal conduct. The process of indictment by secret grand jury proceedings bypasses the filing of a criminal complaint and the holding of a preliminary hearing in municipal court, so that prosecution begins immediately in superior court.

INFANTICIDE

The killing of an infant or many infants. Until modern times, infanticide was an accepted method of population control. It often took the form of abandonment. A few primitive cultures still practice infanticide.

Indicators of Child Abuse and Neglect

CATEGORY	CHILD'S APPEARANCE	CHILD'S BEHAVIOR	CARETAKER'S BEHAVIOR
Physical Abuse	—Bruises and welts (on the face, lips, or mouth; in various stages of healing; on large areas of the torso, back, buttocks, or thighs; in unusual patterns, clustered, or reflective of the instrument used to inflict them; on several different surface areas). —Burns (cigar or cigarette burns; glove or sock-like burns or doughnut shaped burns on the buttocks or genitalia indicative of immersion in hot liquid; rope burns on the arms, legs, neck or torso; patterned burns that show the shape of the item (iron, grill, etc.) used to inflict them). —Fractures (skull, jaw, or nasal fractures; spiral fractures of the long (arm and leg) bones; fractures in various states of healing; multiple fractures; any fracture in a child under the age of two). —Lacerations and abrasions (to the mouth, lip, gums, or eye; to the external genitalia). —Human bite marks.	—Wary of physical contact with adults. —Apprehensive when other children cry. —Demonstrates extremes in behavior (e.g., extreme aggressiveness or withdrawal). —Seems frightened of parents. —Reports injury by parents.	—Has history of abuse as a child. —Uses harsh discipline inappropriate to child's age, transgression, and condition. —Offers illogical, unconvincing, contradictory, or no explanation of child's injury. —Seems unconcerned about child. —Significantly misperceives child (e.g., sees him as bad, evil, a monster, etc.). —Psychotic or psychopathic. —Misuses alcohol or other drugs. —Attempts to conceal child's injury or to protect identity of person responsible.
Neglect	—Consistently dirty, unwashed, hungry, or inappropriately dressed. —Without supervision for extended periods of time or when engaged in dangerous activities. —Constantly tired or listless. —Has unattended physical problems or lacks routine medical care. —Is exploited, overworked, or kept from attending school. —Has been abandoned.	—Is engaging in delinquent acts (e.g., vandalism, drinking, prostitution, drug use, etc.) —Is begging or stealing food. —Rarely attends school.	—Misuses alcohol or other drugs. —Maintains chaotic home life. —Shows evidence of apathy or futility. —Is mentally ill or of diminished intelligence. —Has long-term chronic illnesses. —Has history of neglect as a child.
Sexual Abuse	—Has torn, stained, or bloody underclothing. —Experience pain or itching in the genital area. —Has bruises or bleeding in external genitalia, vagina, or anal regions. —Has venereal disease. —Has swollen or red cervix, vulva, or perineum. —Has semen around mouth or genitalia or on clothing. —Is pregnant.	—Appears withdrawn or engages in fantasy or infantile behavior. —Has poor peer relationships. —Is unwilling to participate in physical activities. —Is engaging in delinquent acts or runs away. —States he/she has been sexually assaulted by parent/caretaker.	—Extremely protective or jealous of child. —Encourages child to engage in prostitution or sexual acts in the presence of caretaker. —Has been sexually abused as a child. —Is experiencing marital difficulties. —Misuses alcohol or other drugs. —Is frequently absent from the home.
Emotional Maltreatment	—Emotional maltreatment, often less tangible than other forms of child abuse and neglect, can be indicated by behaviors of the child and the caretaker.	—Appears overly compliant, passive, undemanding. —Is extremely aggressive, demanding, or rageful. —Shows overly adaptive behaviors, either inappropriately adult (e.g., parents other children) or inappropriately infantile (e.g., rocks constantly, sucks thumb, is enuretic). —Lags in physical, emotional, and intellectual development. Attempts suicide.	—Blames or belittles child. —Is cold and rejecting. —Withholds love. —Treats siblings unequally. —Seems unconcerned about child's problem.

INSTITUTIONAL CHILD ABUSE AND NEGLECT

1) Abuse and neglect as a result of social or institutional policies, practices, or conditions. The rather widespread practice of detaining children in adult jails is one example. Usually refers to specific institutions or populations, but may also be used to mean societal abuse or neglect. (See also SOCIETAL ABUSE AND NEGLECT)
2) Child abuse and neglect committed by an employee of a public or private institution or group home against a child in the institution or group home.

INTAKE

Process by which cases are introduced into an agency. Workers are usually assigned to interview persons seeking help in order to determine the nature and extent of the problem(s). However, in child abuse and neglect, intake of reports of suspected cases is usually by telephone and an interview with the reporting person is not required. Child abuse and neglect workers who do intake must be skilled in getting as much information as possible from the reporter in order to determine whether the situation is an emergency requiring instant attention.

INTERDISCIPLINARY TEAM (See COMMUNITY TEAM)

INTRADERMAL HEMORRHAGE

Bleeding within the skin; bruise. Bruises are common injuries exhibited by battered children, and are usually classified by size:

Petechiae
Very small bruise caused by broken capillaries. Petechiae may be traumatic in nature or may be caused by clotting disorders.

Purpura
Petechiae occurring in groups, or a small bruise (up to 1 cm. in diameter).

Ecchymosis
Larger bruise.

INVOLUNTARY CLIENT

Person who has been referred or court-ordered for services but who has not asked for help. Most abusive and neglectful parents are initially involuntary clients and may not accept the need for services. They may deny that there is a problem and resist assistance. Motivation for change may be minimal or nonexistent; however, skillful workers have demonstrated that motivation can be developed and treatment can be effective.

INVOLUNTARY PLACEMENT

Court-ordered assignment of custody to an agency and placement of a child, often against the parents' wishes, after a formal court proceeding, or the taking of emergency or protective custody against the parents' wishes preceding a custody hearing. (See also CUSTODY)

JEJUNUM

Middle portion of the small intestine between the duodenum and the ileum.

JURISDICTION

The power of a particular court to hear cases involving certain categories of persons or allegations. Jurisdiction may also depend upon geographical factors such as the county of a person's residence. (See also COURTS)

JURY

Group of adults selected by lawyers who judge the truth of allegations made in a legal proceeding. Trial by jury is available in all criminal cases, including cases of suspected child abuse and neglect. Very few juvenile, probate, or domestic relations court cases can be tried before a jury and are instead decided by the presiding judge.

JUVENILE COURT (See COURTS)

JUVENILE JUDGE

Presiding officer of a juvenile court. Often in a juvenile court, there are several other hearing officers of lesser rank, usually called referees or commissioners. (See also HEARING OFFICER)

LABELING
The widespread public and professional practice of affixing terms which imply serious or consistent deviance to the perpetrators and/or victims of child abuse and neglect; for example, "child abuser." Since deviance may suggest that punishment is warranted, this kind of labeling decreases the possibility of treatment. This is unfortunate, because experts agree that 80% or 85% of all child abuse and neglect cases have the potential for successful treatment. Such labeling may also make parents see themselves in a negative, despairing way, and discourage them from seeking assistance.

LABORATORY TESTS
Routine medical tests used to aid diagnosis. Those particularly pertinent to child abuse are:

Partial Thromboplastin Time (PTT) Measures clotting factors in the blood.

Prothrombin Time (PT)
Measures clotting factors in the blood.

Urinalysis
Examination of urine for sugar, protein, blood, etc.

Complete Blood Count (CBC)
Measure and analysis of red and white blood cells.

Rumpel-Leede (Tourniquet) Test
Measures fragility of capillaries and/or bruisability.

LACERATION
A jagged cut or wound.

LATCH KEY CHILDREN
Working parents' children who return after school to a home where no parent or caretaker is present. This term was coined because these children often wear a house key on a chain around their necks.

LATERAL
Toward the side.

LAY THERAPIST (See PARENT AIDE)

LEAST DETRIMENTAL ALTERNATIVE
(See
BEST INTEREST OF THE CHILD)

LEGAL RIGHTS OF PERSONS IDENTIFIED IN REPORTS
Standards for legal rights stress the need for all persons concerned with child abuse and neglect to be aware of the legal rights of individuals identified in reports and to be committed to any action necessary to enforce these rights. According to the National Center on Child Abuse and Neglect *Revision to Federal Standards on the Prevention and Treatment of Child Abuse and Neglect (Draft)*, these rights include the following:

1) Any person identified in a report as being suspected of having abused or neglected a child should be informed of his/her legal rights.
2) The person responsible for the child's welfare should receive written notice and be advised of his her legal rights when protective custody authority is exercised.
3) A child who is alleged to be abused or neglected should have independent legal representation in a child protection proceeding.
4) The parent or other person responsible for a child's welfare who is alleged to have abused or neglected a child should be entitled to legal representation in a civil or criminal proceeding.
5) The local child protective services unit should have the assistance of legal counsel in all child protective proceedings.
6) Each party should have the right to appeal protective case determinations.
7) Any person identified in a child abuse or neglect report should be protected from unauthorized disclosure of personal information contained in the report.

LESION
Any injury to any part of the body from any cause that results in damage or loss of structure or function of the body tissue involved. A lesion may be caused by poison, infection, dysfunction, or violence, and may be either accidental or intentional.

LIABILITY FOR FAILURE TO REPORT
State statutes which require certain categories of persons to report cases of suspected child abuse and/or neglect are often enforced by the imposition of a penalty, fine and/or imprisonment, for those who fail to report. Recent lawsuits have provided what may become an even more significant penalty for failure to report: when a report should have been made and a child comes to serious harm in a subsequent incident of abuse or neglect, the person who failed to report the initial incident may be held civilly liable to the child for the damages suffered in the subsequent incident. Such damages could amount to many thousands of dollars. (See also MANDATED REPORTERS)

LICENSING PARENTHOOD
Proposed method of assuring adequate parenting skills. Various proposals have been developed, including mandatory parenthood education in high school, with a certificate upon completion. Serious advocates compare the process with certification of driving capability by driver's licenses. Many consider the proposal unworkable.

LOCAL AUTHORITY
Local authority refers to two groups: 1) the social service agency (local agency) designated by the state department of social services (state department) and authorized by state law to be responsible for local child abuse and neglect prevention, identification, and treatment efforts, and 2) the community child protection coordinating council (community council). The standards on local authority, as specified in the National Center on Child Abuse and Neglect *Revision to Federal Standards on the Prevention and Treatment of Child Abuse and Neglect* *(Draft)*, include:

Administration and Organization
1. The local agency should establish a distinct child protective services unit with sufficient and qualified staff.
2. The local agency in cooperation with the state department should allocate sufficient funds and provide adequate administrative support to the local unit.
3. The local agency should initiate the establishment of a community council which is to be representative of those persons providing or concerned with child abuse and neglect prevention, identification, and treatment services.

Primary Prevention
4. The local unit and the community council should work together to establish formalized needs assessment and planning processes.

Secondary and Tertiary Prevention
5. The local unit and the community council should work together to develop a comprehensive and coordinated service delivery system for children-at-risk and families-at-risk to be presented in an annual plan.
6. The local unit and the community council should develop standards on the care of children which represent the minimum expectations of the community and provide the basis for the local unit's operational definitions and referral guidelines.
7. The local unit and the community council should establish a multidisciplinary child abuse and neglect case consultation team.
8. The local unit should provide or arrange for services to assist families who request help for themselves in fulfilling their parenting responsibilities.
9. The local unit should ensure that reports of child abuse and neglect can be received on a twenty-four hour, seven days per week basis.

10 The intake services worker should intervene immediately if a report is considered an emergency; otherwise, intervention should take place within seventy-two hours.

11 The intake services worker should ensure the family's right to privacy by making the assessment process time-limited.

12 The treatment services worker should develop an individualized treatment plan for each family and each family member.

13 The treatment services worker should arrange for, coordinate, and monitor services provided to a family.

Resource Enhancement

14 The agency and the community council should assist in the training of the local unit and other community service systems.

15 The agency should promote internal agency coordination.

16 The local unit should implement community education and awareness.

17 The agency should participate in or initiate its own research, review, and evaluation studies.

(See also STATE AUTHORITY)

LONG BONE
General term applied to the bones of the leg or the arm.

LONG TERM TREATMENT
Supportive and therapeutic services over a period of time, usually at least a year, to restore the parent(s) of an abused or neglected child and/or the child himself/herself to adequate levels of functioning and to prevent recurrence of child abuse or neglect.

LUMBAR
Pertaining to the part of the back and sides between the lowest ribs and the pelvis.

MALNUTRITION
Failure to receive adequate nourishment. Often exhibited in a neglected child, malnutrition may be caused by inadequate diet (either lack of food or insufficient amounts of needed vitamins, etc.) or by a disease or other abnormal condition affecting the body's ability to properly process foods taken in.

MALTREATMENT
Actions that are abusive, neglectful, or otherwise threatening to a child's welfare. Frequently used as a general term for child abuse and neglect.

MANDATED AGENCY
Agency designated by state statutes as legally responsible for receiving and investigating reports of suspected child abuse and neglect. Usually, this agency is a county welfare department or a child protective services unit within that department. Police or sheriffs departments may also be mandated agencies. (See also STATE AUTHORITY and LOCAL AUTHORITY)

MANDATED REPORTERS or MANDATORY REPORTERS
Persons designated by state statutes who are legally liable for not reporting suspected cases of child abuse and neglect to the mandated agency. The persons so designated vary according to state law, but they are primarily professionals, such as pediatricians, nurses, school personnel, and social workers, who have frequent contact with children and families.

MARASMUS
A form of protein-calorie malnutrition occurring in infants and children. It is characterized by retarded growth and progressive wasting away of fat and muscle, but it is usually accompanied by the retention of appetite and mental alertness.

MATERNAL CHARACTERISTICS SCALE
Instrument designed to study personality characteristics of rural Appalachian mothers and the level of care they were providing their children. The purpose of this scale is to

sharpen caseworkers' perception of "apathetic-futile" or "impulse-ridden" mothers' personality characteristics for evaluation, diagnosis, and formulation of a treatment plan in cases of child neglect. Some authorities believe this scale has not been adequately validated.

MATERNAL-INFANT BONDING (See BONDING)

MEDIAL
Toward the middle or mid-line.

MEDICAID, TITLE 19 (See SOCIAL SECURITY ACT)

MEDICAL MODEL
Conceptualizing problems in terms of diagnosis and treatment of illness. With respect to child abuse and neglect, the medical model assumes an identifiable and therefore treatable cause of the abuse and/or neglect and focuses on identification and treatment in a medical or other health setting. For child abuse and neglect, some advantages of the medical model are financial support by the hospital, clinic, medical community; accessibility of medical services to the abused or neglected child; involvement of the physicians; and visibility and public acceptance. Possible disadvantages are overemphasis on physical abuse; overemphasis on physical diagnosis to the detriment of total treatment; and isolation from other professional and community resources. (Kempe)

MEDICAL NEGLECT (See CHILD ABUSE AND NEGLECT)

MENKES KINKY HAIR SYNDROME
Rare, inherited disease resulting in brittle bones and, eventually, death. It is found in infants and, because of the great number of fractures the child may exhibit, can be mistaken for child abuse.

MENTAL INJURY
Injury to the intellectual or psychological capacity of a child as evidenced by observable and substantial impairment in his/her ability to function within a normal range of performance and behavior, with due regard to his/her culture. The Child Abuse Prevention and Treatment Act and some state statutes include mental injury caused by a parent or caretaker as child abuse or neglect.

MESENTERY
Membrane attaching various organs to the body wall.

METABOLISM
The sum of all physical and chemical processes which maintain the life of an organism.

METAPHYSIS
Wider part of a long bone between the end and the shaft.

MINIMALLY ACCEPTABLE ENVIRONMENT
The emotional climate and physical surroundings necessary for children to grow physically, mentally, socially, and emotionally.

MINOR (See CHILD)

MIRANDA RULE
Legal provision that a confession is inadmissible in any court proceeding if the suspect was not forewarned of his/her right to remain silent before the confession was disclosed. (See also FIFTH AMENDMENT)

MISDEMEANOR
A crime for which the punishment can be no more than imprisonment for a year and/or a fine of $1,000. A misdemeanor is distinguished from a felony, which is more serious, and an infraction, which is less serious.

MODEL CHILD PROTECTION ACT
Guide for development of state legislation concerning child abuse and neglect and intended to enable legislators to provide a

comprehensive and workable law which will aid in resolving the problem. A draft *Model Child Protection Act* has been developed and is available from the National Center on Child Abuse and Neglect.

MONDALE ACT (See CHILD ABUSE PREVENTION AND TREATMENT ACT)

MONGOLIAN SPOTS
A type of birthmark that can appear anywhere on a child's body, most frequently on the lower back. These dark spots usually fade by age five. They can be mistaken for bruises.

MORAL NEGLECT (See CHILD ABUSE AND NEGLECT)

MORIBUND
Dying or near death.

MOTHERS ANONYMOUS
Original name of Parents Anonymous. (See PARENTS ANONYMOUS)

MULTIDISCIPLINARY TEAM
A group of professionals and possibly paraprofessionals representing a variety of disciplines who interact and coordinate their efforts to diagnose and treat specific cases of child abuse and neglect. A multidisciplinary group which also addresses the general problem of child abuse and neglect in a given community is usually described as a community team, and it will probably consist of several multidisciplinary teams with different functions (see COMMUNITY TEAM). Multidisciplinary teams may include, but are not limited to, medical, child care, and law enforcement personnel, social workers, psychiatrists and/or psychologists. Their goal is to pool their respective skills in order to formulate accurate diagnoses and to provide comprehensive coordinated treatment with continuity and follow-up for both parent(s) and child or children. Many multidisciplinary teams operate according to the Denver Model (see DENVER MODEL). Multidisciplinary teams may also be referred to as cross-disciplinary teams, interdisciplinary teams, or SCAN teams (see SCAN TEAM). However, the Child Abuse Prevention and Treatment Act uses the term "multidisciplinary team."

NATIONAL ASSOCIATION OF SOCIAL WORKERS (NASW)
1425 H St., N.W.
Washington, D.C. 20005
A national organization of professional social workers who are enrolled in or have completed baccalaureate, master's, or doctoral programs in social work education. Members must subscribe to the NASW Code of Ethics, and NASW provides a policy for adjudication of grievances in order to protect members and promote ethical practices.

NATIONAL CENTER FOR CHILD ADVOCACY (NCCA)
P.O. Box 1182
Washington, D.C. 20013
The National Center for Child Advocacy is part of the Children's Bureau of the Administration for Children, Youth and Families within the Office of Human Development Services of HEW. NCCA supports research, demonstration, and training programs and provides technical assistance to state and local agencies with the goal of increasing and improving child welfare services. These services include in-home support to families, such as parent education and homemaker services; foster care, adoption, and child protective services; and institutional care of children. A major project of NCCA is the Child Welfare Resource Information Exchange. (See also CHILD WELFARE RESOURCE INFORMATION EXCHANGE)

NATIONAL CENTER FOR THE PREVENTION AND TREATMENT OF CHILD ABUSE AND NEGLECT
1205 Oneida St.
Denver, Colorado 80220
This center, which is affiliated with the Department of Pediatrics of the University of Colorado Medical School, was established in

the fall of 1972 to provide more extensive and up-to-date education, research, and clinical material to professionals working in the area of child abuse and neglect. The center's multidisciplinary staff has provided leadership in formulating the views that child abuse and neglect is symptomatic of troubled family relationships; that treatment must consider the needs of all family members; and that outreach to isolated, non-trusting families and the multidisciplinary approach are necessary. Funded by the State of Colorado, the HEW Administration for Children, Youth and Families, and private foundations, the center's work includes education, consultation and technical assistance, demonstration programs for treatment, program evaluation, and research. This center also serves as the HEW Region VIII Resource Center.

NATIONAL CENTER ON CHILD ABUSE AND NEGLECT (NCCAN)
P.O. Box 1182
Washington, D.C. 20013
Office of the federal government located within the Children's Bureau of the Administration for Children, Youth and Families (formerly the Office of Child Development), which is part of the Office of Human Development Services of HEW. Established in 1974 by the Child Abuse Prevention and Treatment Act, the functions of NCCAN are to:
1) Compile, analyze, and publish an annual summary of recent and current research on child abuse and neglect.
2) Develop and maintain an information clearinghouse on all programs showing promise of success for the prevention, identification, and treatment of child abuse and neglect.
3) Compile and publish training materials for personnel who are engaged or intend to engage in the prevention, identification, and treatment of child abuse and neglect.
4) Provide technical assistance to public and nonprofit private agencies and organizations to assist them in planning, improving, developing, and carrying out programs and activities relating to the prevention, identification, and treatment of child abuse and neglect.
5) Conduct research into the causes of child abuse and neglect, and into the prevention, identification, and treatment thereof.
6) Make a complete and full study and investigation of the national incidence of child abuse and neglect, including a determination of the extent to which incidents of child abuse and neglect are increasing in number or severity.
7) Award grants to states whose child abuse and neglect legislation complies with federal legislation.

NCCAN is authorized to establish grants and contracts with public and private agencies and organizations to carry out the above activities. Grants and contracts may also be used to establish demonstration programs and projects which, through training, consultation, resource provision, or direct treatment, are designed to prevent, identify, and treat child abuse and neglect. (See also CHILD ABUSE PREVENTION AND TREATMENT ACT and REGIONAL RESOURCE CENTER)

NATIONAL CLEARINGHOUSE ON CHILD NEGLECT AND ABUSE (NCCNA) (See NATIONAL STUDY ON CHILD NEGLECT AND ABUSE REPORTING)

NATIONAL COMMITTEE FOR THE PREVENTION OF CHILD ABUSE
111 E. Wacker Drive
Suite 510
Chicago, Illinois 60601
The National Committee originated in Chicago in 1972 in response to increasing national incidence of deaths due to child abuse. It was formed to help prevent child abuse, which was defined as including non-accidental injury, emotional abuse, neglect, sexual abuse, and exploitation of children, at a time when most programs focused on identification and treatment. The commit-

tee's goals are to:
1) Stimulate greater public awareness of the problem.
2) Encourage public involvement in prevention and treatment.
3) Provide a national focal point for advocacy to prevent child abuse.
4) Facilitate communication about programs, policy, and research related to child abuse prevention.
5) Foster greater cooperation between existing and developing resources for child abuse prevention.

Activities of the committee include a national media campaign, publications, conference, research, and the establishment of state chapters of the committee.

NATIONAL REGISTER

Often confused with the National Study on Child Neglect and Abuse Reporting (National Clearinghouse), which compiles statistics on incidence of child abuse and neglect. A national register, which does not exist at this time, would operate in much the same way and with the same purposes as a state-level central register, but would collect reports of abuse and neglect nationwide. Collecting reports on a national scale would be highly problematic because of variance in state reporting laws and definitions of abuse and neglect. (See also CENTRAL REGISTER and NATIONAL STUDY ON CHILD NEGLECT AND ABUSE REPORTING)

NATIONAL STUDY ON CHILD NEGLECT AND ABUSE REPORTING

Formerly the National Clearinghouse on Child Neglect and Abuse, the National Study is funded by the National Center on Child Abuse and Neglect, Children's Bureau, HEW and is being conducted by the Children's Division of the American Humane Association. The study has been established to systematically collect data from official state sources on the nature, incidence, and characteristics of child abuse and neglect. Participating states receive reports generated from their own data on a quarterly basis so that they can monitor their own reporting mechanisms. At this time, about 40 states are submitting detailed incidence data to the study. It is hoped that the National Study will be able to produce accurate data on the national incidence of child abuse and neglect.

NEEDS ASSESSMENT

A formal or informal evaluation of what services are needed by abused and neglected children and their families within a specified geographical area or within another given population.

NEGLECT (See CHILD ABUSE AND NEGLECT)

NEGLECTED CHILD (See INDICATORS OF CHILD ABUSE AND NEGLECT)

NEGLIGENCE

Failure to act. May apply to a parent, as in child neglect, or to a person who by state statute is mandated to report child abuse and neglect but who fails to do so. Negligence lawsuits arising from failure to report are increasing, and any failure to obey the statutes proves negligence. Lawsuits claiming damages for negligence are civil proceedings.

NETWORKING

Formal or informal linkages of individuals, families, or other groups with similar social, education, medical, or other service needs with the public or private agencies, organizations, and/or individuals who can provide such services in their locale. Formal agreements are usually written and spell out under what circumstances a particular agency, group, or individual will provide certain services. Informal agreements are apt to be verbal and relate to a particular family or case.

NURTURANCE

Affectionate care and attention provided by a parent, parent substitute, or caretaker to promote the well-being of a child and encourage healthy emotional and physical development. Nurturance may also be needed by adults with inadequate parenting skills, or who were themselves abused or neglected as children, as a model for developing more positive relationships with their own children and as a way of strengthening their own self-esteem.

OCCIPITAL
Referring to the back of the head.

OMISSION, ACTS OF
Failure of a parent or caretaker to provide for a child's physical and/or emotional well-being. (See also CHILD ABUSE AND NEGLECT)

OSSIFICATION
Formation of bone.

OSTEOGENESIS IMPERFECTA
An inherited condition in which the bones are abnormally brittle and subject to fractures, and which may be mistakenly diagnosed as the result of child abuse.

OUTREACH
The process in which professionals, paraprofessionals, and/or volunteers actively seek to identify cases of family strees and potential or actual child abuse and neglect by making services known, accessible, and unthreatening. Effective outreach providing early intervention is important for the prevention of child abuse and neglect.

PA BUDDY
Term used by Parents Anonymous for a person who functions like a parent aide in relation to a Parents Anonymous member. (See also PARENTS ANONYMOUS and PARENT AIDE)

PARAPROFESSIONAL
Volunteer or agency employee trained to a limited extent in a particular profession. Since paraprofessionals are usually close in age, race, nationality, religion, or lifestyle to the clientele, they often have a greater likelihood of developing a trusting relationship with a client than do some professionals. The role of the paraprofessional in protective service work is usually to provide outreach or nurturance and advocacy for the family, often as a case aide or parent aide. (See also PARENT AIDE)

PARENS PATRIAE
"The power of the sovereign." Refers to the state's power to act for or on behalf of persons who cannot act in their own behalf; such as, minors, incompetents, or some developmentally disabled.

PARENT
Person exercising the function of father and/or mother, including adoptive, foster, custodial, and surrogate parents as well as biological parents.

PARENT AIDE
A paraprofessional, either paid or voluntary, who functions primarily as an advocate and surrogate parent for a family in which child abuse or neglect is suspected or has been confirmed. The Parent Aide particularly serves the mother by providing positive reinforcement, emotional support, and nurturance, and by providing or arranging transportation, babysitting, etc., as necessary. Rather than serving as a homemaker, nutrition aide, or nurse, the parent aide's function is more like a friend to the family. Parent aides may also be referred to as case aides, lay therapists, or visiting friends.

PARENT EFFECTIVENESS TRAINING (PET)
An educational program developed by Dr. Thomas Gordon and presented in his book, *Parent Effectiveness Training* (New York, Peter H. Wyden, Inc., 1970). The program, taught by trained and certified PET instructors, focuses on improving communication between parents and children by teaching listening skills and verbal expression techniques to parents. The PET course has proven useful for parents who are motivated to change, who are able to give it a consider-

able amount of time, and who can afford the relatively high tuition. For these and other reasons, PET has not proven particularly useful in child abuse and neglect treatment, especially when used as the only mode of treatment.

PARENTAL STRESS SERVICES

Services aimed at relieving situational and/or psychological parental stress in order to relieve family dysfunction and to prevent parents from venting rage or frustration on their children. Service usually begins via a telephone helpline and may include home visits. Workers are usually trained volunteers or paraprofessionals who focus on providing warmth, nurturance, friendship, and resource referrals to the distressed parent. Some parental stress services promote development and use of Parents Anonymous chapters for their clients. Parental Stress Services may refer to specific programs such as in Chicago, Illinois, or Oakland, California, although there is no organizational linkage between them, or this may be a functional description of services provided within a larger agency program.

PARENTING SKILLS

A parent's competencies in providing physical care, protection, supervision, and psychological nurturance appropriate to a child's age and stage of development. Some parents, particularly those whose own parents demonstrated these skills, have these competencies without formal training, but adequacy of these skills may be improved through instruction.

PARENTS ANONYMOUS

22330 Hawthorne Blvd., #208
Torrance, California 90505
Self-help group for parents who want to stop physical, psychological, sexual, or verbal abuse of their children. Because members do not need to reveal their full names, they feel free to share concerns and provide mutual support. Members are accountable to the group for their behavior toward their children, and the group functions like a family in supporting members' efforts to change. With chapters in every state, over 800 in all, Parents Anonymous has been formally evaluated as an effective method for treating child abuse. Unlike most other self-help groups with anonymous members, Parents Anonymous requires that each chapter have an unpaid professional sponsor who attends all meetings to facilitate discussion, provide a role model, and suggest appropriate community resources for members' problems. The Child Abuse Prevention and Treatment Act provides for funding of self-help groups, and Parents Anonymous is one of the few self-help organizations which has received funding from the federal government.

PARENTS' RIGHTS

Besides the rights protected by the Constitution for all adults, society accords parents the right to custody and supervision of their own children, including, among others, parents' rights to make decisions about their children's health care. This plus parents' rights to privacy may complicate investigations of suspected child abuse and neglect and treatment of confirmed cases. Parents' rights may be cited in court in order to prevent the state from taking custody of a child who is in danger in his/her own home. (See also CHILDREN'S RIGHTS)

PARENTS UNITED

Organization name sometimes used for self-help groups of parents in families in which sexual abuse has occurred. Begun in 1972, Parents United is one component of a model Child Sexual Abuse Treatment Program in Santa Clara County, California. (See also DAUGHTERS UNITED)

PASSIVE ABUSER

Parent or caretaker who does not intervene to prevent abuse by another person in the home.

PATHOGNOMONIC

A sign or symptom specifically distinctive or characteristic of a disease or condition from which a diagnosis may be made.

PERINATAL
Around the time of birth, both immediately before and afterward.

PERIOSTEAL ELEVATION
The ripping or tearing of the surface layer of a bone (periosteum) and the resultant hemorrhage, occuring when a bone is broken.

PERITONITIS
Inflammation of the membrane lining the abdomen (peritoneum); caused by infection.

PERJURY
Intentionally inaccurate testimony. Perjury is usually punishable as a felony, but only if the inaccuracy of the testimony and the witness's knowledge of the inaccuracy can be proven.

PETECHIAE (See INTRADERMAL HEMORRHAGE)

PETITION
Document filed in juvenile or family court at the beginning of a neglect, abuse, and/or delinquency case. The petition states the allegations which, if true, form the basis for court intervention.

PETITIONER
Person who files a petition. In juvenile and family court practice, a petitioner may be a probation officer, social worker, or prosecutor, as variously defined by state laws.

PHYSICAL ABUSE (See CHILD ABUSE AND NEGLECT)

PHYSICAL NEGLECT (See CHILD ABUSE AND NEGLECT)

PLEA BARGAINING
Settlement of a criminal prosecution, usually by the reduction of the charge and/or the penalty, in return for a plea of guilty. Plea bargains are sometimes justified by congested court calendars. They are attacked as devices which weaken the intended effect of penal statutes and which reduce the dignity of the criminal justice system. Far more than half of all criminal prosecutions in this country are resolved by plea bargaining.

POLICE HOLD (See CUSTODY)

POLYPHAGIA
Excessive or voracious eating.

PREDICTION OF CHILD ABUSE AND NEGLECT
There are no evaluation instruments or criteria to predict absolutely that child abuse or neglect will occur in specific families. Recently, experts have developed instruments and methods of evaluating the bonding process at childbirth in order to identify families where because of incomplete or inadequate bonding, it can be expected that without further appropriate intervention, child abuse or neglect may occur. Besides bonding, many other indicators can be used to identify families-at-risk for child abuse and neglect, but these factors are rarely sufficiently conclusive to enable absolute prediction. (See also BONDING and FAMILIES-AT-RISK)

PREPONDERANCE OF EVIDENCE (See EVIDENTIARY STANDARDS)

PRESENTMENT
The notice taken or report made by a grand jury of an offense on the basis of the jury's knowledge and without a bill of indictment. (See also INDICTMENT)

PRE-TRIAL DIVERSION
Decision of the district attorney not to issue charges in a criminal case where those charges would be provable. The decision is usually made on the condition that the defendant agrees to participate in rehabilitative services. In child abuse cases, this usually involves cooperation with child protective services and/or voluntary treatment, such as Parents Anonymous.

PREVENTION OF CHILD ABUSE AND NEGLECT
Elimination of the individual and societal causes of child abuse and neglect.

Primary Prevention
Providing societal and community policies and programs which strengthen all family functioning so that child abuse and neglect is less likely to occur.

Secondary Prevention
Intervention in the early signs of child abuse and neglect for treatment of the presenting problem and to prevent further problems from developing.

Tertiary Prevention
Treatment after child abuse and neglect has been confirmed.

Primary, and to varying degrees secondary and tertiary, prevention requires:

1) Breaking the tendency in the generational cycle wherein the abused or neglected child is likely to become the abusive or neglectful parent.
2) Helping a parent cope with a child who has special problems or special meaning to a parent.
3) Helping families cope with long term and immediate situational or interpersonal stress.
4) Linking families to personal and community sources of help to break their social isolation.
5) Eliminating or alleviating violence in our society, particularly sanctioned violence such as corporal punishment in the schools.

A major problem in preventing child abuse and neglect is the stigma attached to the problem and to receiving services from a county protective service agency. Therefore, prevention programs must include community education and outreach. Another problem is that stress is pervasive in our society, and ways must be found both to reduce it and deal with it if child abuse and neglect is to be prevented. (See also EARLY INTERVENTION)

PRIMA FACIE
A latin term approximately meaning "at first sight," "on the first appearance," or "on the face of it." In law, this term is used in the context of a "prima facie case." That is, the presentation of evidence at a trial which has been sufficiently strong to prove the allegations unless contradicted and overcome by other evidence. In a child maltreatment case, the allegations of maltreatment will be considered as proven unless the parent presents rebutting evidence.

PRIVILEGED COMMUNICATIONS
Confidential communications which are protected by statutes and need not or cannot be disclosed in court over the objections of the holder of the privilege. Lawyers are almost always able to refuse to disclose what a client has told them in confidence. Priests are similarly covered. Doctors and psychotherapists have generally lesser privileges, and their testimony can be compelled in many cases involving child abuse or neglect. Some social workers are covered by such statutes, but the law and practice vary widely from state to state. (See also CONFIDENTIALITY)

PROBABLE CAUSE
A legal standard used in a number of contexts which indicates a reasonable ground for suspicion or belief in the existence of certain facts. Facts accepted as true after a reasonable inquiry which would induce a prudent and cautious person to believe them. Also-Please note that the definitions on page 28 of EVIDENTIARY STANDARDS are incorrect. A suggested alternative follows:

PROBATE COURT (See COURTS)

PROBATION
Allowing a convicted criminal defendant or a juvenile found to be delinquent to remain at liberty, under a suspended sentence of imprisonment, generally under the supervi-

sion of a probation officer and under certain conditions. Violation of a condition is grounds for revocation of the probation. In a case of child abuse or neglect, a parent or caretaker who is convicted of the offense may be required, as part of his/her probation, to make certain promises to undergo treatment and/or to improve the home situation. These promises are made as a condition of the probation in which the child is returned home and are enforced with the threat of revocation of parental rights.

PROGRAM COORDINATION
Interagency of intra-agency communication for policy, program, and resource development for an effective service delivery system in a given locality. Program coordination for child abuse and neglect is usually implemented through a community council or community task force or planning committee under the direction of a program coordinator. The functions of these groups are:
1) Comprehensive planning, including identifying gaps and duplication in service and funding policies.
2) Developing interagency referral policies.
3) Educating members to new and/or effective approaches to child abuse and neglect.
4) Problem sharing.
5) Facilitating resolution of interagency conflicts.
6) Providing a forum where differing professional and agency expertise can be pooled.
7) Generating and lobbying for needed legislation.

(See also COMMUNITY TEAM)

PROTECTIVE CUSTODY (See CUSTODY)

PROTOCOL
A set of rules or guidelines prescribing procedures and responsibilities. Originally used primarily in medical settings, establishment of protocols is an increasingly important goal of the child abuse and neglect community team.

PROXIMAL
Near; closer to any point of reference; opposed to distal.

PSYCHOLOGICAL ABUSE (See CHILD ABUSE AND NEGLECT)

PSYCHOLOGICAL NEGLECT (See CHILD ABUSE AND NEGLECT)

PSYCHOLOGICAL PARENT
Adult who, on a continuing day-to-day basis, fulfills a child's emotional needs for nurturance through interaction, companionship, and mutuality. May be the natural parent or another person who fulfills these functions.

PSYCHOLOGICAL TESTS
Instruments of various types used to measure emotional, intellectual, and personality characteristics. Psychological tests should always be administered and interpretated by qualified personnel. Such tests have been used to determine potential for abuse or neglect, effects of abuse or neglect, or psychological makeup of parent or children.

PSYCHOTIC PARENT
A parent who suffers a major mental disorder where the individual's ability to think, respond emotionally, remember, communicate, interpret reality, or behave appropriately is sufficiently impaired so as to interfere grossly with his/her capacity to meet the ordinary demands of life. The term "psychotic" is neither very precise nor definite. However, the parent who is periodically psychotic or psychotic for extended periods and who abuses his/her children has a poor prognosis; permanent removal of the children is often recommended in this situation. It is estimated that well under 10% of all abusive or neglectful parents are psychotic.

PUBLIC AWARENESS (See COMMUNITY AWARENESS)

PUBLIC DEFENDER
Person paid with public funds to plead the cause of an indigent defendant.

PUBLIC LAW 93-247 (See CHILD ABUSE PREVENTION AND TREATMENT ACT)

PUNISHMENT
Infliction of pain, loss, or suffering on a child because the child has disobeyed or otherwise antagonized a parent or caretaker. Abusive parents may inflict punishment without cause, or may inflict punishment, particularly corporal punishment, in the belief that it is the only way to discipline children. Many parents confuse the difference between discipline and punishment. These differences are delineated under DISCIPLINE. (See also CORPORAL PUNISHMENT)

PURCHASE OF SERVICE
Provision for diagnosis and/or treatment of child abuse and neglect by an agency other than the mandated agency using mandated agency funds. The mandated agency subcontracts with the provider agency for specific services with specific clients, but the mandated agency retains statutory responsibility for the case. (See also CASE MANAGEMENT)

PURPURA (See INTRADERMAL HEMORRHAGE)

RADIOLUCENT
Permitting the passage of X-rays without leaving a shadow on the film. Soft tissues are radiolucent; bones are not.

RAREFACTION
Loss of density. On an X-ray photograph, an area of bone which appears lighter than normal is in a state of rarefaction, indicating a loss of calcium.

RECEIVING HOME
A family or group home for temporary placement of a child pending more permanent plans such as return to his/her own home, foster care, or adoption.

RECIDIVISM
Recurrence of child abuse and neglect. This happens relatively frequently because child protective service agencies heretofore have been mandated and staffed only to investigate and provide crisis intervention and not to provide treatment. Most cases where child abuse or neglect results in a child's death have been previously known to a child protection agency.

REFEREE (See HEARING OFFICER)

REGIONAL RESOURCE CENTER
With respect to child abuse and neglect, a regional resource center was funded as a demonstration project in each of the ten HEW regions under the 1974 Child Abuse Prevention and Treatment Act. These resource centers vary in program emphasis, but they all function to some degree as extensions of the National Center on Child Abuse and Neglect in Washington to help NCCAN fulfill the aims of the Child Abuse Prevention and Treatment Act (see NATIONAL CENTER ON CHILD ABUSE AND NEGLECT and CHILD ABUSE PREVENTION AND TREATMENT ACT). Besides regional centers, there are also state resource centers in Arizona, Maryland, New York, and North Carolina; and two national resource centers, operated by the Education Commission of the States and the National Urban League. The regional resource centers are:

Region I (Connecticut, Maine, Massachusetts, New Hampshire, Rhode Island, Vermont)
Judge Baker Guidance Center
295 Longwood Ave.
Boston, Massachusetts 02115
Region II (New Jersey, Puerto Rico, Virgin Islands)
College of Human Ecology Cornell University
MVR Hall
Ithaca, New York 14853
Region III (Pennsylvania, Virginia, Delaware, West Virginia, District of Columbia)
Institute for Urban Affairs and Research
Howard University

2900 Van Ness St., N.W.
Washington, D.C. 20008
Region IV (Alabama, Florida, Georgia, Kentucky, Mississippi, South Carolina, Tennessee)
Regional Institute of Social Welfare Research
P.O. Box 152
Heritage Building
468 N. Milledge Ave.
Athens, Georgia 30601
Region V (Illinois, Indiana, Michigan, Minnesota, Ohio, Wisconsin)
Midwest Parent-Child Welfare Resource Center
Center for Advanced Studies in Human Services
School of Social Welfare
University of Wisconsin-Milwaukee
Milwaukee, Wisconsin 53201
Region VI (Arkansas, Louisiana, New Mexico, Oklahoma, Texas)
Center for Social Work Research
School of Social Work
University of Texas at Austin
Austin, Texas 78712
Region VII (Iowa, Kansas, Missouri, Nebraska)
Institute of Child Behavior and Development
University of Iowa
Oakdale, Iowa 53219
Region VIII (Colorado, Montana, North Dakota, South Dakota, Utah, Wyoming)
National Center for the Prevention and Treatment of Child Abuse and Neglect
University of Colorado Medical Center
1205 Oneida St.
Denver, Colorado 80220
Region IX (California, Hawaii, Nevada, Guam, Trust Territories of the Pacific, American Samoa)
Department of Special Education
California State University
5151 State University Dr.
Los Angeles, California 90033
Region X (Alaska, Idaho, Oregon, Washington)
Northwest Federation for Human Services
157 Yesler Way, #208
Seattle, Washington 98104

REGISTRY (See CENTRAL REGISTER and NATIONAL REGISTER)

REHEARING
After a juvenile court referee or commissioner has heard a case and made an order, some states permit a dissatisfied party to request another hearing before the supervising judge of juvenile court. This second hearing is called a rehearing. If the original hearing was not recorded by a court reporter, the rehearing may have to be granted. If a transcript exists, the judge may read it and either grant or deny the rehearing.

REPARENTING
Usually describes a nurturing process whereby parents who have not received adequate nurturance during their own childhoods are provided with emotional warmth and security through a surrogate parent such as a parent aide. Abusive and neglectful parents are thus given an opportunity to identify with more positive role models.

REPORTING LAWS
State laws which require specified categories of persons, such as professionals involved with children, and allow other persons, to notify public authorities of cases of suspected child abuse and, sometimes, neglect. All 50 states now have reporting statutes, but they differ widely with respect to types of instances which must be reported, persons who must report, time limits for reporting, manner of reporting (written, oral, or both), agencies to which reports must be made, and the degree of immunity conferred upon reporters.

RES IPSA LOQUITOR
Latin expression meaning "the thing speaks for itself." It is a doctrine of law which, when applied to criminal law, means that evidence can be admitted which is acceptable despite the fact that no one actually saw what occurred, only the results. An example in

criminal law would be admitting into evidence in a child abuse case the medical reports of the injured child victim which reflect multiple broken bones and the doctor's opinion that said injuries could not have been caused by an accident. The court using the *res ipsa loquitor* doctrine can convict the person having had exclusive custody of the child without any direct testimony as to how, when, where, or why the injuries were inflicted.

RETINA
Inside lining of the eye. Injury to the head can cause bleeding or-detachment of the retina, possible causing blindness.

RICKETS
Condition caused by a deficiency of vitamin D, which disturbs the normal development of bones.

ROLE REVERSAL
The process whereby a parent or caretaker seeks nurturance and/or protection from a child rather than providing this for the child, who frequently complies with this reversal. Usually this process develops as a result of unfulfilled needs of the parent or caretaker.

SACRAL AREA
Lower part of the back.

SCAN TEAM
Suspected Child Abuse and Neglect team which has as its objective the assessment of a child and his/her family to determine if abuse and/or neglect has occurred and what treatment is indicated. The team usually includes a pediatrician, a social worker, and a psychiatrist or psychologist, but other professionals are often involved as well. A SCAN team or unit is generally located in a hospital or outpatient facility. (See also MULTIDISCIPLINARY TEAM and DENVER MODEL)

SCAPEGOATING
Casting blame for a problem on one who is innocent or only partially responsible; for example, a parent or caretaker abusing or neglecting a child as punishment for family problems unrelated to the child.

SCURVY
Condition caused by a deficiency of vitamin C (ascorbic acid) and characterized by weakness, anemia, spongy gums, and other symptoms.

SEALING
In juvenile court or criminal court practice, the closing of records to inspection by all but the defendant or minor involved. Sealing is provided by statute in some states and may be done after proof is made that the defendant or minor has behaved lawfully for a specified period of years. Note that juvenile court records are never public, as are the records of most other courts; access to juvenile court records is theoretically very restricted, even before sealing. (See also EXPUNGEMENT)

SEIZURES
Uncontrollable muscular contractions, usually alternating with muscular relaxation and generally accompanied by unconsciousness. Seizures, which vary in intensity and length of occurrence, are the result of some brain irritation which has been caused by disease, inherited condition, fever, tumor, vitamin deficiency, or injury to the head.

SELF-HELP GROUP
Groups of persons with similar, often stigmatized, problems who share concerns and experiences in an effort to provide mutual help to one another. Usually these groups are self-directed. (See also PARENTS ANONYMOUS)

SELF-INCRIMINATION
The giving of a statement, in court or during an investigation, which subjects the person giving the statement to criminal liability. (See also DUE PROCESS, FIFTH AMENDMENT, IMMUNITY, and MIRANDA RULE)

SENTENCING
The last stage of criminal prosecution in which a convicted defendant is ordered imprisoned, fined, or granted probation. This is equivalent in a criminal case, to the disposition in a juvenile court case.

SEQUELAE
After-effects; usually medical events following an injury or disease. In child abuse and neglect, sequelae is used to refer to psychological consequences of abusive acts and also the perpetuation of maltreatment behavior across generations, as well as specific aftereffects such as brain damage, speech impairment, and impaired physical and/or psychological growth.

SERVICES
(See EARLY INTERVENTION, EMERGENCY SERVICES, PREVENTION OF CHILD ABUSE AND NEGLECT, SUPPORTIVE SERVICES, TREATMENT OF CHILD ABUSE AND NEGLECT)

SEXUAL ABUSE
In order to encompass all forms of child sexual abuse and exploitation within its mandate, the National Center on Child Abuse and Neglect has adopted the following tentative definition of child sexual abuse: contacts or interactions between a child and an adult when the child is being used for the sexual stimulation of the perpetrator or another person. Sexual abuse may also be committed by a person under the age of 18 when that person is either significantly older than the victim or when the perpetrator is in a position of power or control over another child. (See also CHILD ABUSE AND NEGLECT)

SEXUAL ASSAULT
Unlawful actions of a sexual nature committed against a person forcibly and against his/her own will. Various degrees of sexual assault are established by state law and are distinguished by the sex of the perpetrator and/or victim, the amount of force used, the amount and type of sexual contact, etc. Sexual abuse is one form of sexual assault wherein the perpetrator is known by the victim and is usually a member of the family. (See also CHILD ABUSE AND NEGLECT)

SEXUAL EXPLOITATION
A term usually used in reference to sexual abuse of children for commercial purposes; such as child prostitution, sexual exhibition, or the production of pornographic materials. (See also CHILD PORNOGRAPHY, CHILD PROSTITUTION)

SEXUAL MISUSE
Alternative term for sexual abuse, but particularly reflects the point of view that sexual encounters with children, if properly handled, need not be as harmful as is usually assumed. Its implication is that children are not necessarily harmed by so-called sexually abusive acts themselves, but rather the abuse results from damage generated by negative social and cultural reactions to such acts. (See also CHILD MISUSE AND NEGLECT, INCEST, SEXUAL ABUSE)

SEXUALLY TRANSMISSIBLE DISEASE (STD) (See VENEREAL DISEASE)

SIMPLE FRACTURE (See FRACTURE)

SITUATIONAL CHILD ABUSE AND NEGLECT
Refers to cases of child abuse and particularly child neglect where the major causative factors cannot be readily eliminated because they relate to problems over which the parents have little control. (See also APATHY-FUTILITY SYNDROME)

SKELETAL SURVEY
A series of X-rays that studies all bones of the body. Such a survey should be done in all cases of suspected abuse to locate any old, as well as new, fractures which may exist.

SOCIAL ASSESSMENT (See ASSESSMENT)

SOCIAL HISTORY
1) Information compiled by a social worker about factors affecting a family's past and present level of functioning for use in diagnosing child abuse and neglect and developing a treatment plan.
2) Document prepared by a probation officer or social worker for the juvenile or family court hearing officer's consideration at the time of disposition of a case. This report addresses the minor's history and environment. Social histories often contain material which would clearly be inadmissible in most judicial proceedings, either because of hearsay or lack of verification or reliability. The informal use of such reports has often been attacked as in violation of due process rights of minors and parents.

SOCIAL REPORT (See SOCIAL HISTORY)

SOCIAL ISOLATION
The limited interaction and contact of many abusive and/or neglectful parents with relatives, neighbors, friends, or community resources. Social isolation can perpetuate a basic lack of trust which hinders both identification and treatment of child abuse and neglect.

SOCIAL SECURITY ACT
Established in 1935 as a national social insurance program, this federal legislation includes several sections particularly applicable to child and family welfare:

Title IV-Parts A, B, C, D (Aid to Families with Dependent Children, Child Welfare Services, Work Incentive Program, Child Support and Establishment of Paternity)
Part A, now included under Title XX as services for children, was designed to encourage families to care for dependent children in their own or relatives' homes by providing services to families below a specified income level. As a condition of receiving federal funding for this program, states must provide family planning services. Part B authorizes support to states for child welfare services developed in coordination with the AFDC program to supplement or substitute for parental care and supervision. These services include day care, foster care, and other preventive or protective programs promoting child and family welfare. Part C offers job training and placement for AFDC parents in an effort to assist them in becoming self-supporting. Part D enforces the support obligations owed by absent parents to their children by locating absent parents, establishing paternity, and obtaining child support.

Title V-Maternal and Child Health and Applied Children's Services
Provides a broad range of health care services for mothers and children from low-income families in order to reduce maternal and infant mortality and to prevent illness.

Title XIX-Grants to States for Medical Assistance Programs (Medicaid or Title 19)
Designed to help families with dependent children and other low-income persons by providing financial assistance for necessary medical services. This act is additionally designed to provide rehabilitation and other psychotherapy services to help families and individuals retain or regain independence and self-sufficiency.

Title XX-Grants to States for Services
Provides grants to states for developing programs and services designed to achieve the following goals for families and/or children: economic self-support; self-sufficiency; prevention of abuse and neglect; preserving; rehabilitating, reuniting families; referring for institutional care when other services are not appropriate.

Mandated child protective service agency programs are primarily funded through Title IV-B and Title XX of the Social Security Act.

SOCIETAL CHILD ABUSE AND NEGLECT
Failure of society to provide social policies and/or funding to support the well-being of all families and children or to provide sufficient resources to prevent and treat child

abuse and neglect, particularly for minority populations such as migrant workers and Native Americans.

SPECIAL CHILD

A child who is abused or neglected or at risk of abuse or neglect because he/she has a special problem with which the parent(s) have difficulty coping or because the child has some psychologically negative meaning for the parent. Also referred to as "target child." If this child is abused, the cause may be referred to as "victim" precipitated abuse."

SPIRAL FRACTURE (See FRACTURE)

SPOUSE ABUSE

Non-accidental physical or psychological injury inflicted on either husband or wife by his/her marital partner. Some experts conjecture that husbands as well as wives are frequently abused, particularly psychologically, but the subject of husband abuse has not gained public or professional recognition to the extent that battered wives has. Domestic violence is the term used when referring to abuse between adult mates who may not be married. (See also BATTERED WOMEN)

STAFF BURNOUT

Apathy and frustration felt by protective service workers who are overworked, undertrained, and lacking agency or supervisory support. This is a common problem, and workers who do not leave protective services (see STAFF FLIGHT) or who do not have supervisory support often lose sensitivity to client needs. (Also referred to as Worker Burnout)

STAFF FLIGHT

Continous change of child protective services staff due to staff burnout (see STAFF BURNOUT). This creates the need to provide frequent training for new workers. Informed estimates place the overall national turnover rate of protective service workers at 85% annually.

STAFF SATISFACTION

Structuring a supportive and encouraging environment for protective service workers with regular periods when no new cases are assigned, thereby decreasing staff burnout and staff flight. Supervisors and administrators need to develop programs including the following elements: manageable caseloads, in-service training, participation in and responsibility for agency decision-making.

STANDARD OF PROOF (See EVIDENTIARY STANDARDS)

STANDARDS

Guides developed to ensure comprehensiveness and adequacy of programs or services. Issued by relevant agencies, such as the National Center on Child Abuse and Neglect for state and local level programs and the Child Welfare League of America for member agencies, standards have various levels of authority.

STATE AUTHORITY

State authority refers to the state department of social services (state department) and a state child protection coordinating committee (state committee). As designated in state law, these structures are to accept responsibility for child abuse and neglect prevention, identification, and treatment efforts. The standards on state authority, as specified in the National Center on Child Abuse and Neglect *Revision to Federal Standards on the Prevention and Treatment of Child Abuse and Neglect (Draft),* include:

Administration and Organization

1. The state department should establish child abuse and neglect policies that are consistent with the state law and conducive to state-wide delivery of uniform and coordinated services.
2. The state department should establish a distinct child protection division (state division) to facilitate the implementation of departmental policies.
3. The state department should designate child protective services units

(local units) within each regional and/or local social services agency.
4. The state committee, as required by state law, should be representative of those persons and agencies concerned with child abuse and neglect prevention, identification, and treatment.

Primary Prevention
5. The state division and the state committee should work together towards primary prevention of child abuse and neglect through formalized needs assessment and planning processes.

Secondary and Tertiary Prevention
6. The state division and the state committee should jointly develop a comprehensive and coordinated plan for delivery of services to high-risk children and families.
7. The state division should ensure that those persons who have reason to suspect child abuse or neglect can make a report at any time, twenty-four hours a day, seven days a week.
8. The state division should transmit reports to appropriate authority for assessment of the degree of risk to the child.
9. The state division should operate a central registry that facilitates state and local planning.
10. The state division's operation of the central registry should ensure that children and families' rights to prompt and effective services are protected.

Resource Enhancement
11. The state division should develop and provide public and professional education.
12. The state division should ensure that training is provided to all divisional, regional, and local staff.
13. The state division should conduct and/or sponsor research, demonstration, and evaluation projects.

(See also LOCAL AUTHORITY)

STATUS OFFENSE
An act which is considered criminal only because it is committed by a person of a particular status, such as a minor. If an adult did the same thing, it would not be an offense. For example, a minor staying out after curfew.

STIPULATION
A statement, either oral or written, between lawyers on both sides of a particular court case which establishes certain facts about the case that are agreed upon by both sides. The facts delineated usually involve such issues as the addresses of the persons involved in the case, their relationships to one another, etc.

STRESS FACTORS
Environmental and/or psychological pressures over a prolonged period which are associated with child abuse and neglect or which, without being prolonged, may be the precipitant event. While a certain amount of stress can be useful in motivating people to change, it is generally agreed that there is an overload of stress in our present society, perhaps because people feel decreasingly in control of the forces affecting their lives. Prevention of child abuse and neglect requires both reducing stress in society and helping people cope with it. Environmental stress which may influence child abuse and neglect includes, but is not limited to, unemployment, poverty, poor and overcrowded housing, competition for success, and "keeping up with the Joneses." Psychological stress besides that caused by environmental factors which may influence child abuse and neglect could include such problems as marital discord, in-law problems, unwanted pregnancy, role confusion resulting from the Women's Movement, and unresolved psychodynamic conflicts from childhood.

SUBDURAL HEMATOMA
A common symptom of abused children, consisting of a collection of blood beneath the outermost membrane covering the brain and spinal cord. The hematoma may be caused by a blow to the head or from shaking a baby or small child. (See also WHIP-

LASH-SHAKEN INFANT SYNDROME)

SUBPOENA
A document issued by a court clerk, usually delivered by a process server or police officer to the person subpoenaed, requiring that person to appear at a certain court at a certain day and time to give testimony in a specified case. Failure to obey a subpoena is punishable as contempt of court.

SUBPOENA DUCES TECUM
A subpoena requiring the person subpoenaed to bring specified records to court.

SUDDEN INFANT DEATH SYNDROME (SIDS)
A condition which can be confused with child abuse, SIDS affects infants from two weeks to two years old, but usually occurs in a child less than six months of age. In SIDS, a child who has been healthy except for a minor respiratory infection is found dead, often with bloody frothy material in his/her mouth. The cause of SIDS is not fully understood. The confusion with child abuse results from the bloody sputum and occasional facial bruises that accompany the syndrome. However, SIDS parents rarely display the guarded or defensive behavior that many abusive parents do.

SUMMONS
A document issued by a court clerk, usually delivered by a process server or police officer to the person summoned, notifying that person of the filing of a lawsuit against him/her and notifying that person of the deadline for answering the suit. A summons does not require the attendance at court of any person.

SUPERVISION
1) Provision of age-appropriate protection and guidance for a child by a parent or caretaker. This is a parental responsibility, but in some cases of child abuse and neglect or for other reasons, the state may have to assume responsibility for supervision. (See also CHILD IN NEED OF SUPERVISION)
2) Process in social work practice whereby workers review cases with supervisors to assure case progress, to sharpen the workers' knowledge and skill, and to assure maintenance of agency policies and procedures. Unlike many practitioners in law and medicine, social workers do not generally practice independently or make totally independent judgments. In general, social work supervisors hold Master's degrees, but in some local public agencies these supervisors may be just out of graduate school and have little experience. Since good supervision is a critical factor in reducing the problem of staff burnout and staff flight, it is important for child protective service agencies to provide training and continuing education opportunities for supervisors.

SUPPORTIVE SERVICES
Supportive services are a wide range of human services which provide assistance to families or individuals so that they are more nearly able to fulfill their potential for positive growth and behavior. The concept implies that individuals have basic strengths which need to be recognized, encouraged, and aided. Thus, a wide range of financial, educational, vocational, child care, counseling, recreational, and other services might be seen as supportive if they do indeed emphasize the strengths of people and de-emphasize their occasional needs for help in overcoming destructive and debilitating factors which may affect their lives.

SURROGATE PARENT
A person other than a biological parent who, living within or outside the target home, provides nurturance. This person may be self-selected or assigned to fulfill parental functions. A surrogate parent may nurture children or abusive or neglectful parents who were themselves abused as children and therefore are in need of a nurturing parental model. (See also PARENT AIDE)

SUSPECTED CHILD ABUSE AND NEGLECT
Reason to believe that child abuse or neglect has or is occurring in a given family. Anyone can in good faith report this to the local mandated agency, which will investigate and protect the child as necessary. However, all states have statutes which provide that members of certain professions must report and that failure to do so is punishable by fine or imprisonment. For specific criteria for suspecting child abuse or neglect, see INDICATORS OF CHILD ABUSE AND NEGLECT and FAMILIES-AT-RISK.

SUTURE
1) A type of immovable joint in which the connecting surfaces of the bones are closely united, as in the skull.
2) The stitches made by a physician that close a wound.

SYPHILIS (See VENEREAL DISEASE)

TARGET CHILD (See SPECIAL CHILD)

TEMPORAL
Referring to the side of the head.

TEMPORARY CUSTODY (See CUSTODY)

TEMPORARY PLACEMENT
Voluntary or involuntary short term removal of a child from his/her own home, primarily when a child's safety or well-being is threatened or endangered, or when a family crisis can be averted by such action. Temporary placement may be in a relative's home, receiving home or shelter, foster home, or institution. Temporary placement should be considered only if service to the child and family within the home, such as use of a homemaker or day care, is determined to be insufficient to protect or provide for the child or if it is unavailable. If the home situation does not improve while the child is in temporary placement, long term placement may be warranted. However, authorities agree that too many temporary placements unnecessarily become permanent placements. (See also CUSTODY)

TERMINATION OF PARENTAL RIGHTS (TPR)
A legal proceeding freeing a child from his/her parents' claims so that the child can be adopted by others without the parents' written consent. The legal bases for termination differ from state to state, but most statutes include abandonment as a ground for TPR. (See also ABANDONMENT)

TESTIMONY
A declaration or statement made to establish a fact, especially one made under oath in court.

THREATENED HARM
Substantial risk of harm to a child, including physical or mental injury, sexual assault, neglect of physical and/or educational needs, inadequate supervision, or abandonment.

TITLE IV (See SOCIAL SECURITY ACT)

TITLE V (See SOCIAL SECURITY ACT)

TITLE XIX (TITLE 19, MEDICAID) (See SOCIAL SECURITY ACT)

TITLE XX (See SOCIAL SECURITY ACT)

TORUS FRACTURE (See FRACTURE)

TRABECULA
A general term for a supporting or anchoring strand of tissue.

TRAUMA
An internal or external injury or wound brought about by an outside force. Usually trauma means injury by violence, but it may also apply to the wound caused by any surgical procedure. Trauma may be caused accidentally or, as in a ease of physical abuse, non-acciden-tally. Trauma is also a term applied to psychological discomfort or symptoms resulting from an emotional shock or painful experience.

TRAUMA X
Designation used by some hospitals for a child abuse and neglect program.

TREATMENT FOSTER CARE
Foster care for children with diagnosed emotional and/or behavioral problems in which foster parents with special training and experience become part of a treatment team working with a particular child. Treatment foster care may be indicated for abused or severely neglected children.

TREATMENT OF CHILD ABUSE AND NEGLECT
1) Helping parents or caretakers stop child abuse and neglect and assisting them and their children to function adequately as a family unit. 2) Providing temporary placement and services as necessary for abused or neglected children until their parents can assume their parental responsibilities without threat to the children's welfare. 3) Terminating parental rights and placing the children in an adoptive home if the parents abandon the children or absolutely cannot be helped. Experts believe that 80% to 85% of abusive and neglectful parents can be helped to function without threat to their children's welfare and, more often than not, without temporary placement of the children if sufficient supportive services are available.

Treatment for child abuse and neglect should include treatment for the abused and neglected children as well as for the parents.

Treatment for child abuse and neglect includes both crisis intervention and long term treatment. The mandated agency may provide services directly or by purchase of service from other agencies. Since a multiplicity of services is often necessary, a case management approach to treatment is usually most effective (see CASE MANAGEMENT). Because mandated agencies necessarily focus on investigation of suspected cases and crisis intervention, long term treatment is best assured through use of a community team (see COMMUNITY TEAM).

Both crisis intervention and long term treatment will usually require a mix of supportive and therapeutic services. Supportive services could include homemakers, day care, foster grandparents, parent education, health care, family planning, recreational activities, housing assistance, transportation, legal services, employment training and placement, financial counseling and assistance. Therapeutic services could include psychotherapy, casework, lay therapy from parent aides, group therapy, family or couple therapy, and self-help such as Parents Anonymous.

TURGOR
Condition of being swollen and congested. This can refer to normal or other fullness.

TWENTY-FOUR HOUR EMERGENCY SERVICES
Local services available at all times to receive reports and make immediate investigations of suspected cases of child abuse and severe neglect and to perform crisis intervention if necessary. The mode of providing twenty-four hour emergency services varies in different localities. However, often mandated agency protective service workers are on call for specific evening and weekend assignments. Often the after-hours number rings the police or sheriffs department which then contacts the assigned worker. (See also COMPREHENSIVE EMERGENCY SERVICES)

UNFOUNDED REPORT
Any report of suspected child abuse or neglect made to the mandated agency for which it is determined that there is no probable cause to believe that abuse or neglect has occurred. Mandated agencies may or may not remove unfounded reports from their records after a period of time. (See also EXPUNGEMENT)

VASCULAR
Of the blood vessels.

VENEREAL DISEASE
Any disease transmitted by sexual contact. The two most common forms of venereal disease are gonorrhea and syphilis. Presence of a venereal disease in a child may indicate that the mother was infected with the disease during the pregnancy, or it may be evidence of sexual abuse.

VERBAL ABUSE (See CHILD ABUSE AND NEGLECT)

VERIFICATION OF CHILD ABUSE AND NEGLECT
Substantiation of child abuse or neglect following investigation of suspected cases by mandated agency workers and/or assessment by a diagnostic team. Also referred to as a founded report.

VICTIM-PRECIPITATED ABUSE (See SPECIAL CHILD)

VISITING FRIEND (See PARENT AIDE)

VITAL SIGNS
Signs manifesting life, such as respiratory rate, heartbeat, pulse, blood pressure, and eye responses.

VOIR DIRE
1. Procedure during which lawyers question prospective jurors to determine their biases, if any.
2. Procedure in which lawyers question expert witnesses regarding their qualifications before the experts are permitted to give opinion testimony.

VOLUNTARY PLACEMENT
Act of a parent in which custody of his/her child is relinquished without a formal court proceeding. Sometimes called voluntary relinquishment.

VOLUNTEER ROLES
1) Extension and enrichment of direct services to families by unpaid, screened, trained, and supervised persons who generally lack professional training. Common roles are parent aides, child care workers, outreach workers, or staff for helplines. 2) Development and advocacy of child abuse and neglect programs by unpaid persons through participation on community councils, agency boards, or community committees. Scarce resources in relation to the magnitude of the problem of child abuse and neglect demands that volunteers be used increasingly.

WANTON
Extremely reckless or malicious. Often used in court proceedings in conjunction with "willful" to establish certain kinds of unlawful behavior only vaguely distinguished from careless but lawful conduct.

WARRANT
Document issued by a judge, authorizing the arrest or detention of a person or the search of a place and seizure of specified items in that place. Although a judge need not hold a hearing before issuing a warrant and although the party to be arrested or whose property will be seized need not be notified, the judge must still be given "reasonable cause to believe" that a crime has occurred and that the warrant is necessary in the apprehension and conviction of the criminal.

WHIPLASH-SHAKEN INFANT SYNDROME
Injury to an infant or child that results from that child having been shaken, usually as a misguided means of discipline. The most common symptoms, which can be inflicted by seemingly harmless shakings, are bleeding and/or detached retinas and other bleeding inside the head. Repeated instances of shaking and resultant injuries may eventually cause mental and developmental disabilities. (See also SUBDURAL HEMATOMA)

WILLFUL
Done with understanding of the act and the intention that the act and its natural consequences should occur. Some conduct

becomes unlawful or negligent only when it is done willfully.

WITNESS
1. A person who has seen or heard something.
2. A person who is called upon to testify in a court hearing.

WORKER BURNOUT (See Staff Burnout)

WORK-UP
Study of a patient, often in a hospital, in order to provide information for diagnosis. A full work-up includes past medical and family histories, present condition and symptoms, laboratory, and, possibly, X-ray studies.

WORLD OF ABNORMAL REARING (WAR)
A generational cycle of development in which abused or neglected children tend to grow up to be abusive or neglectful parents unless intervention occurs to break the cycle. The diagram which follows outlines the WAR cycle. (Heifer)

X-RAYS
Photographs made by means of X-rays. X-rays are one of the most important tools available to physicians in the diagnosis of physical child abuse or battering. With X-rays, or radiologic examinations, physicians can observe not only the current bone injuries of a child, but also any past injuries that may exist in various stages of healing. This historical information contributes significantly to the assessment of a suspected case of child abuse. Radiologic examination is also essential to distinguish organic diseases that may cause bone breakage from physical child abuse.

Acronyms

AAP	American Academy of Pediatrics	**PET**	Parent Effectiveness Training
ACSW	Academy of Certified Social Workers	**PINS**	Person in Need of Supervision
		CPS	Child Protective Services
ACYF	Administration for Children, Youth and Families (formerly Office of Child Development), U.S. Department of Health, Education and Welfare	**CWLA**	Child Welfare League of America
		DART	Detection, Admission, Reporting, and Treatment (multidisciplinary team)
		DD	Developmental Disability
ADC	Aid to Dependent Children (Title IV-A of the Social Security Act) (also referred to as AFDC)	**DHEW**	U.S. Department of Health, Education and Welfare (also referred to as HEW)
AF	Alleged Father	**DPW**	Department of Public Welfare
AFDC	Aid to Families with Dependent Children (Title IV-A of the Social Security Act) (also referred to as ADC)	**DSS**	Department of Social Services
		EPSDT	Early and Periodic Screening, Diagnosis, and Treatment
		ER	Emergency Room
AHA	American Humane Association	**FTT**	Failure to Thrive
AMA	Against Medical Advice; American Medical Association	**GAL**	*Guardian ad l item*
		HEW	U.S. Department of Health, Education and Welfare (also referred to as DHEW)
APA	American Psychiatric Association; American Psychological Association		
		IP	Identified Patient
APWA	American Public Welfare Association	**LD**	Learning Disability
		MINS	Minor in Need of Supervision
CALM	Child Abuse Listening Mediation	**NASW**	National Association of Social Workers
CAN	Child Abuse and Neglect		
CAP	Community Action Program	**NCCA**	National Center for Child Advocacy
CDAHA	Children's Division of the American Humane Association	**NCCAN**	National Center on Child Abuse and Neglect
CDF	Children's Defense Fund	**NIH**	National Institutes of Health
CES	Comprehensive Emergency Services	**NIMH**	National Institute of Mental Health
CHIPS	Child in Need of Protection and Supervision	**OCD**	Office of Child Development (now Adminstration for Children, Youth and Families). U.S. Department of Health, Education and Welfare
CLL	Childhood Level of Living Scale		
CNS	Central Nervous System		
	Office of Human Development Services), U.S. Department of Health, Education and Welfare	**OHD**	Office of Human Development (now
OHDS	Office of Human Development Services (formerly Office of Human Development), U.S. Department of Health, Education and Welfare	**PL 93-247**	Child Abuse Prevention and Treatment Act
		SCAN	Suspected Child Abuse and Neglect
PA	Parents Anonymous		

SIDS	Sudden Infant Death Syndrome	**VD**	Venereal Disease
STD	Sexually Transmissible Disease	**WAR**	World of Abnormal Rearing
TPR	Termination of Parental Rights	**WIN**	Work Incentive Program
UM	Unmarried Mother		